ALLEN PARK PUBLIC LIBRARY # 4
8100 ALLEN RD.
ALLEN PARK, 48101
313-381-2425

HELPING ME
HELP MYSELF

ALSO BY BETH LISICK

NONFICTION

Everybody into the Pool

FICTION

Monkey Girl: Swingin' Tales

This Too Can Be Yours

HELPING ME HELP MYSELF

One Skeptic, Ten Self-Help Gurus, and a Year on the Brink of the Comfort Zone

BETH LISICK

WILLIAM MORROW
An Imprint of HarperCollins*Publishers*

HarperCollins books may be purchased for educational, business, or sales promotional use. For information please write: Special Markets Department, HarperCollins Publishers, 10 East 53rd Street, New York, NY 10022.

Designed by Chris Welch

All illustrations by David L. Cooper

Library of Congress Cataloging-in-Publication Data has been applied for.

ISBN 978-0-06-114396-0

08 09 10 11 12 WBC/RRD 10 9 8 7 6 5 4

CONTENTS

INTRODUCTION: SPLITS!

I woke up on New Year's Day feeling like my leg was on fire. It was a lengthy trail of pain, beginning just below my right ass cheek, running along the tendons behind my knee, and wrapping around to the tibialis muscle in my shin. Just wiggling my toes made me see stars. This wasn't the first time I'd awoken with minor injuries and had to reconstruct the previous evening's events from underneath my covers, but I was bathed in a sense of relief knowing that at least I'd spent the whole night in my own home. My husband, Eli, was beside me, stirring from sleep, and there was no sign of a headache, which, considering my bloodstream's cold hard evidence, was itself a tiny miracle.

"I'm injured," I whispered. It was more of a stage whisper, actually. A stage whimper. "My legs!"

Outside was all gray, a low and fuzzy hovering of clouds like the city was being smothered by a particularly fruitful lint trap. I reached for my bedside glass of water, the constant companion of any severely allergic mouth-breather with a deviated septum, and let out a yelp.

"What did I do?"

Welcome to the new year. Same as the old new year.

Eli pulled back the sheet slowly, exposing the pasty specter of my nakedness, which was marked by a plum-sized bruise atop the knob of my knee. He tried inspecting it, but the only way he can see without his glasses on is to stretch back the outside corner of his left eye with his palm until it's a narrow slit. Over the past eight years, I'd seen him do this a thousand times. He touched the knot lightly and I winced.

"And this one," I said, attempting to lift up my right foot. "Ow, ow, ow."

He lay back down and patted my stomach. "If it's any consolation, I've got some chafing around my balls from those tuxedo pants."

The night before had been our New Year's Eve party, the sixth annual. It always felt like a big deal because we rarely have people over. My fault. It's true that when I see those colorful photo spreads in lifestyle magazines in which groups of multiracial friends in colorful clothing are bonding at the Crazy Fondue Party or an Etruscan Bacchanal Dinner, it hurts a little on the inside. It tugs at part of my soul because I will never know the joys of hosting even, say, a Casual Autumn Soup Party, because thinking about entertaining people in my home makes me exhausted. So every year we attempt to absolve all of our negligent hosting sins with this one party.

What happens is that about a week before New Year's Eve we send out an e-mail to literally *every single person we know.* Then I make hundreds of enchiladas, Eli calls the piano tuner, we flip a coin to see who has to clean the toilet, and we put on a talent show. The night before had been a good one. Jennifer Blowdryer, an underground performance artist who prefers to identify herself as "blowsy," sang an a cappella song she made up about a thieving former boyfriend who she thinks is coming back for her but really just forgot his cigarettes. Our friend John, Eli's business partner at his recording studio, played "Night and Day" on the musical straw, and Stallion, an illusionist, martial arts instructor, and couples counselor, lip-synched a painfully long ballad, made even longer and more painful by a skipping CD. For the record, our friends are also payroll processors, elementary school teachers, home stagers, and construction workers, but most of them happen to play drums, write poetry, or make sculptures by casting doll underwear in wax as well. The last of the guests usually leave at about 3:00 A.M., and then, basically, none of them will enter our house for another year.

Eli got up to make coffee, and I looked around our room. Not too bad. There was a gross-looking brown stain snaking across the ceiling from our neglected gutter problem, something we knew about when we moved in seven years ago and hadn't yet taken care of. It was starting to look more and more like we would just wait until the ceiling started physically caving in—until there was an imminent threat—before we would do anything about it. It had to cost a lot of money to fix something like that, and extra money is something we never have. Also, the plaster on the walls was cracked, fractured into spidery legs here and there. But the surfaces were clutter-free. Nothing on the dresser but a pile of illegal firecrackers. Clearly, my preteen habit of shoving things into closets and under the bed to "clean" when people come over was still going strong shortly after my thirty-seventh birthday.

"We forgot to light the firecrackers!" I yelled out to the kitchen.

Eli came in with the coffee and set it on the nightstand. "The house isn't even that trashed. We're definitely getting old."

He climbed in bed with the digital camera so we could review the highlights. At first, the pictures were pretty standard. People, early on, making drinks at the bar we'd set up by throwing a tablecloth over my desk. Couples on the couch shoving chips into their mouths, friends putting their arms around each other by the fridge. Then there was a huge time gap of probably about three hours. After that point, the camera contained only those really short movies that an early-model digital camera will allow you to make. Seven-second clips of our saxophone player/manny friend, red-nosed, singing a Portuguese love song at the top of his lungs.

Everyone was yelling to be heard. None of the ladies was wearing lipstick anymore.

"Okay, here's you hurting yourself," Eli said, pressing the button. The camera moved around the kitchen as a chant went up.

"Splits! Splits! Splits!"

I peered into the tiny frame and saw myself, in a white thrift-store dress I'd hacked from floor-length to knee-length with scissors an hour before the party started, splat down into the splits, in the middle of the floor. First time since the '80s. So that explained the injuries. Or rather, the injuries could be further explained by the sequence of movies that followed, revealing me pulling the same lame stunt over and over again. I'd now identified two issues. One, I was pretty drunk. And two, I am somewhat of a clown. I can't get enough of people going crazy on dance floors, falling down, doing tumbling routines, and otherwise sacrificing their bodies for laughs. Basically, I am both the target market for *America's Funniest Home Videos* and a potential contestant. The problem is that I constantly forget that just because I used to be athletic when I was a teenager doesn't mean I can pull off the same moves now.

In the video, each time I splayed down, my right foot slid forward and my left went back. That's why the top of my left knee was bruised and the right hamstring pulled. Suddenly, an idea struck. I would learn how to do the splits on both sides. From an audience standpoint, it would look a lot better if I could slide down on one side, pop up, and then slide down on the other. Goofier. Plus, more symmetrical and showbizzy. I could bust it out while waiting for the train to make my friends laugh. Or I could work it into my talent show act for next year. *I'll do something involving the splits*, I thought. I lay back in bed, satisfied for a second with my bout of reflection, and took a sip of coffee. Then, as I started imagining how I would train for such a thing, what kind of stretches I could do to accomplish this feat, a scared, empty feeling took hold. A feeling much larger than forgetting to take out the trash cans and only slightly smaller than reading a newspaper article about how Portuguese Water Dogs are able to detect from your breath if you will develop cancer (when these are the kind of dogs your parents have and they always seem skittish around you). I mean, let's reflect a minute: That was now my goal for the new year? My resolution?

Hello, 2006. Hang tight with me for the next twelve months, and come December 31, I will have learned how to do the splits on both sides!

Kind of depressing.

I turned to Eli. "You don't ever make New Year's resolutions, do you?"

"Remember we made one a few years ago? It was something about exercising and being better about answering e-mails."

I vaguely remembered that.

But as I stared at the stain on the ceiling and the screws in the wall that should have been holding the smoke detector for the past few years, I felt like there were a few more things I should accomplish. What if I could just look at everything in my life that was bugging me, everything I wanted to make better, and systematically fix it all? As much as I loathe horn-tooting blowhards, complaining about how lame you are gets kind of old after fifteen or twenty years.

Could it really be so hard to exercise more and have better relationships, an organized home, secure personal finances, a deeper spirituality, and a more consistent parenting style? Maybe it was about time I got inspired in that way I always heard about other people doing. Where they went on diets and joined gyms, made lists and threw out their mismatched socks, created budgets, and promised themselves they would definitely and finally be more patient and forgiving, for real this time. No more road rage and bounced checks. At least six glasses of water a day. Lots of remembering to tell the people in your life how much they mean to you. That type of thing. Could it really be so hard?

They say the first step to helping yourself is admitting you have a problem, but what if your problem is with self-help?

In my stable, modest family, the entire idea of self-help was an embarrassing topic, like sex or Hitler. Self-help was meant for the addicted and abused and neurotic, right? And those stray hippie navel-gazers with too much time on their hands. It couldn't have been meant for regular people who were doing okay. I mean, back in 1969 when Thomas Harris wrote his iconic self-help manifesto *I'm OK, You're OK*, the goal—if I'm interpreting the title correctly—was being okay. And if you already were okay? Great! You were done. You could defrost your TV dinner, go see *Midnight Cowboy*, and listen to Joni Mitchell's *Clouds* without having an existential crisis. I just don't think self-help's target market used to be defined as "everybody." Being okay with yourself was supposed to be a blessing.

I'd gone through my whole life being okay with being okay. And though I'd never read a single self-help book before this year, I always liked picturing a world where the self-help movement had ended right there, with everyone feeling overwhelmingly, satisfyingly okay. A world where phrases like "competitive enlightenment," "killer abs," and "dress for success" didn't exist.

Unfortunately, it seems like nobody wants to feel just okay anymore. Perhaps evolution is pushing us into becoming hyperbolic über-creatures, but it feels like I'm constantly surrounded by people wanting to get better and better, and it was hard to admit that that might include me. The list of things I could improve about myself was a long one, but how does a skeptic dive into the world of self-help?

I know I'm not alone on this. Surely my friends and I weren't the only people who used to sit around at 2:00 A.M. watching Tony Robbins infomercials for amusement.

"Look at the size of his head!" we'd scream.

"Did he just say, 'Make your life a masterpiece!'?"

Between Mr. Robbins, Jim and Tammy Faye Bakker, and Susan "Stop the Insanity!" Powter, I was bombarded, during some very formative years, with slick images of cheesy, large-headed gurus with porcelain veneers telling me how to be more like them. *No, thank you.*

I was aware there was a slice of my skepticism that was pure immaturity. Like when you stop going to church when you're eighteen because you can't understand how anyone could call herself a member of the Catholic Church if she believed in abortion, birth control, and equal rights for women. But then you find out that most Catholics you know do believe in those things. Somehow, they're able to stick with the church anyway because of the other things it offers them (delicious communion wafers, promise of eternal life, etc.). So maybe I needed to think about self-help the same way. If I chucked out the pabulum, detritus, and shit-crockery, maybe there would be a few choice nuggets to pluck out and drop into my invisible life-force pouch.

And speaking of confusing self-help jargon, I decided I didn't want my gurus to be fringe players who advertised their workshops by stapling flyers to telephone poles near the laundromat. I had grown up in the Bay Area, and the allure of the "alternative" world was waning. I could already take my kid to the park and encounter two separate Wiccan potlucks in progress—I didn't want to be chanting and dancing and burning things in order to get my household budget in order. I wanted to test out the big guys, the ones who sell millions of books and go on talk shows. The pros. That way, if I didn't quite get what they were saying, I would have to admit to myself that millions and millions of others apparently did. I figured it would do my cynicism a world of good to try to understand mainstream self-help and try not to get entangled with debunking the entire industry as a series of scams and shams. All

I wanted to do was look for clear advice on how to fix some stuff by universally recognized experts.

So, on January 1, 2006, I hobbled out of bed and got into the shower. As I stood under the pathetic spray of warm water, I instantly envisioned how much better my experience would be if I simply replaced the showerhead that had been clotted with mineral deposits for years. I decided to pick twelve things I wanted to improve in my life, find an established guru in each field, and devote one month to each of them.

To quote Mr. Ralph Waldo Emerson from about eight score and six years ago: "The sinew and heart of man seem to be drawn out, and we are become timorous, desponding whimperers." Not me. I was going to take care of some business, starting with washing the frosting out of my hair. I didn't want to whimper anymore. At least not this year.

DISCLAIMER

Caution: Results May Vary

HELPING ME HELP MYSELF

January

A LESSON IN CRINGE-STIFLING

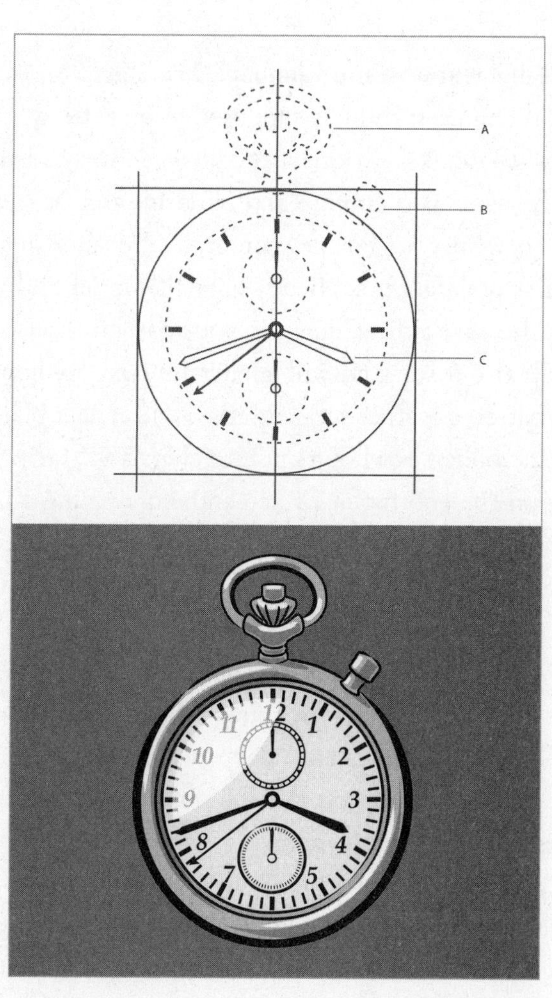

Technically, you wait until January 2 to start your resolutions, right? When everything is supposed to be getting back to normal, when banks are open and mail delivery resumes, that must be when you jump in and blindside this nascent, unsuspecting year with your hot new program. Because, if you're like me, the first of January is already shot. It's noon and you're just getting in the car to drive down to your parents' house to collect your four-year-old son and will spend the next six hours sinking into their battered leather sofa with the central heat blasting while emptying a wooden bowl of its potato chips and staring at a football game on the enormous TV screen before eating a half-pound of ham and polishing off the rest of the See's candies. See what I'm saying? You can't attempt anything new or revolutionary under those circumstances.

My dad, who's gearing up for triple bypass surgery later this month, is filling Eli in on the game using some of his favorite phrases like "barn burner" and "deep yogurt." Eli's not much of a football fan, but he can get into the novelty of it during holiday gatherings. My son, Gus, is momentarily content, doing a connect-the-dots book on the coffee table in front of me as I watch this football coach get more and more agitated. My first thought is: *I'm glad it's not me he's yelling at.* Then it dawns on me that I've been hearing a lot lately about "personal coaches" and "life coaches." It's usually in the context of a joke, or one of those newspaper lifestyle features you can't quite believe is real. One of those stories where it seems like the journalist is just interviewing her friends and passing it off as a trend. But maybe I should find a coach to help me. The thought of it makes my scalp tingle, but it might be time to admit that if I put my mind to it, anything could happen. I'm already doing okay, so I've got nowhere to go but up, right? It could even be entirely possible that by the end of the year I will actually be able to say it—"life coach"—without using a cartoon voice or making air quotes with my fingers.

"I need a life coach," I practice saying to the TV.

There are supposedly 30,000 certified life coaches in the world right now, and lord knows how many unlicensed practitioners lurking about on Craigslist, which means that each time I say those words with a sneer I am essentially hocking a giant loogie on a group of people who are only trying to help (and I'm sure some who are preying on your insecurities, which can be found in *any* profession, including dentistry, landscaping, and the small but influential army of body waxers). I'll start with opening my heart a little and trying not to be mean for sport. Being mean, as I've learned from Gus and quite a few blogs, is one of the easiest things in the world.

The first time I ever heard of a life coach was a couple of years ago. Some guy I'd met at a party, the kind who introduces himself as "an entrepreneur," was carrying on about a dinner party he'd thrown to which he'd invited everyone in his employ—"my people," he'd said. I was a little hung up on the reality of it anyway, a dinner party for the eight people who work for you—not for you at your company, but just, you know, the housekeeper, the accountant, the pool guy, and the like. The staff. (How did I even meet this person?) He said he had wanted to invite everyone "from his life coach to his housekeeper" but wasn't sure if his housekeeper would feel awkward, because she didn't speak that much English, or—"and I know this is terrible to say," he conceded—if his life coach would feel "insulted" to be invited to a dinner party that included the housekeeper.

Quality problems.

I went on to quiz him, in a not unkind manner, about what he and his coach did together as I tried to wrap my mind around it. You pay this person to help you achieve your goals. You are so focused on yourself and your quest for fulfillment and happiness that you hire a professional to motivate you. You're okay, but you want to be the *best* you can be, and you have a very specific idea of what constitutes this Ultimate You. The corners of my mouth were involuntarily turning downward as I spoke, nearly twitching as if they were being pulled by strings. Interesting that I have none of these reactions when people tell me they are in therapy. I have heard of life coaching being called "the new therapy," and supposedly it's much more popular with men because of the bro-friendly nomenclature.

Just hanging with my coach. We're coming up with a game plan!

But why am I so critical of someone who's trying to improve his life? Do I think if I don't keep up, I'll be the last loser standing? Part of it is that the intimacy of having a personal coach freaks me out. I can barely get a pedicure without feeling ridiculous for imposing my feet upon someone for twenty minutes. How could I dump my whole life in someone's lap?

It's not that I don't have a plan. What I want to do is spend the year putting some well-known self-help programs to the test, but I am lacking any semblance of an entry point. Do newbies really just walk down the self-help aisle at the bookstore and pick up whatever looks appropriate? For something so monstrously popular, it sure is difficult to get hooked up. Where's the pusher willing to give me the first one for free?

January is passing slowly. I try to eat well and get plenty of sleep while waiting for inspirational lightning to strike, but the rotting front steps to my house, the books on the shelf that I haven't read, the way I get out of breath playing with Gus, are nagging signs that I've got to improve. As a matter of fact, I've started seeing signs everywhere, as if the universe is somehow in on my experiment with me. There are weird coincidences and synchronicities, a phenomenon first brought to my attention in the following dialogue from the 1984 cult classic *Repo Man*.

Miller: A lot o' people don't realize what's really going on. They view life as a bunch o' unconnected incidents 'n things. They don't realize that there's this, like, lattice o' coincidence that lays on top o' everything. Give you an example; show you what I mean: Suppose you're thinkin' about a plate o' shrimp. Suddenly someone'll say, like, "plate," or "shrimp," or "plate o' shrimp" out of the blue, no explanation. No point in lookin' for one, either. It's all part of a cosmic unconsciousness.

Otto: You eat a lot of acid, Miller, back in the hippie days?

Miller: I'll give you another instance: You know how everybody's into weirdness right now?

The first plate o' shrimp incident happens on January 3. My mom gets me a sweater for Christmas every year, and when she asked me what I wanted, I'd told her it would be nice to have a black hooded one that zips up the front. Saint that she is, she looked absolutely everywhere, and when she couldn't find it, she got me an off-white pullover one instead. Now I'm walking Gus home from preschool, wearing my new sweater, thinking about how I still want a black one. This one is so nice, cashmere and very ladylike, but I know it's only a matter of time before I ruin it. I am hard on clothes. Buttons practically fly off my shirts, shoe soles get worn down at warp speed, and holes appear in the knees of my jeans almost as frequently as they do in Gus's. So there I am walking along, a vision of the kind of sturdy sweater I want in my mind, when I see a piece of balled-up fabric in an agapanthus bush. I reach down, unfurl it, and am astounded to see almost exactly the type of sweater I was picturing.

"Gus!" I say. "This is amazing! I was just thinking about this sweater, and here it is!" The thing is sopping wet, but I snatch it up. It looks like my size, and I could wash it.

"I put it there for you," he says. And even though he's got the *I know that you know I'm lying* face on, I am reminded once again why Hollywood makes so many psychological thrillers featuring small children possessed by supernatural forces.

A few nights later, after I put Gus to bed, I turn on the TV. I'm not a big TV watcher, and even as I'm turning it on I'm thinking, *Why am I turning on the TV? We only get three channels and all of them are fuzzy.* Plus, it's Tuesday, which means there's no chance of catching an episode of *America's Next Top Model.* I stand in front of the screen, mostly a snow flurry, but the audio is clear. I'm drawn in by the announcer, who sounds like a great friend to have. I've always been fascinated by voice-over actors, those disembodied beings carrying urgent messages to your ears. The voice speaks about creating the life you want, finally taking the time to become the person you are really meant to be. *That's what I'm doing!* And what's he selling? Mattresses. Didn't the Sleep Train (where, coincidentally, my mattress is from) used to have kind of an "All aboard! *Woot-woot!* Catch a ride on the Sleep Train!" type approach? Is this personal fulfillment angle a new campaign?

And what about that box of free books left in front of the neighbor's house when they moved out on the first? The box I rifle through and discover *Passages: Predictable Crises of Adult Life* by Gail Sheehy, Dr. Benjamin Spock's *The Pocket Book of Baby and Child Care*, and *OK Words: A Good Book About the Good Life from I'm OK, You're OK* (all of which I pile into my bag after opening OK

Words to a page that says: "'I am like that' does not help anything. 'I can be different' does"). And how do I explain all the life coaches I'm suddenly meeting?

I was invited to give a talk at a fund-raising luncheon for an upscale private school in Marin County. God only knows how they found me, but I'm glad they did. The honorarium was generous and included chauffeur service to and from the school by a sweet mom in a big black SUV. As I arrived at the pastoral campus, located on thirty-five acres near the town of Corte Madera, the children were testing out special pedal carts the school had just purchased for them so they could cruise out to their fields and harvest their organic crops. There was a lovely lunch for a few hundred parents, and then I gave a reading, trying hard to edit out material that didn't seem so tame now that I was delivering it in an elementary school gymnasium.

During the Q&A session, I made a comment, mostly to get laughs. "So if anyone knows a good life coach . . ." I knew it was a lazy way to make a joke, like saying "mime" or "David Hasselhoff," but people laughed a lot. A bit too much, really. Post–coffee and dessert, I received no fewer than five business cards, either from actual life coaches or from people referring me to their life coaches who were alternately outstanding, incredible, inspiring, powerful, or intuitive. Many more parents told me that they knew life coaches and could get me the information if I needed it. I definitely needed information. When did personal coaching become so rampant? Granted, I did happen to be in Marin at a private school with its own organic farm, but a few days later, when I spoke at a book club in my hometown, one of the members also turned out to be a life coach. And I'd just heard that a friend I haven't seen in a while, a radical gay punk rock dad, also recently became a coach.

The month is slipping by. Feeling lost, I decide to go on a fast, one I'd read about called "the Master Cleanse." Maybe that would be a decent way to begin my year of self-improvement without having to make any phone calls or ask anyone for favors. Clean colon = clean slate. An equation as old as time. The start is a little rocky, but by day five I'm in the groove of drinking cayenne-laced lemonade all day and having my asshole open like a faucet each morning to release a nasty yellow bile that I'm told by a website is "built-up toxins."

The wrench in the gears comes on day six when I happen to pick up one of my Christmas presents, David Rakoff's book of essays *Don't Get Too Comfortable*. Hmmm. Looks like he's written a very hilarious essay about going on a fast. Okay, forget it. Scratch writing about a fast if someone better than you has already done it. Actually, I decide, let's scratch the fast entirely. What's the use now? To add insult, he also claims his twenty-day fast is the shortest one out there, and here I was doing a wimpy ten. I immediately go out and get Indian food. Clearly, my heart is nowhere to be found in this project yet. The only thing I learn is you don't eat two pieces of tandoori chicken, a lump of sag paneer, and a sheaf of garlic naan on an excavated stomach. Cramps and more faucet-butt follow.

I admit that I need some guidance. All I've been doing is walking around with an ever-increasing sense of self-awareness, which I'm finding debilitating. One last stab at running interference is made when I get my hearing tested and put a coaster under a wobbly table leg in the kitchen. When I find out my hearing is fine, I make a mental note to try to speak more quietly. Nice work.

The next morning, I hightail it to the bookstore. Here I am walking down the self-help aisle on purpose for the first time in my life. It makes my insides feel bad, and I don't think it's just my digestive system kicking back into gear. The problem is that instead of thinking that all those smiling faces and soothing colors and jacked-up titles are trying to help me, I feel like a bigger loser. Weak and clichéd. Like I should be drinking a glass of chardonnay while sitting on a swiveling bar stool at the island in my friend's kitchen saying, "I don't know, Joan. It's all just too much sometimes. I need some help, but I don't know how to ask for it."

Eventually, I see something. A book I decide to purchase for the six-burrito price of $24.95. It's the latest by Jack "Chicken Soup for the Soul" Canfield. The reason this one stands out is because I recognize his face, but not in a bad *please change the channel he's scaring the children* way. Last year I introduced myself to Jack and his wife at a publishing party. Jack Canfield happens to be the father of one of Eli's oldest friends, which is about as bizarre as finding out that your friend's dad is the biggest sitcom star in Canada or happens to be a notorious serial killer. No disrespect intended, it's just that's how far removed I feel from his world. Our friend didn't grow up in the same house as his father, so I don't know much about Jack personally, but at least I have some sort of connection to go on. Jack seemed friendly enough when I met him, and after years in the self-help biz, he's earned the nickname "America's Number-One Success Coach."

His new book is called *The Success Principles: How to Get from Where You Are to Where You Want to Be*. Jack is on the cover, kind of a silver fox character, leaning jauntily onto the capital letter *T* in the title. I like imagining the photo shoot. He'd be leaning on a podium or a plant stand against a blue screen, all the while knowing there was a master plan to Photoshop it out so it looks like he's leaning into a wide open space of possibility, the only support coming from his very own title.

The endorsements on this thing are positively mammoth, with extra emphasis on the word "positive." Fifty glowing reviews from my boyfriend Tony Robbins to Wally Amos of Famous Amos cookies to the former president of Reebok. There are television producers, the CEO of Discount Tire Company, and a twelve-time national gold medalist in Olympic-style tae kwon do known as "Ninja Grandma," all praising Canfield for his wisdom and mastery of life.

I know better than to judge a book by the hyperbole of its

endorsements, but I am willing, as Marcia Martin, transformational coach and former vice president of est, blurbs, to "get ready for the ride of my life." The book is touted as being the next best thing to having Jack as your personal guide, so I'm ready to strap myself in and floor it.

As I'm waiting in line to buy it, I read the dedication. "This book is dedicated to all those courageous men and women who have ever dared to step out of the dominant culture of mediocrity and endeavor to create the life of their dreams. I honor and salute you!"

My cynicism falls away. He means people like me, the ones taking the road less traveled. Just as I'm thinking, *Why, thank you, Jack! Thanks for the kudos!* it dawns on me. Reading this type of book is exactly something I've always associated with the dominant culture of mediocrity. That's not enough to deter me, though. I swipe my credit card so violently, I am forced to repeat the action nearly a half dozen times before the cashier steps in and bails me out.

"I guess I need some help, huh?" I chuckle awkwardly, gesturing to the book.

"Everybody needs a little help," she responds gently, not making eye contact.

Plate o' shrimp.

The sheer amount of braggadocio in the introduction is highly amusing, especially as I huddle underneath a rainbow afghan in my freezing cold living room, wisps of my hair being blown by the wind-tunnel effect created by the quarter-inch gaps in my ancient wooden-framed windows. Somebody drunk is rifling through the recycling containers on the side of my house as I read:

> My success includes earning a multimillion-dollar net income every year for over the past ten years, living in a beautiful

> California estate, commanding speaking fees of $25,000 a talk. . . . I get to socialize with CEOs of Fortune 500 companies; movie, television, and recording stars; celebrated authors; and the world's finest spiritual teachers and leaders. I have spoken to the members of Congress, professional athletes, corporate managers, and sales superstars in all the best resorts and retreat centers in the world—from the Four Seasons Resort in Nevis in the British West Indies to the finest hotels in Acapulco and Cancún. I get to ski in Idaho, California, and Utah, go rafting in Colorado, and hike in the mountains of California and Washington. And I get to vacation in the world's best resorts in Hawaii, Australia, Thailand, Morocco, France, and Italy. All in all, life is a real kick!

I settle into my couch, the one with the stuffing peeking out of the armrests that my ex-roommate's ex-girlfriend's neighbor put out on the street six years ago, and fight the urge to slam the thing shut. Good for you, Jack.

Though sifting through the golf metaphors is rough at first, I start to fall for Canfield's earnest, conversational voice. When he advises me to start each day saying, "I believe the world is plotting to do me good today," it takes some reconditioning to realize he doesn't really mean, "Get a load of this hellhole we're living in!" And that is refreshing. It almost feels alternative to me, revolutionary. Jack asks me to think about the personal work I'm going to be doing as similar to what it's like getting your kitchen remodeled. You have to live with the upheaval and chaos for a while, but in the end, when you see your dream kitchen, you'll be happy you went through the whole process.

Boy, it's hard to relate. I haven't even had a dishwasher since I moved out of my parents' house twenty years ago. A dishwasher. The idea hits me like a skillet in the face. I really want a dishwasher. I think I want a dishwasher more than anything else in life.

Now I simply have to focus on how to get one. The only obstacle standing between me and that dream is money. Jack has a few ideas about that.

Early in his career, he says, he created an enormous replica of a $100,000 bill and affixed it to the ceiling over his bed for inspiration. It's go time! I set down the book and walk over to Gus's yogurt container full of crayons and start drawing, digging a humble one-dollar bill out of my wallet as a reference point. After a few minutes, I cut it out and look at it. Of course it looks dumb. We don't have a ladder tall enough to reach our ceiling, so I tape it on the wall next to my side of the bed. Then, taking another suggestion, I write myself a check for a million dollars and put it in my wallet. On the memo line, tongue gently touching cheek, I enter the words "Life Purpose." I already imagine pulling this check out and showing it to my friends for laughs, but deep down I kind of mean it. It feels sort of like voodoo.

Jack moves on to affirmations. He says we must create these for ourselves and repeat them often. In the beginning of his career, his affirmation was:

> God is my infinite supply and large sums of money come to me quickly and easily under the grace of God for the highest good of all concerned. I am happily and easily earning, saving, and investing $100,000 a year.

Too bad I am such a knee-jerk Godophobe. As boring and predictable as the Godophiles, I get all bunched up when people start throwing around the word *God,* even if it's clear they only mean it as a code word for "a force that is bigger than me." You know how celebrities always thank God (after their agents) during award acceptance speeches? Well, I am pretty sure that I have officially heard as many people making fun of celebrities for thanking God as I have heard God being thanked at this point. Screw it. I can be different.

Even though I don't believe in one supreme and all-knowing being, I get Jack's gist and decide to spare the judgment. I applaud myself for making this leap, one I know I will have to make again and again to survive in this deity-heavy self-help world.

Some more simple advice Jack has is to greet every interaction in your life with the question: "What opportunity does this present to me?" Tomorrow I'm going to start substituting this for the more familiar "What does this person want from me?" and "Dude, you better not take my parking space." I spend the next few days attempting to find opportunity when purchasing produce and meats and when asking the neighborhood cat lady to stop throwing cardboard boxes, speckled with maggots and dried chunks of Friskies Senior Savory Beef, into our garbage can. I make an effort to smile more at people, not knowing if I should expect the opportunity to come in the form of a discount, recipe suggestion, or knock-knock joke.

While I'm filling up my car with gas, two teenage boys ask me if I will buy blunts for them. I take the opportunity to decline politely, presenting them with the opportunity to call me a "motherfucking white bitch" in front of Gus, who is fiddling in the nearby squeegee bucket. That, in turn, presents me with the unexpected opportunity to say in a strange shaky voice that is beyond my control, "Well, I certainly am white, that's true, but I'm not really a bitch. Ask anyone!"

I'm admittedly a little more frazzled than usual because my dad is going in for his surgery tomorrow. Even though it's supposedly a common procedure, he's sixty-eight and not in the greatest health. And then there's the fact that his own mother died directly following her open-heart surgery, one of the first ever performed. Most of all, I hate thinking of him all unconscious on a table, chest opened up, surgeons making wisecracks about him being fat like they do on hospital shows. Sometimes I wonder if doctors really talk that disparagingly about their patients, or if maybe they've started doing it to be more like their TV counterparts.

In an unprecedented moment of boldness that afternoon, I decide to call the Chicken Soup headquarters to see if I can coax some free e-coaching out of Jack. Perhaps some direct mentoring will do me good. I explain my project and even tell them that one of Jack's sons is a friend of mine. I am given a contact name to e-mail, a task I take care of promptly.

The next day, Gus and I go down to San Jose to visit my dad in the hospital. Eli feels bad that he can't come, but he's working. In shorthand, Eli is a workaholic, but when you're trying to get a small business off the ground, there's no other way around it. He takes whatever work comes his way—jazz, bluegrass, folk, reggae, rock—he records it all at his Oakland studio (which, in a nice synchronicity, happens to be called New, Improved Recording) any day of the week during any given twelve-hour period between 9:00 A.M. and 2:00 A.M. At this point, he hasn't had a day off in nearly three weeks.

The hospital smells like steamy Band-Aids and Mr. Clean. Gus hates it, but my mom distracts him with a game of Go Fish while I wander down the empty corridor to find my dad. I walk in the room and I'm shocked. He looks amazing, better than he has in months. His skin had taken on an odd grayish tone, like a pile of soggy newspapers, which is completely gone now. He clutches a giant, red, stuffed heart pillow to his chest like a kid. When he asks what I've been up to, I try to explain myself.

"I've decided to see if I can improve my life by following the advice of America's best-known self-help gurus."

He knows me too well. He thinks I'm joking! Even while severely medicated, he replies, "But seriously. Don't you ever wonder how nice it might be if you actually did try to improve your life?"

"God, Dad!" I huff. "Why do you think I'm actually doing it?" I unconsciously pull the stuffed heart from his chest and keep my focus on it while I talk. "Do you think I'm going to dedicate a year of my life to something that's a joke? Don't you think I wish I could fix my gutters? Pay my bills? Start exercising so I don't wind up . . . ?" Oops. I quickly apologize. I don't need an expert to tell me that I should definitely stop lapsing into teenage behavior, especially when someone I love is hooked up to several machines and has tubes threaded into each orifice.

With only a few days left in January, I turn off the light that night and lie in bed worrying. It's 1:00 A.M., and Eli is not home from the studio yet. I roll toward my $100,000 bill and envision big piles of dishwasher-shaped money falling from the sky. Then I get out of bed and pick up *The Success Principles* again.

I see a lot of myself in Canfield's chapter succinctly titled "Ask! Ask! Ask!" Most of my reasons for not asking for help or favors are in there: fear of rejection, not wanting to be seen as a bother, and my favorite, the almighty pride. I immediately get up the courage to send another e-mail to Mr. Canfield's office. "Get your head out of the sand and ask, ask, ask!" he exhorts. His coterie of fans, including Olympic bobsledders, chiropractors, supermodels, and Colonel Sanders, cannot all be wrong.

What I learn from this chapter is that I have been asking for Jack's help the wrong way. I need to ask as if I truly expect to get it. I need to assume that he will agree to help me. The best advice of all is that I can't be afraid to ask repeatedly. I fire off another e-mail about getting some free e-coaching.

What I've noticed is that a lot of the people Canfield uses as examples of success are other success and empowerment coaches, speakers, and authors. Many of the heartwarming stories end with phrases like "and now he has the time to spend building an airplane in the basement of his 7,000 square foot mansion." (That's an actual quote.) There is clearly money to be made in the inspiration business. Perhaps if I am able to inspire all the people who have previously doubted self-help, I can be in Mr. Canfield's club. I will never learn to golf, however. It is not one of the action items in the "101 Goals" binder I spent the morning making. Number one:

dishwasher. Number thirty-three (as far as I've gotten): learn to make good pork chops. Do I need to aim higher?

The old cynical me gets super-excited when I finally run into some really out-of-touch bullshit on page 170. Vinod Khosla, who is the founding CEO of Sun Microsystems, is quoted as saying, in reference to his goals for spending time with his family: "I track how many times I get home in time to have dinner with my family; my assistant reports the exact number to me each month."

And principle twenty-five stinks. "Drop out of the Ain't It Awful Club and surround yourself with successful people."

I have always found inspiration in people who wouldn't necessarily be described as "successful." What about the people who just aren't equipped to survive that well in a world that focuses on luxury goods, earning potentials, and superstars?

The next night I decide to spend some time before bed doing what Canfield calls the Mirror Exercise. I am supposed to look in the mirror and tell myself that I've done well that day. I am instructed to stay focused only on the positives. The example of Jack's own mirror exercise is excruciatingly detailed, step-by-step throughout the day, so I follow suit. My bathroom mirror is dirty. I clean it. Then I begin:

> Beth, I want to appreciate you for the following things today: First of all, you got up at 9:00 A.M. even though the last time you remembering looking at the clock from your chamber of insomnia it was 3:15. When Gus came into your room and demanded that you go into his room and find his glass of water, you sprang out of bed and went to go look for it instead of yelling at him. You only drank one cup of coffee instead of two and treated yourself to a piece of buttered toast even though you suspect that wheat makes your asthma flare up. You got to your office and refrained from wasting time/making self feel dirty by reading self-aggrandizing blog posts

by people you have met once or twice. When you walked out into the hallway and you and another woman reached the bathroom at the same time, you used the men's restroom so that she could use the women's. When there was no toilet paper, you wiped with the toilet seat cover (actually more of a light blotting) instead of the paper towels because there have been plumbing problems in the building and you know that you are not supposed to flush paper towels down the toilet. (I guess you could have put the paper towel in the garbage can like they do in some countries you have visited, but you don't know when the trash will be emptied again.) You went out to lunch with your friends and only told one critical story about someone, but it was the same one you told yesterday at lunch, to a different person, so that is probably minus points. But maybe plus points for recycling the story instead of putting a new unflattering story out in the world. You read a few chapters of your latest self-help manual before leaving on time to pick Gus up from school. You stayed and played on the playground even though you were sick to your stomach. You made Gus a healthy dinner, played trains with him, gave him a bath, and got him into bed by 8:00 P.M. Then you fell asleep in his bed because you were exhausted from not sleeping last night. When you woke up, the house was dark and quiet. Eli has since come home and gone to sleep. The two of you did not speak today except briefly on the phone to see who remembered to write the check for the Target gift card for the preschool teacher's baby shower. Neither of you did. And now you are standing here at 1:30 A.M. looking at yourself in the mirror. It is still dirty. You missed a few spots.

Jack says that it's not unusual to have a number of reactions the first time you do the Mirror Exercise. He says you might feel silly, embarrassed, or "like crying." Jack knows a lot.

It's not until his chapter "Keep Your Eye on the Prize," where he talks about how important the last forty-five minutes of the day are, that I actually remember an experience I have had with something he writes about—"imprinting." Supposedly your unconscious mind processes late-night information up to six times more often than other things you experience during the day. That's why, if you go to sleep right after watching the late-night news, you're likely to dream about discovering mutilated body parts that have been shoved inside an Igloo cooler and buried underneath the floorboards of a meth lab.

My senior year of high school my friend Nicole and I got ahold of a performance-enhancing audiocassette for athletes. We were on the track team and extremely competitive. Neither of us can remember where this "visualization" tape came from, but her stepdad was an orthodontist who dabbled in jazz and aviation, so clearly he is the prime suspect. We would listen to it before big track meets, sort of embarrassed by ourselves, but curious to see if it would work. I remember lying on my taupe-carpeted bedroom floor, looking up at the popcorn ceiling, listening to a soothing male voice guiding me through the set of actions I would take the next day, encouraging me to see myself winning my event. And it's true that that year, 1987, I broke my high school track team's long-jump record. That record still stands to this day. I actually think the tape might have worked. So what if I spent a few minutes each night "imprinting" about having a dishwasher or maintaining an orderly home?

Though I don't know much about self-help yet, remembering this story hammers it home that for any of these programs to work, I have to be committed. I have to believe. The other night I missed my train back home and went looking for someone to give me a ride across the Bay Bridge. I waited for an acquaintance to close up the bar she works at, and then we walked back to her truck. She told me her father recently died and he was her only family. She laughed and said she was basically "raised by wolves."

An artist and a bartender, she is still trying to figure out what path to take in her life. She seemed sad and overwhelmed. When I mentioned the life coach thing, she didn't even flinch.

"Oh yeah, I had one of those for a while."

"You had a life coach?" She seems so normal.

"Yeah. It didn't really work out, but at first I thought he could help me get my shit together."

The thing is, of course she's normal. And because she's normal, she is just looking for ways to improve her life, even though the obstacles, including asking for help from an outside party, can seem insurmountable. If you pay someone a fistful of dough to help you make your life better, when it doesn't get better it's easy to write the whole thing off as a scam or simply "not for you."

By the way, good time to mention that a few friends have expressed concern that I will become "brainwashed" by this whole experiment.

When I wake up the next morning, I have an e-mail from the Chicken Soup HQ! Unfortunately, it says that due to the newness of the e-coaching program, they are not able to offer it to me for free. So now I have to either pony up the $300 or trust that reading Jack's advice truly is the next best thing to in-person coaching. I decide to skip the e-mail mentoring and keep reading.

Another e-mail from the desk of Jack Canfield arrives! I've been added to their mailing list. This one is pitching a new film called *The Secret*, something Jack says "may be the most exciting worldwide film event in history." It is also noted that due to third-party contractual restrictions, users in Australia, New Zealand, and Papua New Guinea will not be able to watch the movie or purchase DVDs at this time. Sounds . . . controversial.

I'm starting to feel better by actively using my good attitude to look for possibility and opportunity instead of being cowed by all my perceptible problems and faults. Last night I tried employing Jack's advice of simply asking for what you want. Eli and I were at an after-party-type thing for the San Francisco Sketch Comedy Festival and found ourselves standing next to comedians from a prematurely canceled HBO series that I loved. Normally, I would never strike up a conversation with semifamous people. I usually get intimidated and pretend not to recognize them, mostly to cut down on awkwardness, but also as a sign of immaturity on my part. I once was told Céline Dion was having dinner at the table next to me, and I refused to sneak a peek at her for the entire two hours I was there. *You guys probably get stared at all the time,* I thought, *so I'm going to pretend I have no clue who the fuck you are.* Exhilarating, though pretty sophomoric. And this was different. These were relatively obscure comedians whom I actually admire.

Eli plays no such games. He asked two of the writer-actor guys what they were currently working on, curious if there was anything we could look forward to watching. Now, I'm sure living in Los Angeles puts people on the defensive about their careers, but I thought it came across pretty clear that we were asking them as fans, not to judge what kind of work they were getting. Anyway, they didn't seem to want to talk to us that much after that, but one of the guys mentioned a comic book he was writing for. That's when it dawned on me. I was putting together a reading at the Hammer Museum at UCLA the following month, and I needed actors to read from "fan fiction" stories—stories that people write starring their favorite characters from comic books. If he was into comics, maybe he'd like to do it.

"Just tell him about it," Eli said, nudging me. "You never know."

So I gave him the lowdown, telling him what a fan I was, and tried graciously to pose the question of whether he'd like to take part. He didn't seem that enthusiastic and mumbled something about possibly being out of town for WonderCon, the big comic book convention, but he gave me his e-mail address and turned away. Of course I didn't e-mail him. Baby steps.

A couple of nights later, our new DVD from Netflix comes. I had forgotten that on one of those nights when I'd sat in front of the computer with a large goblet of wine, I had lined up about fifty movies in our queue. The one that arrives is a documentary of three comedians touring the country, playing in rock clubs as opposed to two-drink-minimum Laugh Factory comedy clubs. One of the featured comedians is the guy whose e-mail address was still sitting in the pocket of my jeans.

"Did you e-mail him about the show?" Eli asks. "What did he say?"

I duck down in my seat like I'm anticipating a smack in the face. "I never e-mailed him."

"What about your new, improved life?"

If we were on a reality TV show, I would do that thing people do where they firmly flip the bird, in your face, all stony and silent, letting the finger do the talking, but instead I just ignore him. A bit later in the movie, when they show a scene at the comedian's house, it turns out he has an entire room devoted to his massive comic book collection. Walls of them! Then a few minutes later, they show him comic book shopping while on tour.

"You have to e-mail him," Eli says. "The museum show is all about comic books, isn't it? He wouldn't have given you his e-mail address if he wasn't interested."

Maybe getting this movie in the mail is a sign about an opportunity being presented to me.

The next day I spend at least fifteen solid minutes crafting a solicitous e-mail to the comedian. How I don't want to bother him, but after I saw the film, I was compelled to contact him. I even mention that he met me with my husband so he isn't weirded out that I might be trying to stalk him. I hit Send. And then I never hear back.

I take a look at his e-mail address again: partybummer@____.com. I realize that this is probably the address he gives out to annoying people at parties. As in "what a party bummer it was having you ask me for my e-mail. Please write me at this address, which may or may not be real, but is silently insulting you." Prescreened. So I guess I did learn a lesson. Not about getting what you ask for, but rather how to prescreen your e-mail for idiots who are bothering you at a party while you're trying to talk to your friends. That's a pretty smart trick. So I just registered the address youreharshingmybuzz@yahoo.com. If you want me to ignore you, shoot me an e-mail.

But seriously, the real party bummer is the rejection. I go back to Jack's chapter "Ask! Ask! Ask!" He writes, "How do you go about bouncing back from rejection? When do you decide that maybe your idea/project is actually not interesting?" Harsh.

Jack says that when you get rejected you can turn the beat around and expect something better to come of it. The irony is not lost that if I keep getting rejected by Jack Canfield, the more ammunition I will have that this self-help stuff is bunk, that visualizing what you want doesn't really work. But in wanting the self-help project to succeed, I also need to succeed. Jack writes:

> Everyone wants financial abundance, a comfortable home, meaningful work they enjoy, good health, time to do the things they love, nurturing relationships with their families and friends, and an opportunity to make a difference in the world. But too few of us readily admit it.

That is definitely part of my problem. It goes against my nature to admit that I want all those things. So I accept this rejection and wait for something better.

February

A CAREER-DEFINING MOMENT

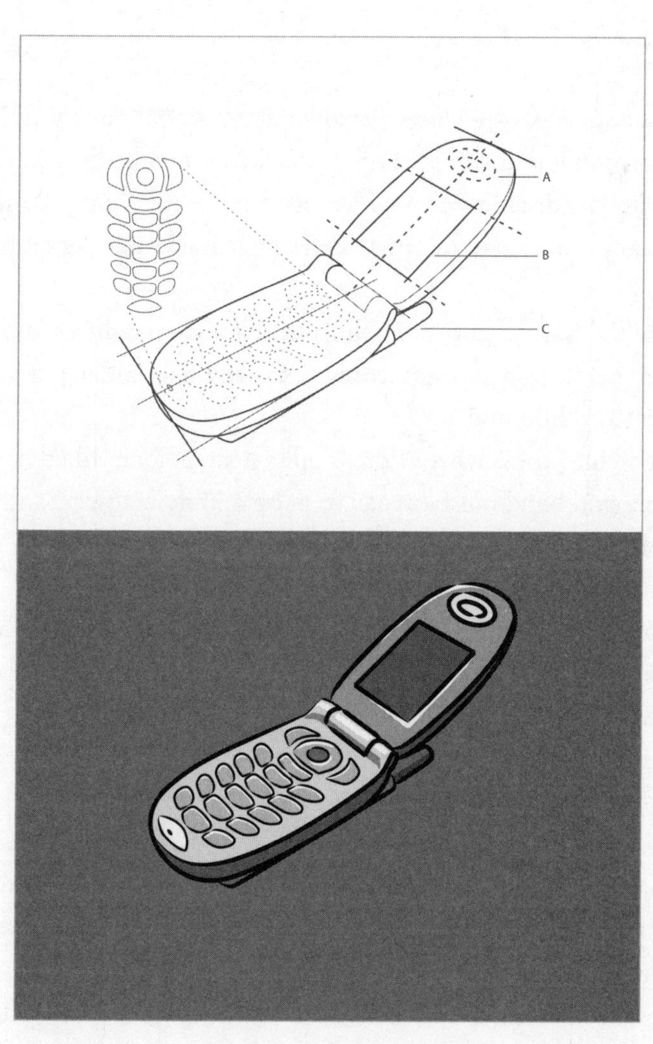

The car is making a *chunka-chunka* noise. For about a week, I've been doing that thing where I just turn the radio up extra loud while I'm driving because we don't have any money to fix it. Finally, I decide to tell Eli. I know he'll make sure I get it to the shop.

"Okay," I say, "I guess we can put it on the credit card, but I can't take it in tomorrow morning because I have a banana job."

This stops him midshave.

A "banana job" is where I dress up in a large, foam-filled banana costume and hand out bananas to people in downtown San Francisco. I did it once a few years ago and wrote a story about it for my last book.

"Wait. You're doing another banana job?" The way he says it makes me defensive.

"Well, yeah. Why not?"

"I just thought, you know, you already used it for material. Why would you do it again?"

"It's a job!" I sputter. I'm flustered. My whole approach to the banana suit was to embrace the ridiculous nature of it, to enjoy the liberation of not being ashamed of it, but here I am second-guessing myself.

It's true that we desperately need any income we can get, but maybe Eli has a point. If I'm trying to have a career as a writer, and I'm still not positive if I am, maybe I should spend more time networking and hustling for writing jobs. Maybe I should finally curb my proclivity for accepting whatever random employment falls in my lap and *focus*. But the banana job pays $25 an hour. That's more than I get paid to write most of the time. Plus, I do enjoy the work.

"I could never do that," people would say to the banana, huffing past me with weird, sad smiles on their faces as I held a piece of fruit in my outstretched palm.

"You couldn't pay me enough to do that job," they'd mumble, just loud enough for me to hear.

Being the banana made me feel like I had a special talent, like I was doing something a lot of people couldn't do. Couldn't or wouldn't. It's a tough call, but I'll argue that many people who say they *could* dress in a banana suit but just choose not to, actually could not even physically subject themselves to the (perceived) humiliation of the job.

But what was I doing exactly? With my career. I was happy with what I'd managed to accomplish so far. I had published a few books, made a record with my band, written a weekly nightlife column for eight years, and toured all over the United States and Europe as a spoken-word performer. Weren't these the years that I should be building something solid out of that? Something I could live on? What were my goals? I thought it was borderline farcical to be a freelance banana the first time around at age thirty-four, and now look at me. I mean, sure, when I'm sixty I can take it up again, because everybody knows that nothing could be funnier than a senior banana. But it was obvious that I could not have, nor did I want, a full-fledged banana career.

Eli's pulling his shirt on, a blue T-shirt that used to feature an iron-on appliqué of a rainbow, back when we first started going out. Now the rainbow is gone, melted and shredded by the dryer. It's just a few silvery specks sprinkled across his chest.

"Well, I guess you should probably take it. Did I tell you I'm finally going to quit teaching?"

Uh-oh. In addition to working at his studio, Eli teaches recording about fifteen hours a week at a nearby technical college. Even though we still have to pay for our own health insurance, his teaching paycheck is the only steady income we have. About once a month he can write himself a check from his business, but the overhead is pretty high because there is a never-ending stream of new equipment to buy and obscure vintage gear to be repaired. Still, he's been starting to feel like he has to make the leap. He wants to put all of his time and energy into New, Improved to see if it will fly. Intellectually, it makes sense. Financially, it's spooky.

"I totally understand," I say. "I just wish one of us was normal."

"Hey!" he says, changing the subject. "New month, huh? So what is it? What are you going to fix now?"

I glance over at my $100,000 bill. Have I fixed anything yet? I mean, besides the kitchen table.

Given the preceding conversation, I don't want to say what I'm about to say. "I think I'm supposed to be, uh, working on my career."

"Well, that's great. Your career is basically just being yourself."

I love this man, but I can't let him get away with it. His unique perception of me also includes repeated purchases of underwear for me in a size small.

"You mean kind of like Paris Hilton?" I reply, trying so very very hard to fart on cue. It's not happening, so I make the sound with my mouth instead.

"Hey!" A great idea has just struck. "Just think how much more fun the world would be if every time someone said, 'Paris Hilton,' a loud farting honk could be heard in the distance. Like a new kind of punctuation."

These are the kinds of moneymaking ideas I'm good at coming up with.

Careening through my late thirties, my only proven vocation is foraging for multiple $100 or $200 paychecks, so that hopefully at the end of the month I will have enough dough to make my half of the bills. But I never do. I'm on a career path where I stare longingly at paper towels in the grocery store and almost start crying when the woman in front of me at the checkout buys $534 of stuff that fits into three bags. Last week my friend told me about someone's $15,000 bathroom remodel, and my endocrine glands started dumping adrenaline into my bloodstream. I got the shakes. I wanted to make a citizen's arrest.

I have set aside the month of October to delve into the sorry state of my personal finances, but it's obvious what I need to do right now. I need some serious career counseling or I'll be writing the final chapters of this book from my childhood bedroom after moving back in with my parents.

I check around and decide to consult one of the masters of American business coaching, Stephen Covey, author of the megabestseller *The Seven Habits of Highly Effective People: Powerful Lessons in Personal Change*. When I get on the BART at 7:30 the next morning, wearing Easy Spirit shoes with Velcro closures for my long day of banana distribution, I start reading.

In the first few pages, Covey talks about the last two hundred years of "success writing." I always placed the genesis of that stuff in the 1950s, but it becomes clear that what I'm thinking of is the more recent glut of books with "quick fix" solutions to life's problems. In the previous 150 years, this genre focused on character ethics like integrity, humility, patience, simplicity, and modesty. All those things associated with Benjamin Franklin's autobiography (not to be confused with a collection of Franklin's satirical writings entitled *Fart Proudly*.) Covey says what he's found is that there are basic principles of effective living and that people can only experience "true success and enduring happiness as they learn and integrate these principles into their basic character."

I scope out the train. We're a bunch of commuters looking alternately glum and tired, anxiety-ridden, engrossed, annoyed, or reasonably satisfied. The only people who look overtly happy are the Down's syndrome guy and his minder, whispering in each other's ears about something awesome as the train disappears underground.

I am feeling kind of moved and embarrassed. What an old-fashioned idea to strive to have a strong and humble character. Who does that anymore? Is it wrong to look to a self-help book to help you improve your character? What feels like my inner core is telling me it's pretty weak. Let's say I was reading a novel and the situation and characters in that story inspired me to strive to be a better person (not the reason I usually read)—that would be infinitely more palatable to me. This nakedly didactic "how-to" stuff seems strictly for losers, yet if it's making me feel something in my guts, I must be, in some regards, one of those losers. Why is my ego so resistant to accepting it?

When Covey says that after World War I the focus in success writing (I will now take off the ironic quotes) moved away from character and toward personality, he's onto something. Like one long infomercial, the self-help genre shifted toward accentuating things like smiling, looking happy, thinking positively, and a host of bumper-stickerific adages like "Whatever the mind of man can conceive and believe, it can achieve!" He seems to be saying, in not so many words, that a lot of the new books are bullshit. And I'd like to think he might make a farting sound, at least in his mind, when one of his nine children or forty-seven grandchildren mentions Paris Hilton's name. Yes, Covey is a serious Mormon. More on that later.

He emphasizes not coming across as cheesy and slick, because we would automatically distrust him. He knows he would essentially be a fraud. So maybe I was getting a little ahead of myself beginning with Jack Canfield, whose philosophy seems to take the Seven Habits as a springboard. Covey sums up those who focus on the personality ethic, as opposed to the character ethic, with the Emerson quote "What you are shouts so loudly in my ears I cannot hear what you say." As I'm reading this, in a nice trick of synchronicity, a crazy guy wearing wrist guards made of orange juice cans gets on board the train and starts shouting something about a "conflagration situation" in a female passenger's "bagineous regions." He's yelling and pointing at her crotch. It's excruciating to watch. I step off, the mulchy smell of wet paper and damp sweaters wafting around me, thinking about paradigms.

Covey urges us to understand them and to recognize when they need to shift, but I can't figure out what in my life could change as drastically as Copernicus trumping Ptolemy by revealing that the sun, not the earth, was the center of the universe. Having a clean closet? Paying off my credit card?

Part of the Seven Habits master plan is to simply start acting like you are the kind of person who has your shit together, remembering not to put personality before character.

I always thought your character was something you were born with, but according to Covey, it is a composite of your habits, things that are so ingrained in you they are often difficult to determine. He throws four habits out there—procrastination, impatience, criticalness, and selfishness, which sound pretty familiar to these ears. These are also the things that give us a sense of pseudosecurity, or to use Canfield's term, they can make up our "comfort zone." We need to understand that independence is not supreme, that interdependence is what is valuable. This is a huge problem for me because I am resistant to taking other people's advice, especially advice that claims to work for everybody else. But I guess I am just like everybody else. This is an idea I need to get used to because being interdependent is how Covey says I will achieve the greatest success.

Finally, on page 51, I get to the first golf reference! I knew these guys had a special club.

So here is a summary of the Seven Habits, described with the least amount of sarcasm possible.

HABIT 1: Be Proactive The basic idea here is that you are responsible for your own life. Don't be the kind of person who is in a crappy mood because it's too windy outside or your co-worker prattles on about her baby shower and it's enraging. Bring your own weather with you. You can't control how other people treat you, but you do have the power to control your response to them. Always remember: in this life, you get to be you. I don't know if Covey would endorse this part, but whenever somebody is a jerk to me, I always think, *At least I am me, while that asshole has to spend his whole life being him.*

HABIT 2: Begin with the End in Mind Imagine your funeral will be three years from today. What do you want people to say about you and your life?

A huge cliché, but take a minute to actually visualize it. *She could do the splits on both sides.* This immediately makes me think of a friend of ours who was struck and killed by a car while riding his bike to work a few years ago. Matthew Sperry truly was an exemplary person—kind and passionate, creative and committed, fair and funny and smart. An exceptional bass player, he made music with Tom Waits and MacArthur genius Anthony Braxton, as well as all the hotshots on the Bay Area new music scene. He even donned raccoon makeup and got a fancy new haircut for his onstage role in the San Francisco production of *Hedwig and the Angry Inch*. When he was killed, leaving behind his wife and two-year-old daughter, there was a huge emotional outpouring, as you'd expect when someone so beloved dies tragically and young. But losing Matthew was different. To this day, a large community of people continue to honor his memory with concerts and reference him in conversation almost as frequently as if he were alive. It sounds harsh, but he really was a better person than most people are. It's uncomfortable to think about how, if you died, would there still be people five years from now talking about how enjoyable or inspiring you were?

Part of this habit is developing a personal mission statement, essentially a personal philosophy about who you want to be and what you want to do. Live a principle-centered life instead of one centered around yourself, pleasure, an enemy, your spouse, or your friends. Principles are deep fundamental truths that, unlike people, won't steal your car, call you fat, or wake up handcuffed to you in a strange bed wearing a rubber mask.

HABIT 3: Put First Things First This one kind of threw me because there are a lot of "charts" and "quadrants" involved in this chapter, as well as diagrams and a spreadsheet. My brother, who works in advertising, has always told me to stop listening immediately the minute someone throws up a PowerPoint slide with complex human interactions boiled down to an *x* and *y* axis, but I give Covey the benefit of the doubt. Mostly because he did it first—twenty years before it got debased to sell spray-on salad dressing.

HABIT 4: Think Win-Win You will succeed by using the Golden Rule. Seek out mutually beneficial arrangements in all of your human interactions. "It's not your way or my way; it's a better way, a higher way." Work from a paradigm of abundance instead of one of scarcity. There is plenty for everybody, and if you're the kind of person who is afraid to tell people about an amazing hole-in-the-wall sushi joint because you're scared they will ruin it for you, then you have a gaping hole in your character pants.

HABIT 5: Seek First to Understand, Then to Be Understood Be an empathic listener. Don't read your own autobiography into other people's lives. If someone says, "I'm way over budget on my $15,000 bathroom remodel," don't say, "Sorry about that, Chad. My house is infested with black mold spores, but I feel ridiculous complaining about it after reading this morning's article about the boy with no legs who crawled across the desert to flee Mogadishu." Try to remember that for Chad, hiring a lazy and incompetent contractor is his own personal Guernica.

HABIT 6: Synergize Generate a new force field of awesomeness by incorporating differing opinions and ideas to create a third alternative to the either-or mentality. Covey gets kind of hardcore on this one and says that if you can't learn to work with differences around you, you are boring, uncreative, and insecure. Synergy may sound like a frightening word only used by politicians, capitalists, healers, and coaches, and well . . . that's probably still true.

HABIT 7: Sharpen the Saw This is the habit of renewal. Get exercise for your physical well-being, pray or meditate for your spiritual well-being, read and write to expand your mental well-being, and renew your social/emotional well-being by using habits 4, 5, and 6. Treat other people well, listen to what they're saying, and affirm them. This George Bernard Shaw quote sums it up nicely: "This is the true joy in life—the being used for a purpose recognized by yourself as a mighty one; the being a force of nature, instead of a feverish, selfish little clod of ailments and grievances complaining that the world will not devote itself to making you happy."

So. You can go ahead and call it the cheesy deep thoughts of a cultish Mormon grandpa, but I think it sounds pretty good. I'm still having a hard time, though, not being a little irked about the very idea that people have to be given guidelines on how to live their lives. Not that there shouldn't be standards, but it seems counterintuitive to make them a commodity.

I decide what I need to do is go see Stephen Covey in the flesh, so I register for his next speaking engagement, popping a make-believe Dilaudid under my tongue as I charge the $699 on my credit card. And that's the "early bird" price. At this point, I have received some money to document my year of self-help in print. After paying off debts, I vow to use the rest of the money for research. A booming voice in my head, echoing from some long-ago situation that was surely uncomfortable, is reminding me, "You gotta spend money to make money." If I simply read self-help books, I'm not going to have the full experience. So now I'm signed up for the Twelfth Annual International FranklinCovey Symposium.

Who's Franklin anyway? Maybe Covey's silent partner. I imagine a loose cannon Mennonite drinker who is constantly crashing company cars and trashing hotel suites. Covey's people probably work hard to keep his name out of the papers. I enjoy this version for three or four minutes before moving on.

FranklinCovey. I do recognize the name and logo from some mall-like situation—maybe the new complex in Emeryville that is supposed to evoke an "urban village" feeling. As if you are wandering out onto Main Street to hear ye olde town crier at the Banana Republic before dining at Fuddruckers. It dawns on me that I have just spent close to a month's income on something I associate with Sunglass Hut.

My first collateral material arrives a few days later. It reads:

> This year's theme is Sustained Superior Performance: Lead, Focus, Win! Almost all organizations want to achieve and maintain superior performance. In practice, however, few

actually do. This year's theme recognizes the critical role leaders' [*sic*] play, at all levels, in engaging people throughout their organizations, and focusing their best efforts toward the achievement of their organization's most important goals.

- You will learn the foundations of long-term organizational performance and growth from Jack Welch, the man *Fortune* magazine names "Manager of the Century." He will share how General Electric was able to sustain superior performance during his tenure as CEO, and you will learn how to apply these principles in your organization.
- FranklinCovey senior consultants will share new findings about the three key "drivers" of superior execution learned from FranklinCovey's work deep within the operations of hundreds of organizations, the analysis of data from hundreds of thousands of individual respondents, and the results of deep interviews with the members of more than 1,000 teams.
- Stephen R. Covey, author of the best-selling business book of all time, *The 7 Habits of Highly Effective People,* and his newest best seller, *The 8th Habit—From Effectiveness to Greatness,* will discuss key ways in which you can find your own "voice" or unique contribution within your organization and help others to make theirs.

And at the bottom: "Dress code is business casual."

I start to panic.

In the days preceding the conference I toy with the idea of thrifting some appropriate business casual slacks and sensible working-lady shoes. Maybe I could wear my Easy Spirit banana shoes and a smart blazer. I imagine creating a persona whom I could name Deb or Trish, a woman who is looking to build her team of marketing consultants back at the industrial furniture wholesaler or really whip those clowns in accounts receivable into shape. In the end, though, I realize if I am going to take this somewhat seriously, I should go as myself. When asked to fill in the space indicating my employment position, I went for it. "Beth Lisick," I typed. "Position: President."

I get a round-trip ticket to Chicago for $289 and arrange to stay with my sister-in-law's family. They live in the Old Town neighborhood, which is about a half hour by public transport to McCormick Place, but by not staying at the official conference hotel, the Hyatt, I'm saving $460. Feels highly effective. When I arrive at their house Monday evening, my hosts gently hint around that they'd rather not be included if I were to write about this experience. They are both lawyers and incredibly smart, but hopefully I can say this: thanks for the delicious steak dinner, Stephen and Susan. You're the best.

Day One The next morning, I oversleep and get to the convention center a half hour late. Still, it's only 7:30 A.M. when I arrive; there's a full half hour of continental breakfast and networking time before the opening remarks. The place is packed with close to a thousand people. Instantly, I understand that "business casual" is simply code for "khaki pants and a braided leather belt."

I feel relieved that the seminar is so large, absolving me of any intimate contact with other people. Still, I feel awkward. Like I don't fit in. I've chosen to wear a pair of gray pants and a black blouse, but it devastates me that I cannot mask my inner slacker even when I've pulled my hair back into a neat ponytail and gotten my toes done. There is just something slouchy and unkempt that resides very deeply in my DNA. Something that says, "I probably use the copy machine for personal use and don't refill the paper tray when I'm done." But you know what? I have always been a paper tray refiller. As anyone knows, if you are refilling the paper tray, you are not sitting at your desk doing work.

I move through the clusters of people holding coffee cups and consulting their conference schedules, trying to catch snippets of conversation. "Your team is going down!" I hear a young guy with floppy blond hair say to his female co-worker. High-five. Then I realize that most people are attending the seminar with other employees from their companies. Everybody seems to have a convention buddy except me.

I sit down by an escalator with my coffee and watch everyone. Now I wish I were staying in the hotel. I've read about these things called "business conventions" where Frank in accounting and Maria in marketing decide to consummate the last seven months of flirting by the oversized popcorn barrel after having too many kamikazes at the piano bar. I want to be in on the joke when the guy with the Lexus whom everybody hates gets drunk and calls a local escort agency but passes out before the arrival of his date, who then wakes up everyone else on the floor by pounding on his door with the heel of her open-toed platform jelly. I want to be where the action is, but will try to remember Habit 2 and forgo those self-centered desires with the big picture in mind.

Idea: new catchphrase for FranklinCovey T-shirts.

I give the lady at the registration table my name, and she hands me a black laptop bag emblazoned with the FranklinCovey logo and those of the event's sponsors, one of which is Executive Book Summaries, a company that condenses business books down to their essentials, which usually comes in at about eight pages. Basically Cliff's Notes for busy entrepreneurs.

Even just putting the name tag around my neck feels strange. BETH LISICK, PRESIDENT. Whenever I'm given a name tag, for any social occasion, I won't wear it. Someone will hand it to me, and I put it in my pocket every time. Even when I was writing a column and would be given backstage passes at clubs, I would put the thing in my pocket. Then, if someone needed to see it, I would pull it out, show it to them, and put it back in my pocket. It always felt like bragging to walk around with an all-access pass stuck to your body. But especially in this case, I recognize it's just me being childish. Everyone else is wearing a name tag. If I don't put mine on, it will look like I'm trying to be different, that I have trouble being interdependent. If I accomplish anything in these two days, I want to make it okay for myself to wear a lanyard. Paradigm, get ready to shift.

As luck would have it, the first person I see when I walk into the Grand Ballroom is Stephen Covey, sitting at one of the tables by the door. At least I think that's him. Dressed in a dark suit with a high waxy shine on his bald head, he is holding forth at a table full of attractive women. [Insert polygamy jokes here.] All the tables close to the front are filled, so I find one with an empty chair midway back. My tablemates are two stereotypical white "nerds," their chambray shirts tucked in but slightly billowing over their relaxed-fit waistlines, cell phones clipped to their belts, one of which is braided. To the left of me is a young black woman with short hair, showing her co-workers, three middle-aged white ladies, the new FranklinCovey planner she just bought out in the lobby. (All items from the FranklinCovey store are priced at a 20 percent discount throughout the conference!)

I watch a tall, angular man with glasses, about forty, stroll slowly across the floor, hands clasped in front of him, head lolling this way and that. Every few seconds his small mouth opens as wide as it can and he booms out a greeting. "Welcome!" he yells. "Welcome, gentlemen!" He wanders into our vicinity and expels a mighty "Good morning to you all! Welcome!"

He's bad. Robotic. It's as if somewhere in his training he was told to perform this task but didn't make the connection that when the time came, he would actually be addressing real people. I start laughing, not only because this is the exact kind of behavior I expected to see from a "Lead, Focus, Win!" seminar, but because I am suddenly reminded of a production of *A Christmas Carol* I was in during winter break in seventh grade.

Throughout the rehearsals, the boy playing Scrooge would walk over to where the fireplace was going to be and busy himself with throwing some fake logs on it. Then he would fake-warm his hands on it. Every rehearsal, same thing. It looked more like he was doing a rapid cat's cradle with an invisible piece of yarn than lifting logs.

On the night of the show, as I stood there dressed in a ruffly white blouse, black vest, and corduroy knickers, Scrooge got up and harrumphed over to the fireplace, which was now actually a prop we could all see. And he proceeded to do the exact same thing he had done time and time again in rehearsal. He trod the boards across the stage, leaned down a bit, not very close to the fireplace at all, and, while delivering a curmudgeonly monologue, started rolling his hands around, not unlike someone trying to unwrap foil from a hot potato in slow motion.

Of course I burst out laughing right there in the middle of the performance, cementing the fact that I would never have what it takes to be a real thespian. All I could think of were the people in the audience. If you were sitting there and didn't know that his stage direction said "tend to the fire," you would have had *no idea* what that boy was spazzing out for.

This was a pivotal moment in my life, an effective lesson in personal change. A paradigm shift of sorts. For the past twenty-five years, I have thought of that incident at least once every month whenever I see someone going through the motions without really being alive or present. I often catch myself fake-tending a fake fire. So I think of it again when I see this guy roaming around pressing the flesh, his stage direction of "creating a warm feeling on the convention floor" painfully obvious.

A pleasant, prerecorded female voice comes over the sound system and says, "The general session is going to begin in five minutes." Slightly sci-fi. Some light alternative rock is playing, too low and too current for me to identify. A woman in a soft tan suede jacket and chocolate brown suede gauchos saunters by talking into her BlackBerry. I flip through the bios of the instructors and see lines like "Andy is a Master Gardener with a passion for homemade salsa" and "Blaine and his sweetheart live in a country home near Salt Lake City, Utah, where he relishes his time as a deliberate dad."

The pleasant voice returns. "The general session is going to begin in one minute." I count it down. Exactly sixty seconds later, the lights dim, the crowd of a thousand hushes, and the unmistakable first notes of the song "My Sharona" kick in. *Ba-na-na-na-NA-na Na-na-na-na-NAH-na.* Out onto the stage walks the professional greeter, who unfortunately is just as mechanical and stiff when addressing a large crowd. *Oh my little pretty one! Pretty one!* This isn't going so well. Or, rather, this is going exactly as I might have imagined it.

He asks us to stand as the Chicago Honor Guard and a brass quartet "post the colors." Two giant screens alternate between displaying the action onstage and playing B-roll of an American flag waving in the breeze. Robot Man is possibly a holograph. He quickly introduces Bill Bennett, resident of Salt Lake City and the president of the Organizational Solutions Business Unit for FranklinCovey, whose bio states that he once successfully moved his former company from a loss position to consistent profitability over five quarters while achieving 44 percent revenue growth. Let's hear it for Bill! Bennett is a likable guy, a clean-cut white guy with a slight lisp who promises that over the next two days we will each experience at least one "career-defining moment" that will lead to "sustained superior performance." I look down at how my name tag is hanging around my neck and feel pretty good already. I like Bill. If I had any doubts that this conference was for me, Bill lets us know that it is for anybody. And everybody. Whether you are a fourth-grade teacher or a Boy Scout troop leader or an athletic coach—even, Bennett says, if your job is "making sure that pieces of mail are delivered appropriately"—this $699 conference, not including airfare, hotel, and evening meals, is for you. He then introduces the keynote speaker, Jack Welch, who has been named CEO of the Century. Before he leaves the stage, Bennett reminds us that FranklinCovey's goal is to "enable greatness in people and organizations everywhere." I can't help but be struck by the language. He says he wants to help me to be great. I want to find out how sincere he is.

"*I'm coming up, so you better get this party started!*"

The music is cranked for Jack's entrance. I think of the episode of *The Office* in which David Brent dances between cubicles singing this exact same song to his employees. I look at my plate and think, *Irony omelet with irony sauce on the side.*

Straight off, it's easy to see why people love Jack Welch, especially in the Dilberty business world where there are millions of conformists to every renegade. In a sit-down Q&A session with FranklinCovey associate Jennifer Colosimo (whose bio states she has thirteen years of value-based change management under her belt!), Mr. Welch presents the kind of sound-bitey tough talk that people love. Some gems include:

"You need to find something that really turns your crank, and things will fall into place from there!"

"I get a hell of a kick out of it!"

"Let 'er rip!"

"No more jackass leaders!"

His voice is quickly getting raspy.

"Screw it!" he goes on. "It's ass-backwards!"

Every time he lets loose with one of these zingers, the audience hoots and hollers.

I am not surprised to learn that he now provides "color commentary" for the Boston Red Sox. He gets a big cheer when he talks about how he never understood the business models for many companies during the dot-com boom.

"I couldn't explain why some kid in Palo Alto needed a BMW in order to sign with a company."

More laughs and applause.

You would think he was doing a headlining set at McCrackers in the strip mall. In the end, though, he tells Jennifer, as the FranklinCovey logo quivers on a screen above them, that the way to get recognized is by the "reflected glory of your people." The takeaway: treat your employees well and they're going to make you look good. So for me, it means "Treat yourself well and you will make yourself look good"?

It's now time for our "break-out sessions," and I choose to attend one called "Take Your Life Back with Judy Henrichs." Briefly, the hour-and-ten-minute session explains the "see do get" method of achieving your dreams. First, we need to change our paradigm so that we can have a vision of what we want. Then, with our behavior, we do things to make that happen, thereby getting the desired results. You want coffee, so you buy the beans, grind them up, and drink it. Or something. Also, spunky, flame-haired Judy wants you to know: "My husband, Fred, is the most wonderful man in the world. Sorry, guys! Title's taken!"

During the break, I get a text from my sister-in-law's brother Daniel, asking me if I want to go to a Cubs game with him. Hell yes. Only seven more hours to go.

For my next break-out sesh, I choose one called "Championing Diversity" because I really don't want to go to "Build Compelling Scoreboards" or "The Six Most Important Decisions Teens Will Ever Make." The best thing about this session is that I sit next to Kelanie Simonson from Madison, Wisconsin, who describes her job as "an event coordinator for a group of industrial laundries." She is super-nice with an indelible Wisconsin accent and has taken this workshop because she doesn't work with any people of any color, or really know any at all, and it disturbs her. The retired police chief who facilitates the session seems like a cool guy but has this familiar elementary school teacher's habit.

"People have very, very long what? Long *memories*. Our memories are very, very what? Very *long*, that's right. Now, when Bruce Banner turned into the Hulk, it was because he became very what? He became very *angry*, that's right."

In the end, I learn that the first reason to embrace diversity is because it is the right thing to do. And number two? It's the law of the land. And our nation was founded to give equal opportunity to whom? To everyone. That's right.

It's lunchtime. I walk back to the ballroom and see that McCormick Place is already getting ready for the next incoming seminar: "The Society of the Plastics Industry Inc. presents NPE, The International Plastics Showcase." That might be where the real party is.

Things improve dramatically when I arrive back in the ballroom later in the day for the cocktail party to find plates of fried mozzarella sticks, spicy wings, *and* potato skins. It's as if T.G.I. Friday's is catering the whole thing. (No jalapeño poppers or blooming onions, though.) I pile up my plate, get a beer, and sit next to Susan Sandberg, a FranklinCovey instructor from Dayton who teaches leadership skills in the U.S. Air Force. She tells me, "It's not a big deal to teach a dog to roll over. You've got to teach a dog to teach a dog to roll over!" This breaks the ice for our other tablemates, a veterinarian and her office manager from the western Chicago suburbs, to regale us with their highlight reel of stupid things that pets have eaten that look really cool in X-rays. Such as the pit bull who swallowed a steak knife, the cat who ate the candle snuffer, and the snake who swallowed three lightbulbs. We're having a good time carbo-loading and talking about our kids, but I tell them I've got to leave to go to a baseball game.

"Cubs?" the veterinarian asks, barely able to get the word out without looking like she's going to barf up her mini-quiche. "Cubs fans are horrible."

I look at the office manager a little helplessly.

"The worst," she says. "Idiots."

"Sox," the vet says definitively and looks at her pal for backup.

"Sox," the other one says.

I pull a Covey and consciously decide to brush off their bad attitudes. My "maturity continuum" has now progressed to the point where I understand loyalty to sports teams.

"Great meeting you guys!" I smile and head out to the ballpark.

They curse me behind my back.

At one point, deep into the game when the Cubs are down 6–1, a combination of beer, agitation, and perhaps an increasing need to stay warm catalyzes the crowd into a chant of "Let's go, Cubbies!" *Clap-clap-clapclapclap*. I think of my grandfather, who died when I was eleven. He was from Illinois and went by the name of Cubby, which was given to him by his fellow coal miners, most of whom were black, because when he took off his goggles, he had prominent white circles around his eyes. Cubby Lisick, Coal Miner.

A sense of despair mounts as I think about the very real work he did versus this personal growth "work" I am paying over a thousand dollars to do. My parents were the first in their families to go to college, and here I am, flying halfway across the country to hammer out my "personal mission statement." It seems like the curse of a certain class, having the free time and energy to devote to your "emotional bank account" and "synergistic communication." Not that I want to romanticize my grandfather's life, though by all reports he had a good one. He was also, apparently, somewhat of a "real-life Archie Bunker," as my dad would joke, right down to his favorite chair and a slight aversion to dark-skinned people. He probably could have used a "Championing Diversity" seminar more than Kelanie, but that doesn't mean he wasn't a good man, even if he never spent a second analyzing his "circle of concern."

Daniel returns with the greatest hot dog I've ever had and internal order is semi-restored. When we get back to the house, I pass out. Constantly monitoring the vital signs of your life is a chore. Though when I did my chores as a kid, I got an allowance. Hopefully, what I get in return will be enough to pay myself back for the seminar and plane ticket.

Day Two I arrive at the convention center a little before 8:00 A.M. in order to get a good seat for the keynote address by Stephen Covey. I'm prepared for a little magic this morning. When I walk through the doors of the ballroom, I am handed my very own hardcover edition of *The Eighth Habit*, Covey's newest book, which is the topic for the lecture. I notice that symposium sponsor Executive Book Summaries has already summarized this 406-page book into a 350-word column in its brochure. Maybe the books aren't flying off the shelves once people realize they can get the gist in a few tidy paragraphs.

As soon as Covey walks onstage, I realize that this is not the man I saw yesterday sitting at the table. This man has a hypervitality about him that is slightly otherworldly. Like he might possibly be emitting a messianic high-pitched buzz at all times. So either Steve has a super-fan totally biting his style, or perhaps a sanctioned Saddam Hussein–style decoy has been employed for security purposes. I scan the room for the fake Covey and his harem.

One of the first things Covey says is that our legal system is totally screwed up and that most lawyers are not happy or fulfilled people. Cheers all around the room as people bond in their hatred of lawyers. Then he references a nice chat he had the other day with Nelson Mandela before giving this advice to companies: "We need to stop looking at people as an expense, and things, which have no power of choice, as assets." Big applause from those present who agree with this statement. Namely, people.

He asks us to think of a defining moment in our lives when someone had faith in us but we didn't believe in ourselves. True leadership, he says, is unleashing what is already inside people.

I feel like I have a few of these stories, tales of getting encouragement when I was flailing and most needed it. Not being a true rugged individualist, I'm not the type to toil away at an endeavor that is showing absolutely no signs of life. How do people do that? All those geniuses with a vision who die miserably and later get independent films made about them starring actors who are far more attractive than they were in real life, all set to a moving score composed by the lead singer of a defunct indie rock band. The only reason I'm still writing now is because a few people took the time to encourage me.

There's a small press in San Francisco called Manic D Press. About ten years ago, the editor, publisher, and sole employee, Jennifer Joseph, wanted to collect the little poems and stories I had been reading in bars and put them into a book. I thought she was out of her mind, but she convinced me that it was a good idea, that people would want to read it. When she was too hugely pregnant to attend a writing conference in Birmingham, Alabama, she sent me instead. One evening a few of her authors were scheduled to do a reading at a cocktail party that had some fancy writers and publishers in attendance. Yet another historic combo of cheese cubes, white wine, and poetry. After we finished, the poet James Tate, who has won both a Pulitzer and a National Book Award, came up to me and said he really liked one of my poems. Huh. He had just been asked to edit the *Best American Poetry* anthology and was wondering if my poem had been published. (I later found out that to be in those books the piece has to have been previously published somewhere.) An editor of a literary magazine was standing there and said he was about to go to press with a new issue. He said he could publish it first and Tate could pull it from his magazine for the anthology.

I didn't even consider myself a writer at the time, but when James Tate called my thing a poem and put it in a book called *Best American Poetry*, making this my first-ever published piece of writing, I realized that there were obviously not a lot of rules in this literary world, and it became less daunting to me. I can relate to what Covey is saying. A few people helped me do a little unleashing just by believing in me at the right time.

Covey is now talking about how he arm-wrestled Oprah, as he invites someone to come up onstage and take him on. I wish I were sitting closer. As they grapple, he goes about calling the guy, a hulking six-foot-five dude named Jerry, a loser, a wimp, and a wuss. This is a bit confusing. It looks like he's demonstrating the power of psyching people out, but having read his book, I think he is probably trying to show Jerry that Jerry has the power not to let his opponent psych him out. It's just uncomfortable, this seventy-four-year-old man with a silhouette like a Grecian urn, breathing hard and hissing nasty things into another man's ear onstage, his facial expression nearing the throes of ecstasy. In the end, Covey triumphs and relishes the win.

We watch a short film to learn about the concept of becoming a "trim tab." Something about the lingo here feels a bit culty, but then I quickly learn that a trim tab is a small part attached to a ship's rudder that determines the ship's course. The idea is that you may feel small and powerless, but if you work within your circle of influence, you can effect change.

"Could there be a synergistic partnership in Iraq?" Covey later asks. I wonder for a second if he could possibly be against the war when he seems so conservative. There's all that stuff in *The Seven Habits* about listening to all sides and working from a paradigm of abundance, but when I looked up a profile of him in *USA Today*, it said he told Colombian president Alvaro Uribe, when asked how Habit 4—"Think win-win"—might apply to terrorists: "You have to hunt them down and kill them. It's win-win or no deal. In this case, it's no deal."

We watch another short film. In fact, in the back of my copy of *The Eighth Habit*, there is a DVD containing a whopping sixteen inspirational companion films, none of which is the trim tab one or this one, entitled *Masterpiece*. (Note: Tell filmmaker friends about the hot market for inspirational films.)

"If life were a painting and you were the artist, what would you paint?" the narration begins. "What colors would you choose?" We see a montage of happy, noble, or peaceful-looking people. A few minutes later, it ends dramatically: "This is your life. Paint a bold picture. Make it a masterpiece."

A masterpiece? That's Tony Robbins's line. I wonder if Stephen ripped that line off from Tony or vice versa. These guys. Or maybe, somewhere in the basement of a Calvary Church in El Paso or a Dale Carnegie Training Institute in Naugatuck, there is some lesser-known inspirational speaker whose lawsuit against the powerhouses is being squelched.

And though he is careful to leave out religious references in his books and his philosophy has been criticized as Mormon propaganda, Covey wraps up the speech by saying that he gives all the credit and all the glory to God, and the fruit of service is peace. Cascading standing O.

It's time again for the break-out sessions, and I head to a biggie: "Building Your Personal Mission Statement." One of my favorite moments of the whole conference comes when the instructor actually begins the session with the phrase "Are you all ready to rock and roll?" If only he had broken into a quick air-guitar lick. In this workshop, we get to break into small groups and do some chatting about our governing values. I talk with a woman whose name tag says she works in "The Executive Office."

"Hey, does that mean you work in the White House?" I ask.

"Yeah," she says. "I work in the Department of National Intelligence." She wears a gold crucifix around her neck.

"That's so cool," I say.

"Eh," she replies, "it sounds exciting, but it's really pretty boring."

The instructor screens *Masterpiece* again. Paint a bold picture, etc.

Now we have to come up with our own mission statement, which is basically a few sentences summing up what you value and how you can contribute to the world.

After an hour of tooling and honing, the mission statement I come up with is (go ahead and laugh): I will live my life with honesty, humor, and patience. Using my gifts of compassion and leadership, I will help others feel good about who they are. I will try to be an example.

Sounds honorable, doesn't it? Yet it doesn't feel quite like *me*. Is there a way to participate in this world without sounding like you're a zombie drinking the Kool-Aid? Last one out of my comfort zone, please turn off the lights.

Break-out session number two, "Achieve Extraordinary Results in Student Achievement," is basically a friendly commercial for the

A. B. Combs Leadership Magnet Elementary School in North Carolina. It is the first school in the world to be based on the Seven Habits. The hallways have names like Covey Way and Synergy Street. Look it up.

Led by Covey's brother, Dr. John Covey, and his wife, Jane, breakout session number three, "The Eight Habits of a Highly Successful Marriage: An Emerging Market Opportunity," is packed when I walk in. The most surprising thing is when the adorable Jane Covey, a tiny, attractive lady who looks like she might know how to tap-dance, says, "If you're in a relationship with another man or another woman . . . we don't try to define it and get political." Basically, Jane is letting everyone know that the Mormons might be down with the gays after all.

Unfortunately, when *Masterpiece* is screened for the third time that day, I become suspicious about the bold picture I am supposed to be painting. All those scenes in the film of watercolors and oils. Swirls of color and brushstrokes. I'm not naive. My UC Santa Cruz education showed me how they can hide a picture of a naked lady in a liquor advertisement. I've seen the deodorants shaped like penises. It makes me wonder if *Masterpiece* isn't simply an expedient way to subliminally deliver some messages about the Latter-Day Saints. Or perhaps give you an unexplainable urge to purchase a Franklin-Covey planner.

I walk out of there exhausted. I wish I had a convention buddy to have a cocktail with, someone with whom I could unwind and rehash the many bizarre moments of the day. I see the Stephen Covey clone walking toward me, shiny head, immaculately dressed in a dark suit and tie, three women flanking him. In my head, I say, *I've got your number, buddy.*

Before I walk out of McCormick Place, I ask the concierge at the Hyatt for directions to the el stop.

"We really don't recommend that anyone walk to the station," he says somberly.

I look out the glass windows, into the overcast afternoon. "Really? It's dangerous?"

He ominously repeats himself. "We don't recommend that people walk to the station."

Huh.

"But if I were going to walk, I would just head out the door and curve on around Cermak Street. Right?"

"Yes," he says. "But we don't recommend it."

"Okay," I say. "I don't want to upset you, but I am going to walk."

He and the porter look at each other. Then he says, "Well, try not to look like a tourist."

I walk along the sidewalk, next to a steady stream of traffic, on the lookout for trouble. I suppose people like me, walking along a scarcely populated stretch from a convention center to a train station, have been harassed and possibly even mugged. Still, it doesn't seem likely. It's light outside, there are a lot of cars around, and I'm too cheap to take a cab. What was it that Covey said earlier? If you know something but don't act on it, you can't say you really know it at all.

I come upon a set of tracks, but it doesn't look like there's a station here. If I pulled out my map, I could see what the cross street of the station is, but I was told in very serious tones not to look like a tourist. I pull out my map anyway.

A woman walks up behind me and I ask her where the Red Line is. "It's just right there," she says, pointing a couple blocks ahead. "You coming from McCormick?"

"Yeah," I say. "They told me not to walk and not to look like a tourist."

"And look at you," she laughs, gesturing to my map. "You're doing everything they told you not to do."

Does this make me a Jack Welch–style renegade or simply an idiot?

Clouds are gathering overhead as I decide to go to Wicker Park to get something to eat. Mostly, I want to visit Quimby's, a great independent book and comic store that hosted readings for me years ago. At the shop, I buy a bag of cool stuff I've never heard of before and ask a lady on the street to point me in the direction of Old Town.

"You don't want to walk," she says, collecting her dog's poop off the sidewalk. "But it's that way."

But I do want to walk. All I want to do is walk. I have absolutely nowhere to be for the next sixteen hours, and that conference kind of did a number on me. Being around such altruistic, motivated people makes me feel like an aimless slacker. On a deserted stretch, I see a leather bar with a skull and crossbones on the door. It looks familiar, like somewhere I'd been years ago while on tour with Sister Spit, a spoken-word road show that took eleven queer writers and performers, and me, from San Francisco through thirty U.S. cities. I stride past in my modest business casual outfit, imagining the ghost of myself years earlier, playing pinball at last call and wearing two flimsy slips for a dress. Am I really better off now? Any more proactive? Focused? It starts to rain.

Finally, I come upon something that looks like a neighborhood. Can you still call it a neighborhood if the only stores are chains and the houses are new condo developments? There is a Gap, an American Apparel, a Starbucks, a Borders, and a Container Store. What Covey was saying today is that every employee, no matter how negligible their position may seem, can make a difference by being a "trim tab." I stop at the window display at the Crate & Barrel. It's a table for six, set up for a dinner party with a red-and-white theme. I imagine the design meeting where someone excitedly pitches a new idea.

"Let's do an edgy twist on the classic red-and-white-checked tablecloth. Take a picnic theme and really tear it a new asshole!"

Maybe, in that atmosphere, that employee is a trim tab. Someone who cares and is trying to make a difference. Next to each water glass and patterned highball on the place settings are individual-sized, stainless-steel cocktail shakers with red accents. I repeat: each guest gets his own individual cocktail shaker to match his place setting. Looking at it makes me want to kick in the plate-glass windows, collect all the shakers, and hurl them into passing traffic. I think there's something morally wrong about it. Using my new definition of character, I realize I must not have any, because after the emotion of the decision has passed I don't have the ability to carry out the decision. Scowling at the display, I continue walking, slowly becoming drenched. What I should figure out is why these stupid flashes of anger momentarily debilitate me. Is it because I could never imagine a world in which any person should be willing to purchase a set of six individual-sized cocktail shakers? You'd think I would be used to it by now. Hating desperate consumerism is part of my paradigm, like the girls who hate the Cubs. And it's going to be hard to change that. What would Covey tell me to do about the things I kind of enjoy hating?

I fly home the next morning, using the dead time in the air to decompress. I don't feel like reading or writing or watching a movie. I just sit there for a few hours listening to music on headphones, watching the familiar ballet of humans in flight. A head-ducking, butt-brushing, glance-stealing good time. While listening to a particularly pretty song with no lyrics and watching Storm Troopers march across the screen of my neighbor's laptop, I am overcome with a low surge of self-empowerment. I suddenly think: *If I want to be a professional writer, I can. I can do it!* It fades out as I close my eyes and drift.

A few days later, the marketing director at the Fruit Guys calls me. She wants to know if I'm available for three more upcoming jobs. She says the company will throw in a complimentary crate of fruit, which will be delivered to my door every other week for as long as I work with them. I check my calendar and realize there's not another paycheck in sight.

"Great," she says. "I'll see you at the Gap headquarters at 8:00 A.M. Bring the banana suit."

March

HUG IT OUT

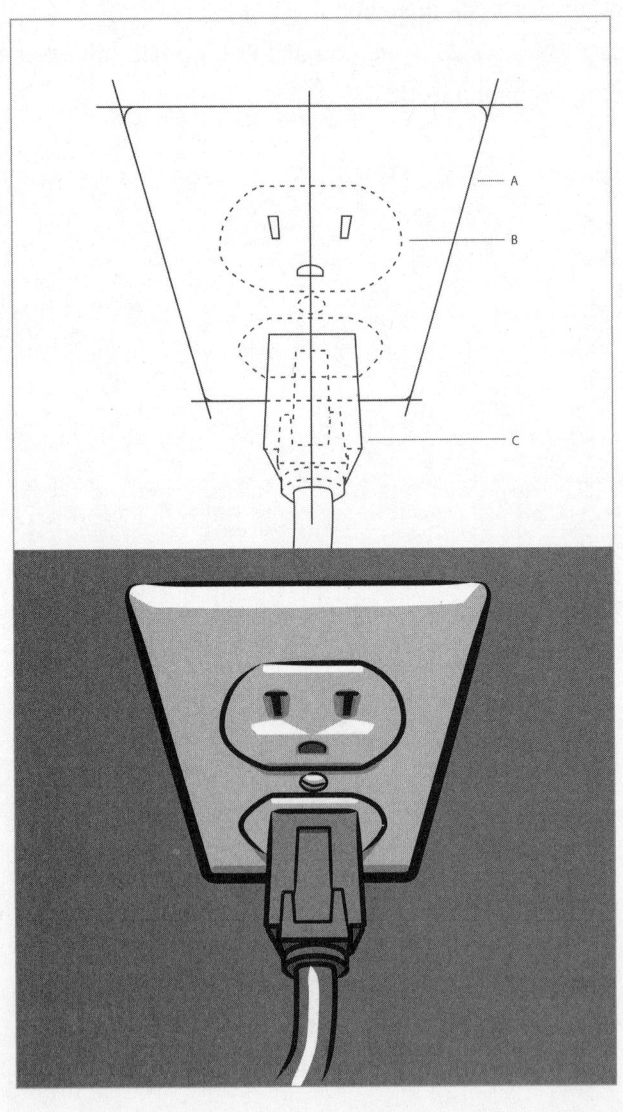

I just found out that our former babysitter has been apprehended by the FBI. My friend Angela called and said, "Did you hear about Briana? The FBI thinks she was involved in some environmental activist arson thing in Seattle a couple years ago. They arrested her and made her surrender her passport and everything."

"How did you find out?" I said, having a hard time picturing Briana blowing up a university horticulture building. She plays Balkan violin and always looks a little sleepy. "Did you talk to her?"

"No, there was an e-mail sent out a few days ago. I didn't see your name on there, but I saw Eli's. He didn't tell you?"

And here is the crux of it.

I'd like to think that Eli and I have the most majestic marriage ever, that this particular chapter would be an area where I need the least amount of advice, that communication breakdown is far too trite a marital problem for us to actually have, but certain facts can't be denied. Most of our conversations take place between 11:00 P.M. and 9:00 A.M., while we are lying in bed or someone has a mouthful of toothpaste. Many more are simply e-mailed. And it would be incorrect to imagine that we are simultaneously getting ready for bed or waking up together, like some couple in a soap commercial, because five nights out of seven, sometimes more, one of us is already asleep when the other one gets home. It's sort of unfortunate, and entirely likely, that a conversation like the following will occur at 2:00 A.M.

(Sound of Eli opening the bedroom door, which makes a bunch of noise during the winter months because the increasing dampness in our home causes the wood to swell.)

Me (groggy from sleep): Hi, honey.

Eli: Hi.

Me: How was your thing?

Eli: Good. I'll tell you about it tomorrow. I am so fucking tired.

Me: Okay. Did you remember to ask Alex if he can come over and look at the toilet?

Eli: Shit. I forgot. I'll do it tomorrow. Were you able to pick up that gear from the Electronic Musician office?

Me: Shit. I'll do it tomorrow. What's your schedule like?

Eli: Same as today, except I don't have to go in until eleven.

Me: Oh, cool. We can have breakfast.

Eli: Well, I really have to write that review in the morning, 'cause my deadline is Thursday. Do you have your thing with Tara tomorrow?

Me: Yeah. Hey, how come you didn't tell me that Briana was wanted by the FBI? Did you get that e-mail?

Eli: Yeah. Can you believe that?

Me: I can't believe you forgot to tell me.

Eli: I haven't seen you. Did you get someone to watch Gus on Friday?

Me: I tried Joel, but he can't do it. Did you know Pete had to go to rehab because supposedly he's been smoking crack off and on for six years? He stole a bunch of stuff from his roommates.

Eli: Wow, that's terrible. Did I tell you that Deerhoof might open for Radiohead?

Me: Really? That's so cool.

Eli: My mom is coming out next month.

Me: Oh, good.

(Brief silence.)

Eli: I am so fucking tired.

Me: Me too.

(*End scene.*)

It's not that we don't know how to communicate, it's just that everything we say to each other is condensed to the essential information. In one way, our relationship works precisely because we hardly ever get to hang out. Whenever we do, it's like winning twenty bucks on a scratcher. Fairly thrilling. Every couple of weeks we'll find each other sitting on the couch with a stack of Netflix and a bottle of wine and not be able to believe our good fortune.

"I thought you had a thing!"

"It got canceled!"

"Are we really awake and in the house at the same time?"

"Let's not even check our e-mail!"

Being apart so often also adds an interesting twist to that other popular snag of marital life—intimate relations—because doing it can often take on the air of hooking up with some perfect stranger who magically knows all the right moves and doesn't mind your stubble. Or sometimes, when he needs to unwind after one of his fourteen-hour days but I've gone to bed early, I tell him he can just come in and do it to me while I'm sleeping.

"Do whatever you want," I'll say.

"Are you sure?"

"Yeah. Just don't wake me up."

So, you know. We cope.

The problem is, when I try to think of what self-help guru is known for his work on male-female relationships, only one comes to mind. I don't even know his name until I look it up, but I know his face, his schtick. He has appeared on every talk show ever created and wrote what is reputed to be the bestselling book of the last decade.

John Gray, PhD, is the man behind the raging bestseller *Men Are from Mars, Women Are from Venus*, as well as books such as *Mars and Venus Starting Over, Practical Miracles for Mars and Venus, The Mars and Venus Diet and Exercise Solution*, and the 1994 audiocassette *Understanding Martian and Venusian*. I put my $5.99 down for a used copy of the classic *Men Are from Mars, Women Are from Venus* and send Eli a dorky e-mail. "Help is on the way!" Five minutes later, it bounces back because his in-box is full.

If you Google around, you'll find that lots of opinionated people don't care for John Gray. I don't know anything about him personally yet, but I have to admit I have a huge problem with his thesis statement: men are like *this*, and women are like *that*. As long as I can remember, perhaps since first reading "The Lockhorns" in the Sunday comics section, I have never believed it. A woman can come home drunk while her husband is burning the dinner too. I know mine is not a popular opinion, at least according to most magazines, sitcoms, and greeting cards, but if Gray truly is the most popular relationship expert *ever*, he's got to have something to offer even me.

His detractors spend most of their time taking him to task for the quality of his credentials. In an excoriating profile in the book *SHAM*, journalist Steve Salerno attempts to whittle Gray's immense forest of self-actualization down to a tiny toothpick. By referring to the schools Gray attended as a "nonaccredited correspondence college" and a "diploma mill" and pointing out that the Swiss Maharishi European Research University he went to is best known for its "emphasis on levitation," Salerno more than makes his point. He also indulges in a bit of harmless gossip, revealing that Gray was once married to fellow motivational sexpert Barbara

DeAngelis (imagine the pillow talk—or don't), who herself was previously married to Doug Henning, the late inspirational magician who was famous for perching atop a rainbow while wearing a super-wicked mustache. But when Salerno ridicules Gray's stint of celibacy, saying, "It's not often that experts on human sexuality spend the better part of a decade as celibate monks," he goes overboard on the snide-itude, even for me. There's just something boring about calling someone a dipshit over and over and over. I'm trying to be more creative about it.

To get some balance back, I contact Carol Queen, a compassionate and influential writer, speaker, and educator who has a doctorate from the Institute for Advanced Study of Human Sexuality in San Francisco. In an e-mail to me, she writes:

> The process of understanding and honoring one's own sexuality might very well include a period of withdrawing from sex with other people. Whether Gray was truly sexually abstinent during his time out of relationships or had a nourishing autoerotic life I do not know, but neither—certainly the latter—would disqualify a thoughtful, informed person from usefully teaching others about sex. What commonly *does* make an expert's teaching suspect is his or her inability to understand that other people might have other, different experiences and needs from sexuality, and this is a problem with many more "sexperts'" work than just John Gray's. Gray's great genius is actually his ability to say, at the right time and in the right way, what a culture mired in sex-role stereotypes and confusion wants to hear.

Apparently, Queen is not so hot on Gray, either. However, I'm curious to find out what he is saying that resonates with millions of people. I go to his website, and my question is beginning to get answered.

Top 5 Things Only Women Understand:

- Why bean sprouts aren't just weeds
- Taking a car trip without trying to beat your best time
- The difference between beige, off-white, and eggshell
- The inaccuracy of every bathroom scale ever made
- Other women

Um. This is going to be tough.

Men Are from Mars, Women Are from Venus begins with an anecdote about Gray's wife, Bonnie, being "torn" during the delivery of their daughter and desperately needing more pain pills. Already juicier than I thought. When he comes home and finds Bonnie irritable, he turns on his heel to start walking out the door, something he admits he used to do whenever he got angry. On this day, he is ultimately capable of stopping himself. He returns and holds her. She weeps in his arms. He learns a life lesson. Another woman, Gray writes, would have instinctively known that all his tore-up, pill-jonesing wife needed was a hug, but he couldn't see it because he's a man. He had to be shown the way.

Maybe he was stressed out because he had a week-old baby and his wife was crabby, but so far he sounds like a total dick. (Perhaps he's exaggerating his faults to prove something later?) The introduction then moves on to cite a few examples of couples that Gray has helped over the seven years of researching this book, people he has saved from the rocky shores of divorce by teaching them that, guess what, men and women are different. According to him, men and women "think, feel, perceive, react, respond, love, need, and appreciate differently."

A lot of people might hear this information and say, "He's made millions by discovering that men and women are different?! Well, no shit, Sherlock!" but it's going to be an uphill battle convincing me. The world could be divided into two groups so many better ways—by whether they enjoy the films of Oliver Stone or prefer Tabasco over Krystal hot sauce—but as a woman who doesn't like to shop, has no interest in diamonds, and would rather fuck than hug, I'm not fit to be lumped onto a planet with Gray's version of Venusians. (Or it could also be that, as my friend Jan has said, "Beth is kind of a man.")

Just as I'm about to write the guy off completely, he says it is perfectly normal to experience role reversal, where women relate to more masculine qualities and vice versa. Okay. Let's give it a shot. I'm about to let John Gray show me how to "keep my love tank full."

Just to keep me on my toes, I am going to refrain from using the term "blatantly misogynistic" while referring to this book. It's so exasperating to be trying my hardest to read with an open mind but page after page becoming more and more stupefied. Going in, I wanted to be able to say, "Shut up, snobs! John Gray has some decent advice!" but by chapter 2 things aren't looking good. What is this?

> A man's sense of self is defined through his ability to achieve results. . . . Even their dress is designed to reflect their skills and competence. Police officers, soldiers, businessmen, scientists, cab drivers, technicians, and chefs all wear uniforms or at least hats to reflect their competence and power.

Or *at least hats!*

> Venusians have different values. Rather than building highways and tall buildings, the Venusians are more concerned about living together in harmony, community, and loving cooperation. Relationships are more important than work and technology. . . . Venus is covered with parks, organic gardens, shopping centers, and restaurants.

It feels like there's a knitting needle slowing entering my brainpan, but he goes on:

> [Venusians] may even change outfits several times a day as their mood changes. . . . To share their personal feelings is much more important than achieving goals and success. . . . This is hard for a man to comprehend. He can come close to understanding a woman's experience of sharing and relating by comparing it to the satisfaction he feels when he wins a race, achieves a goal, or solves a problem.

On and on it goes, reading like a fairly decent piece of satire. Breathing deeply, I tell myself that he is just trying to help, that his words of wisdom have been celebrated around the globe. And he is certainly full of suggestions on how to keep a Venusian happy. Or as he puts it, "There are a variety of ways a man can score points with his partner without having to do much." Take, for example, some highlights from the section "101 Ways to Score Points with a Woman" (many of which involve television-watching etiquette).

24. Give her four hugs a day. . . .
28. If she washes your socks, turn your socks right side out so she doesn't have to. . . .
33. Wash before having sex or put on a cologne if she likes that. . . .
56. Drive slowly and safely, respecting her preferences. After all, she is sitting powerless in the front seat. . . .
63. Offer to sharpen her knives in the kitchen. . . .
80. When listening to her, reassure her that you are interested by making little noises like *ah-ha, uh-huh, oh, mmhuh,* and *hmmmm*. . . .
99. Eat lightly on romantic occasions so that you don't become stuffed and tired later.

Gray definitely likes to keep the pimp hand strong. Without even getting into the catastrophe of the gender roles (*man drives! woman cooks!*), it makes me confused about what kind of couple would need this advice. Yes, it is nice to be hugged, and it is great when your loved one does something thoughtful for you, but it is so dismal that there is a bestselling guidebook spelling this out for you. Plus, Eli and I *always* eat too much on romantic occasions. Overeating together *is* a romantic occasion. Being too full and tired to have sex is funny. In what cartoon world is there a disappointed woman storming around in her lace teddy because Bill helped himself to too much carbonara again and is now refluxing acid and moaning on the couch with a softy?

He finishes the list off with the capper, the hall-of-famer:

101. Leave the bathroom seat down.

Besides the fact that he can talk about his wife's vagina being torn up but is so genteel as to call the toilet seat a "bathroom seat," it has always seemed to me that toilet seat touching is an equal opportunity activity. Why should a man be the only one to have to touch it? As with a light switch, the approaching party should be responsible for rendering the object of their use in the desired position. (I always wondered when in my career I would stoop to weighing in on the world's oldest debate, and now I have. And while I'm at it: stop peeing on the seat, ladies.)

Finally, after many laughs, I get to something of real value in chapter 12, "How to Ask for Support and Get It." Gray writes, "On Venus, their motto is 'Love is never having to ask!' " while on Mars, he notes, "if you want support, you simply have to ask for it. Men are not instinctively motivated to *offer* their support, they need to be asked." He says the best way for a woman to ask for a man's help is to have appropriate timing and a nondemanding attitude and to be brief and direct.

If you can just edit out the dumb parts, this is actually good advice. It sounds so basic, yet I violate it all the time. When I want Eli to do me a favor, I always say something like, "Hi. I'm totally exhausted right now, and I'm not sure I'm going to get back home in time to start dinner and then pick up Gus at four because BART is running behind schedule, so I probably won't get back to the East Bay until late and then I wanted to stop by the post office . . ." when all I'm really trying to say is, "Can you pick up Gus from school?" I realize that what I think I'm doing by explaining is letting Eli know that I'm justified in asking for help, but all I'm doing is being annoying. Progress! It's a relief to have finally found something helpful.

There are a few rules about asking, though. Gray points out that when asking men for help, women shouldn't use the words *can* or *could*. It's the magic "w" words *will* and *would* that will have him feeling more capable and trustworthy. He admits that when his wife asks him, "Can you change the baby's diaper?" he feels "resentful" and "controlled," as if there is hostility and distrust behind the question, but if she says, "Would you change the baby's diaper?" he suddenly feels appreciated. He writes:

> When a woman says, "Could you do this for me?" I get kind of honest and say, "I'd rather not."

God, that poor woman.

I decide to test this out on Eli, anyway. Just to see if it works. I pick a chore that can be a struggle for both of us: waking up early in the morning to get Gus's breakfast. Ever since he was born, we have traded off mornings, only straying from that schedule if one of us has an extreme illness of the up-all-night-in-the-bathroom variety. If somebody stays up late watching a movie or drinks too many beers at a show, too bad. If it's your morning, you get up.

At about 6:15 A.M., a few hours after he'd crawled in bed with us and commandeered most of the real estate, Gus starts kicking me in the ribs.

"Hey, Mommy. I think I just farted, but I didn't feel the fart come out of my butt."

"Oh, cool," I say. My standby. I use it almost as much as "Good job!"

Now's the time. I could step out onto the cold hardwood floor and trudge into the kitchen, or I could pull a John Gray. I roll over, rub Eli's shoulder, and say, "Honey, would you get Gus his breakfast this morning?"

"Isn't it your morning?"

I feel bad waking him up, but in the name of the experiment, I go on. "Yes, but would you do it today?"

To my amazement, he gets out of bed and I fall back asleep, sleeping the sleep that only the truly manipulative can sleep. This is terrible. Did I just do that with my language? Gray might come off like a jerk, but he's certainly down with the psychology of semantics. Or maybe Eli is just a sweetheart.

What Gray explains is that a man hears the manipulation among the iterations of reasons *why* a woman needs help, and a man doesn't like to be manipulated. So let's get this straight: it's manipulative to explain why you need the help, but not manipulative to phrase the question in a way that caters to a man's desire to be thought of as useful. It's so sick, but apparently it works. Another tip is to remain silent after you have made your request, thereby allowing the man to work through his resistance. Also, ladies, learn to take no for an answer.

> If you ask him to run to the market and buy salmon for dinner when he is busy watching the news, you can expect he's probably going to say no. It will be music to his ears when he rejects your request and you *graciously* say, "No problem."

This leads us to Gray's chart called "How Women Can Score Big with Men." This shows us how many points a man will give us for doing or saying the correct thing in a given situation. Watch out, however, because Venusians can also accumulate penalty points.

> When a woman prepares a meal for a man, he gives her one point or ten points, depending on how she is feeling toward him. If a woman secretly resents a man, a meal she may cook for him will mean very little to him—he may even give her minus points because she was resenting him.

Gray's point system works like this. If the man gets lost while driving and the woman doesn't make a big deal about it, she can earn ten to twenty points. If he loses his keys and she doesn't look at him like he is irresponsible, she can get ten to twenty more. Another ten to forty points can be tallied if she "really enjoys having sex with him" (doesn't say whether she has to be conscious). What the accumulation of points earns you, I'm not quite certain, but obviously there is some subjectivity at play, as evidenced by the bold subhead earlier in the book that says "A Wealthy Woman Needs More Permission to Be Upset."

Mostly what a Venusian should work on is pumping up her Martian because "deep inside every man there is a hero or a knight in shining armor." Sounds like lyrics to a pretty good power ballad. Gray hammers the point that what a man wants is for his partner to appreciate him and not make him feel stupid when he makes mistakes. But this should apply to everybody, right? If this book were subjected to the Executive Book Summaries crew from the Franklin-Covey seminar, all they'd need to do is print out little strips of paper that say, "Don't be a jerk to the person who loves you most." And then they could put them inside cookies. (Note: New marketing concept of gluten-free fortune cookies with self-help advice on them.)

Thinking that some of Gray's fairy dust might have been lost in merely reading his words on the page, I decide to check his speaking schedule. He is, after all, one of the most sought-after motivational speakers in the world.

There's a listing on his website for something called the Smart Marriages seminar in Atlanta. It sounds a bit like a "Family Values" or "Pro-Life" situation, a name barely masking its conservative nature, but it fits into my schedule and I sign up. Unlike a similar event in San Francisco, it probably won't have break-out sessions on polyamory or BDSM and a merchandise showcase by Good Vibrations. There likely won't be anyone from the Church of Satan officiating at impromptu nuptials after getting his beard groomed by a trussed-up vixen who also happens to work at the DMV.

The seminar is actually a weeklong affair, but I plan to attend the closing weekend, making sure I'll catch the back-to-back lectures by Gray on Sunday. Compared to many seminars out there, it's a bargain at only $325, but I also have to shell out $450 on the plane ticket and figure out where to stay. There are hotel rooms available for around $100 a night, but that means I'll again be spending a total of $1,000. This part of the self-help world is discouraging. I like to travel, and I want to experience the purported genius of these gurus firsthand, but any perceptible benefits are being undermined by my poor attitude about parting with what little money I have. I go back to the Seven Habits and decide that this can be a win-win situation. Once I see John Gray in the flesh, I will likely have a hard time making fun of him. I will find something useful. And it will be good to take all this negativity and chuck it, just like I recently did with all my underwear that was older than Gus. I still had some from the '90s.

Hopefully, one day, the entrance to the Marriott Marquis in downtown Atlanta will be used as the set for a sleazy, *Barbarella*-style fantasy film. I come upon this architectural delight after exiting the subway station, my back plastered with sweat, my bangs sticking to my forehead in the muggy air. It feels like I am in "the future" as seen from the early '70s. There is a monstrous golden ball hanging low over a fountain as I walk up the paved roundabout. Suspended, hovering. It's like an enormous pendulum waiting for a push.

It's early Friday evening, and quiet. According to my schedule, the dinner banquet should be in full swing, with guest speaker Scott Stanley doing a talk called "Skating to Where the Puck Is Going to Be." The sports metaphors continue to mount like bogeys on a fairway bunker. All of the banquets at the seminar are an additional cost, so I've opted out of them, choosing instead to fill up on the complimentary nuts and candies placed around the convention floor, which is completely deserted. As I take some time to peruse the tables and booths, a theme quickly emerges: Christianity. Bookmarks and stickers and magnets quoting biblical verse are everywhere. There are banners made of felt, always a sure sign that the Jesus people are nearby. So now I'm getting an idea about what constitutes a smart marriage. I fill my bags with pamphlets, flyers, and more snacks and notice a box brimming with official conference totes. The black-and-white bags are courtesy of Chick-fil-A, the fast-food chain given a special shoutout at the FranklinCovey seminar for being closed on Sundays to observe the Sabbath.

I head back upstairs to the lobby, bummed out. Years ago, I would have been delighted to land in the middle of a conservative Christian conference, imagining an overripe grab bag of bad hair, tacky jewelry, and uptight optimism to use as fodder. But just as I hadn't wanted to tackle Mormonism when trying to sift through the Seven Habits, I am not keen on skewering Christians. I am trying to be productive here, not rehash a litany of mean-spirited insults about Bible-thumpers. I even decide to pray. Pray that when I take the glass elevator twenty-three floors up to my room, it will be empty.

Did I mention my roommate? Yeah, I'll have a roommate. A complete and total stranger who will be sleeping a few feet away from me on the other bed in the same hotel room. There's no other word for it except *awkward*.

In order to help people save money and also foster friendships between seminar attendees, the Smart Marriages website offers the free service of hooking up solo parties at the hotel. Same sex, of course. And I'm pretty sure they'd rather you not be gay with each other. The problem is that I couldn't commit to booking a room for myself, so when I finally buckled and filled out the form looking for shared accommodations, I received a curt reply suggesting I look into a designated "overflow hotel" because all 1,663 rooms at the Marriott were booked. I stalled and sure enough, an opportunity presented itself. (Thank you, Jack Canfield. And no matter how much self-help I do, I don't ever want to forget the good luck I've always had with procrastination.) I got an e-mail from someone whose roommate had bailed at the last minute owing to a death in the family. Perfect. (And I'm sorry for her loss.) It turns out my roommate would be the editor of a marriage magazine, who requested that I be "fragrance-free" if possible. She signed her e-mail "Blessings!"

The room is beautiful, and empty, though surprisingly, not the least bit fragrance-free. The place smells of essential oils and slightly putrid fruit. It puts me right at ease. One of my main anxieties going in was worrying about any conceivable odor I could possibly emit that would set off my roommate's sensors. With whatever this is she has going on fragrance-wise, it is apparent I will be in the clear.

I open the chest of drawers to put some of my clothes away, but they're all stuffed full. Every single one of them. It's true that she has been here all week and that I'd only be sticking around a few days, but I was paying for half the room. However, as the editor of a marriage magazine at a marriage convention, she probably knows she can pull rank. I shudder thinking that she may have Googled me after our e-mail exchange. Had she seen the photo of me dressed as my alter ego Carole Murphy, a lesbian comedienne prone to duct-taping her leather chaps on?

I open the closet, and this is when I first get a true sense of her. The first garment I notice is a two-piece, rust-colored velour ensemble with a healthy amount of fringe. And next to it, a royal blue windbreaker warm-up suit, the kind often seen paired with gold jewelry and some fancy shoes. And she does have some fancy shoes, some strappy gold numbers, perhaps a size six or so. Part New Age healer, part grandma-on-the-go.

On my pillow is a note, executed in a lovely, loopy cursive script. "Welcome, Beth!"

Before I leave, I write one for her pillow. "I made it, Sheila!"

Then I go to the bar. To say there is no one in the bar is a bit of an exaggeration because there is, of course, the bartender. And then I arrive, making two of us.

"Man, I can't believe there are over two thousand people in this hotel right now and I'm the only one in the bar," I say, ordering a drink.

The bartender is a big guy, at least six-five. Young.

"Yeah, it's weird. Friday night." He scans the deserted tables while giving the cocktail shaker a rattle. "It's usually only like this if there's some kind of Christian conference going on, but I think this is just a marriage seminar."

"Well," I say, "this one doesn't explicitly say it's Christian, but I think it pretty much is."

He laughs, throwing his head back. "So they're all doing their drinking up in their rooms where no one can see them!" He wants to high-five me about this, so I comply, lamely hitting the side of his hand on my approach. We try again with greater success.

I had planned on scaring up some conversation over beverages, but it's nearly 10:00 P.M. The entire hotel is dead. I decide to get a snack somewhere in the neighborhood, walking out onto the sci-fi set alone. It's still warm out, and the streets are empty. I call Eli to say hi, but when his voice mail picks up, I remember that he's at a concert. Though I haven't been able to find much inspiration yet in Atlanta, there's some in the story of why Eli is where he is tonight. It also relates to Jack Canfield's success principle of simply asking for what you want.

Eli has done some recording with his friends who are in a great band called Deerhoof, a group that's been playing shows in small San Francisco clubs since the early '90s but has recently gained a bigger audience and a lot of critical success. Their booking agent was contacted to see if the band would be available to open for one of the biggest acts of the last decade, Radiohead. Just one date, at the Greek Theater in Berkeley. Their agent wrote back and said that they would love to play the show. Everyone was excited. Then Radiohead's people rescinded the offer, saying that the band would not be using any opening acts because of the complicated logistics of their own setup. Too much equipment, not enough space onstage, no time for another band to break down. Plus, the tickets had long sold out, so having an opener wasn't necessary at all from a sales standpoint. That's when the members of Deerhoof decided to sidestep normal protocols and write a very heartfelt e-mail in their own words. They told Radiohead how much their music had meant to the band over the years and how honored they felt to even be considered. They described their small setup and explained that they would be willing to work within any constraints if there was any possibility of the opening slot working out. Very quickly, they received a response. Deerhoof was on the bill not only for Berkeley but for Los Angeles and San Diego as well. The two bands ended up getting along so well, Deerhoof was invited to do another tour with Radiohead in Europe and the U.K. To me, this is Covey's habit of being proactive at its best. Not sleazy, not manipulative, just knowing what you want and doing what you can to get it. So Eli is seeing Radiohead for free, celebrating with Deerhoof, while I am trolling Atlanta for a hot meal.

I wind up at sort of an Irish pub place. It's the only business downtown that looks inhabited, besides the overpriced fusion restaurant across the street. I sit at the bar and end up talking to a young photographer named Robert from Dallas. He's tall, thin, a little tipsy. He says he's in town doing work for a magazine that he describes as "a plastic surgery– and dentistry-related periodical."

"I don't even know how to respond to that," I offer. "Though I am in town for a conservative Christian marriage conference, so I guess that's pretty weird, too."

He looks a little confused as I try to explain my yearlong project. The intersection of my sincerity, curiosity, revulsion, and sheer desire to actually improve my life is a difficult one to navigate, let alone explain to a stranger. He tells me he just spent all day photographing a team of cosmetic dentists, financed by a company that has put him up at the Ritz and given him tickets for tomorrow's matinee of the musical *Chicago.* The world is a trip, we agree, in that beautiful, easy way that complete strangers can. He's a cool guy, and before I leave we make tentative plans to have dinner the next night.

"I might have to cancel if something really wild comes up over at Smart Marriages," I joke, giving him my number.

It's late when I get back. I can hear Sheila breathing, deeply and evenly, just a few feet away. Boy, this is uncomfortable. I should have just splurged on my own room. There is a sliver of light coming through the curtains, and I squint my eyes to check her out. She is lying on her back, and her little feet are pointing straight up underneath the sheet, creating two triangles. She looks like an elf. She is so very tiny. It's dark, and I've had a few drinks, but really it appears as if she stands about four-foot-nine. Please don't let her wake up while I'm staring at her.

I notice a new note on my bed.

> Hi Beth! I've got to get up early for an interview. Hope I don't wake you! See you tomorrow!—Sheila

I sleep tentatively, quietly, remaining in the same position all night, facing the wall. When I wake up in the morning, she's gone. The shower is still wet, and the bathroom smells like toothpaste (and essential oils). I notice she has a gray hair pick, as opposed to a comb. The strange thing is, while most people would proceed to flesh out their image of her with curly hair, I don't. I happen to own the exact same gray hair pick even though my hair is bone straight. We bought it once to pick out Eli's tight curls into a fluffy halo for a Halloween costume, and it has somehow remained long after all my combs have been lost. I've been using it for years instead of spending the fifty-nine cents on a new comb. I take my identical gray pick out of my bag and place it parallel to hers on the side of the sink. What I am trying to communicate to her by doing this, I don't know.

Outside the window, far below and in the distance, I can see a huge rainbow flag. It's Gay Pride weekend, and it dawns on me that the fact the Smart Marriages crew booked their seminar this particular weekend is probably no accident.

I try not to get too bent out of shape about the exclusion of any gay topics. I do notice that John and Jane Covey, whose marriage workshop I attended in Chicago, gave their presentation earlier in the day. I had been so pleasantly surprised by Jane's disclaimer that the ideas in their workshop could be used no matter what kind of relationship you were in, whether you were married or not, or in a relationship with another man or another woman, that I wonder if she has been so bold as to say the same thing here.

I grab some coffee and decide which of the morning sessions I should go to. Out of the eighteen options, including one called "Marketing Chattanooga Style," I pick a ringer: "Internet Sex Addiction." Facilitated by Dr. Mark Laaser, the session is packed and incredibly engrossing for Laaser's personal story alone. He's a pastor who was addicted to porn for twenty-five years, had affairs and hired prostitutes, and is now an advocate for sexual addiction in the church (or rather, an advocate for creating awareness about it). He reveals he once met a sex partner playing online euchre.

"Where are they going to go?" he says of the addicts. His face is creased with what seems like a permanent sadness, the look of someone who has seen a lot of disappointment. "They either go to the culture and make a bad situation worse, or they remain in silence and Satan has a field day."

He's not without humor and is incredibly honest, almost pathologically so. When speaking about a famous client whom he counseled for sexual addiction after the man had spent over $3 million on prostitutes and slept with nearly three thousand women, he said, "It's a name you would recognize instantly, but I can't tell you who it is, which bothers my narcissism. But you can get the idea that I am such a wonderful therapist that even big Hollywood stars come to me for treatment." Also discussed is a company called Covenant Eyes (coming from Job 31:1: "I have made a covenant with my eyes") that will detect every keystroke made on your computer to keep addicts on the straight and narrow. The only other notes I have are that he pronounced Joaquin Phoenix's name as "Jockin" and made a reference to, yes, golf.

After a quick lunch at a Texas BBQ chain restaurant, I attend the afternoon session called "Fighting for Sexual Intimacy." A woman behind me with beauty-queen hair and a giggle in her voice asks her friend, "Are you exuberantly joyful today?" to which her friend responds, "Of course. But I am also joyfully exhausted!" I think of the bartender and picture the empty box of wine in their room. They laugh, then go on to recount a nine-year-old's recent treadmill accident, proclaiming it "a horrific ordeal for the ministry." I'm intrigued and want more, but unfortunately the lecture begins. For the first time in recorded history, no one seems to want to talk about sex. The instructors have us form separate groups, men and women, and brainstorm ideas for "making one another feel good." Answers include helping with household chores and buying scented candles. When one man says he would like his partner to be "adventurous," a flurry of titters and *tsk-tsks* break out.

I go up to the room for a nap, hoping that I won't have to face Sheila yet. I fall asleep quickly but am awakened about fifteen minutes later by the sound of the door opening. I sit up in a panic, but then decide the best thing to do is lie back down, be still, and fake it. As she enters, I breathe deeply and slowly, a trick I sometimes use to get myself to fall asleep when I have insomnia. There is just no way I can have my first conversation with a total stranger upon waking up from a drooling afternoon nap. Luckily, she has only come up to do something quick, a misting of oils perhaps, and I hear the door click shut. Less than twenty-four hours to go. Maybe I'll never even meet her. A few minutes later, I get a text message from Robert.

> Cosmetic dental photographer wants to know if self-help queen is free for dinner.

We decide to meet at the bar of the overpriced pan-Asian-Italian place around the corner from our hotels. When I get there, he's talking to another solo traveler, a psychologist from Phoenix in town for a convention. The three of us decide to eat dinner at the bar, which really spares Robert and me the pressure of the datelike situation we've created. It's a relief not to be sitting at a table for two in the candlelit glow of a modernistic urban fusion restaurant.

When we decide to go out for a drink after dinner, I suddenly remember a bar that my friends from Atlanta have talked about, the Clermont Lounge. It started out as an upscale supper club in the '50s and is now the city's oldest strip joint, famous for its rowdy "nontraditional" dancers. We hop in a cab and head down to Ponce de Leon Northeast and spend the next two hours drinking beers and watching our favorite lady, Blondie, crush the empty cans between her boobs. (Like Chick-fil-A, the Clermont is also closed on Sundays.) I keep my eye out for any Smart Marriages conventioneers throwing dollar bills onto the bar, but there seems to be only one possible candidate. He's around sixty, clean-cut and gray-haired, wearing his best go-to-meetin' clothes. I keep staring, trying to imprint his face in my mind so I can give him a thumbs-up in front of the "Reptiles in Love: Escape Your Primitive Brain" booth tomorrow, but he spends the night nose-deep in cleavage.

Later, when I call Eli, it hits me how lucky I am. I can tell him about my funny "date" the same way he used to tell me stories from the road when he was on tour with his band. He doesn't act jealous or weird. He laughs. He appreciates the absurdity of it, like any of my friends would. Our marriage may not be perfect, but I feel like we're definitely from the same planet.

(Un)fortunately, another late night out means another missed opportunity to meet Sheila. Though I'm sure she'd have some interesting insights on the seminar, it's better this way. We are phantom roommates leaving behind only our scents, letting our gray hair picks speak volumes about the potential bond we could have.

Today is my big John Gray day. I'll be attending two back-to-back sessions with him, one a plenary keynote address called "Mars/Venus Makeover: Get Your Mojo Working!" followed by a seminar, "Mars/Venus Communication Skills."

After the ballroom fills up, Diane Sollee takes the stage. Sollee is the founder and director of the conference and of the Coalition for Marriage, Family, and Couples Education in Washington, D.C., and she appears to be somewhat of a Mars/Venus groupie. She stammers excitedly, so tickled to introduce Gray.

As he comes onstage, she remains by his side, clasping his arm, gushing about how lucky we all are.

"He cares so much about us that he keeps on working!" They're holding hands now, beaming into the audience. "He's a generous genius!"

"How many of you have read my book?" Gray asks coyly. The ballroom becomes a sea of arms. I take a second to look around. For the first time I notice how ethnically mixed this conference is, like Christianity itself, I suppose. What seems to hold this group together is a stolidly middle-class feeling. Sensible shoes, not too flashy. The laptops are all PCs. A lot of people are drinking diet soda for breakfast.

"And if you haven't read my book," Gray continues, "thank you for coming. That means I'm going to sell some more books!" He pauses, creating a cavern of dramatic silence, and then puts his fingertips together underneath his chin and does a yoga bow.

He says his new book is a diet and exercise book and then reveals why he's qualified to write it.

"I just had my testosterone levels checked, and I have the testosterone of a twenty-five-year-old man!" There is a swell of applause, to which he answers, "My wife is very happy about that!"

I can't help but notice that on the table behind him, beside a vase of flowers and a couple bottles of water, are a few jars and canisters. Looks like the set of an infomercial.

As Gray begins his talk, his image appears in close-up on the two big screens on either side of the room. The first thing I notice are his eyes, which seem to me to have been nipped and tucked a bit. He's a small man, slightly built, about five-foot-seven, with blondish, blow-dried hair. Gray appears a little out of place at first in his fancy suit, like a seasoned statesman arriving to a potluck dinner given by his minions. Or maybe like the life coach at the dinner party with the housekeeper. He has an easy smile, though. He's clearly happy to be here.

The mood turns serious as he launches into a harrowing tale. He says that when he was on his honeymoon he received a call from his mother saying that his father was missing. They later found him dead, in the trunk of his car, presumably killed by a hitchhiker he had picked up. The next time he saw his father's car he felt compelled to crawl inside the trunk, so he could experience a taste of what his father had felt in the last few hours before he died of heat stroke. Once inside the trunk, he saw how his father, in a desperate attempt to escape, had punched one of the brake lights out to get air and yell for help.

He then realized, to his horror, that if his father had just put his hand through the hole he'd punched out and reached around, he could have pushed the button to release the trunk and free himself.

The audience is stunned. People are covering their mouths with their hands, shaking their heads slowly.

That was the moment, Gray says, that he knew he wanted to "stand outside the box and help people get out of that box."

The focus of Gray's new work is brain chemistry, the essential reason, he says, that males and females are different. Men store more serotonin than women do, he says. Women have low serotonin, which translates to low blood sugar.

"It's why you crave your chocolate!" he says and gets a knowing laugh. I like chocolate as much as the next lady, but I hate how he makes me feel predictable. I bet he'd never guess in a million years that I don't own a comb or a brush, though.

Diane Sollee had urged him to do "the purse thing" when she introduced him, so now he decides to do it. He goes out into the audience and asks a woman to borrow her purse, then he asks a man for his purse.

"Your wallet," he clarifies to a guy sitting up front.

Hoisting up the bulky purse, he exclaims, "This is Venus!" Then he holds up the compact wallet and says, "And this is Mars!" Big belly laughs all around. *These ladies and all the crap they cart around!*

"Isn't it nice being a guy?" he asks the guys, explaining that the Martian gene is one that makes you never want to do anything that you don't have to. "We're streamlined. But for women, little things mean a lot."

He explains that the main thing tearing apart marriages today is stress. Everyone is stressed out. If we can learn how to balance our blood sugar, he says, we won't fight as much. Women need oxytocin, which they can get simply from being touched. I flash back to his "four hugs a day" rule. If you'll notice in Italy, he says, they may eat a lot of carbs, but the women are happy because men are whistling at them all the time!

I try not to think of the time I was in Italy when a toothless eighty-year-old man pretended he couldn't hear me, then when I moved closer, grabbed my head and stuck his tongue down my throat. But what a relief to know he found me attractive!

He says his new book will be called *Mars and Venus Collide*. The crowd overwhelmingly approves. In it, he'll be teaching people how to "sustain the feeling just before arousal." Racy. And then he elucidates what is on the table behind him.

Gray steps back to reveal his new line of nutritional supplements for men and women, eight years in the making. He is racing toward the finish but wants to make sure all of the information is covered. He's getting a little frantic as his voice gets more hoarse.

He says one of the drinks contains rice bran and aloe vera, which is a gentle colon cleanser, acidophilus for healthy flora, and molasses, which is full of "brain minerals, minerals for the brain."

We can purchase these miracle products at the back table along with nine CDs of visual guidance, with which we will receive a free two-week supply of the supplements. He has been doing research with German scientists and has discovered that what we need is calcium oratate and zinc oratate. Also lithium oratate, which produces serotonin. Did you know that El Paso has the lowest crime rate in the country and the highest lithium content in its water? The reason so many kids are autistic now is because there are too many heavy metals in our environment. He would never give his kids medication for ADD and ADHD—he would give them his special formula and see the results unfold.

"I'm getting excited here," he concedes, breathlessly.

Though the easy assessment would be that he's getting all jacked up thinking about how much money he's raking in, I honestly think he is excited because he believes he is helping people. Gray's invested a lot of time and money and energy into his new venture, a breakfast drink made with super-amino acids, nonpasteurized whey protein, Tibetan goji berries, and omega-3s that comes in a delicious chocolate flavor.

"If I were you, I wouldn't wait, because it is going to sell out!"

He ends his talk to a huge round of applause and then strides back to the merch table.

"If anyone is leaving, you're a miracle. I love you. See you in Denver." The site of the next conference.

But not me. I'm not leaving. Though his song and dance, and my note-taking of such, have pretty well exhausted me, I am in for another two hours. After a five-minute break, he's back onstage for "Mars/Venus Communication Skills." I settle into my padded hotel banquet chair.

Gray starts out by giving a little tip to the ladies. "When you're talking to a guy, keep repeating the names of who you're talking about, because we have to go behind the curtain for a second and think." Couples look at each other and laugh as if to say, *Oh, how Judy prattles on about those friends I can't keep straight.*

It soon becomes clear that there is no real concept for this talk. It is John Gray being John Gray, dispensing some amusing Lockhornsian anecdotes.

He talks about how he likes to drive fast, how he's never gotten a ticket from a male cop because he's got a silver tongue. "I pull the Mars/Venus card all the time," he says. "I say to the officer, 'This is a pretty nice car I've got here, huh?' He understands why I would need to drive it fast."

"Listening to a woman's problems has never been a man's job," he says, historically speaking. Women are supposed to talk to other women about their problems.

"A hobby for a man is anything a woman thinks is a waste of time, money, and energy."

He is most passionate about health and longevity, so this is where the lecture goes back to. He is really putting the "man" back in "manic" now.

Some advice:

- Stay away from diet drinks and partially hydrogenated fats.
- The cholesterol-lowering drug Lipitor causes Alzheimer's.
- By the way, Americans are all loving people.
- We need to look at other cultures. For instance, Afghan men are still fathering children at one hundred, women are still having periods at seventy.
- Your body gets filled up with cortisol when you get stressed,

and you have to find a way to get that cortisol out of your body. In the olden times, you would get stressed out if you were running from a bear, but by running away, you were burning off the cortisol.

- You don't need red wine, you need grape skins. And you don't really need grape skins, you just need my product!

"Sherry!" he calls to a woman at the back of the room. "Make me a Lemon Cleanse!"

Sherry comes onstage and absolutely floors us by revealing that she is a mother of seven and grandmother of five. She looks younger than me.

He says he is working with the government to develop a program for war veterans because of all the post-traumatic stress syndrome. The war is a dopamine provider. The soldiers get home, and they are abusive and depressed.

A woman who sounds kind of drunk wants the floor. She stands up and starts yelling. Gray graciously lets her say her piece, which is mostly unintelligible to me, but is something about how not all soldiers are wife-beating depressives and we need to support the troops.

His energy is really starting to soar now.

"I want everybody to get up, and I'm going to show you how I exercise. Stand up, everybody!"

We put aside our papers and pens. The woman next to me smiles and stretches her arms up into the air. The couple in front of me takes the opportunity to exchange a big bear hug. Gray smiles out into the audience, and everyone I can see is smiling right back at him. Big gum-baring smiles. I wish I could see it from his point of view, all the necks craning back and the beaming, like at a rock concert or in a congregation.

"What I want you to do is start shaking." He bends his knees a little and puts his hands in front of himself and starts shaking his hands like you do when there're no paper towels in the gas station restroom.

"Just shake. Just shake now. You're not going to *believe* how much energy you'll have when you're done."

We're told not to breathe through our mouths because mouth-breathing doesn't burn fat.

"In three minutes you'll feel the tingling of more energy. I've been doing yoga since I was four years old. I made the first yoga video on planet Earth! But this is the only type of exercise I do now."

He takes us around the world while we shake. We go to China and bang on imaginary gongs. We go to Africa and pound our invisible drums. In South America, we march in a pretend Carnaval parade, and then it's back here to the Native Americans, where we shake out a fake rain dance.

"I've been around the world twenty-five times," he exclaims, still shaking. I assume he's speaking literally. "I'm high as a kite right now!"

Gray finally allows us to sit down. We are all out of breath, but I have to admit I do feel energized. This is the *only* way he exercises now? He tells us another way to get rejuvenated: any of us in his "financial bracket" can stay at his wellness center in northern California. I can't imagine who in this room is in his financial bracket. He speaks of the oxygen therapy he does, the fact that you can stay in his hot tubs for a really long time and not get pruny because his water is so pure. The words continue tumbling out of his mouth.

"I'm buying lakes in Alaska because the water is so toxic everywhere else!"

"Don't use Splenda! It is chlorinated sugar! Go to mercola.com to find out about its hazards! Use stevia! It's natural!"

"My wife is constantly confronting a world wanting to make women into men!"

"These testosterone women, we used to call them feminist women."

"Give men credit whenever possible. Don't let him be wrong!"

When the monologue has finally ceased, he heads, sweating, back to the merch booth. A mob surrounds him as his fans clamor for autographs.

"Mr. Gray," I shout, like a reporter at a press conference. He looks in my general direction, and I say, "Should a woman get her testosterone tested if she identifies more with Martians? Or what if you don't feel like you're from either planet?"

He laughs and points to the products on his table. "We've got what you need right here!"

I wander out of the hotel and collapse into a waiting minivan. My friend Jan's childhood friend Andrea is going to let me stay at her house tonight. In the backseat is another friend who will also be staying the night.

"Hi, you guys," I say, getting in. "I feel really weird right now. I just heard John Gray perform a live infomercial, and I've been surrounded by Christians for the past few days."

"Uh," Andrea says, stopping me short, "before you say anything else, this is my good friend Terri. She is just coming back from a Christian camping retreat in western Tennessee."

"Oh, God. That was lame," I say. "Believe me, I have nothing against Christians. . . ."

"No! Don't worry," Terri says. "Our church is kind of different."

Andrea explains that Terri lives with members of her church in a communal house in the Mission District and that they are devoted to living their lives as Jesus did. Ascetic living, helping others, all that. Terri also teaches writing workshops at San Quentin. We all end up having a great time together back at the house, along with Andrea's husband and their three daughters. We eat a big dinner and play board games. Their suburban life looks pretty good. Homey, regular. Definitely more normal than mine.

I wake up the next morning before dawn to catch my flight. Even though I'll be back in California before noon, I won't see Eli for another two weeks. He'll be leaving just before my flight touches down to go work on a record at someone else's studio in Phoenix. I call him from the airport when I get in.

"So Gus is okay? You dropped him off at school all right and everything?"

"Yeah, he's great. He had some daddy time, and now he'll have a few weeks of mom time."

"I want some daddy time!" I say.

But in a way, I'm happy he won't be around. Dealing with his schedule is stressful, always trying to figure out which nights that week, if any, he'll be home for dinner. Organizing people to watch Gus when Eli is working at night and I also have to be somewhere. At least for the next two weeks I'll know that I can't count on him for anything. In classic Mars/Venus stereotyping, I feel like I come across as a nag, always asking about his schedule so I can figure out when we can be together. I flash back to the anecdote in Jack Canfield's book about making a goal about how many nights you have dinner with your family. How cheesy it sounded at the time. I guess you can only go with the flow when it's actually flowing.

I don't want to be a sad sack about it, though. We've been together for nearly ten years now, so maybe this is our flow. Not so much a flow of gentle streams as the adventure of waves, the depth of a well, the comfort of a whirlpool, with the occasional downward spiral of a toilet being flushed. But at least it's a toilet with a seat that will always be acceptable in whatever position it lands.

April

SHAPE UP AND SHIP OUT

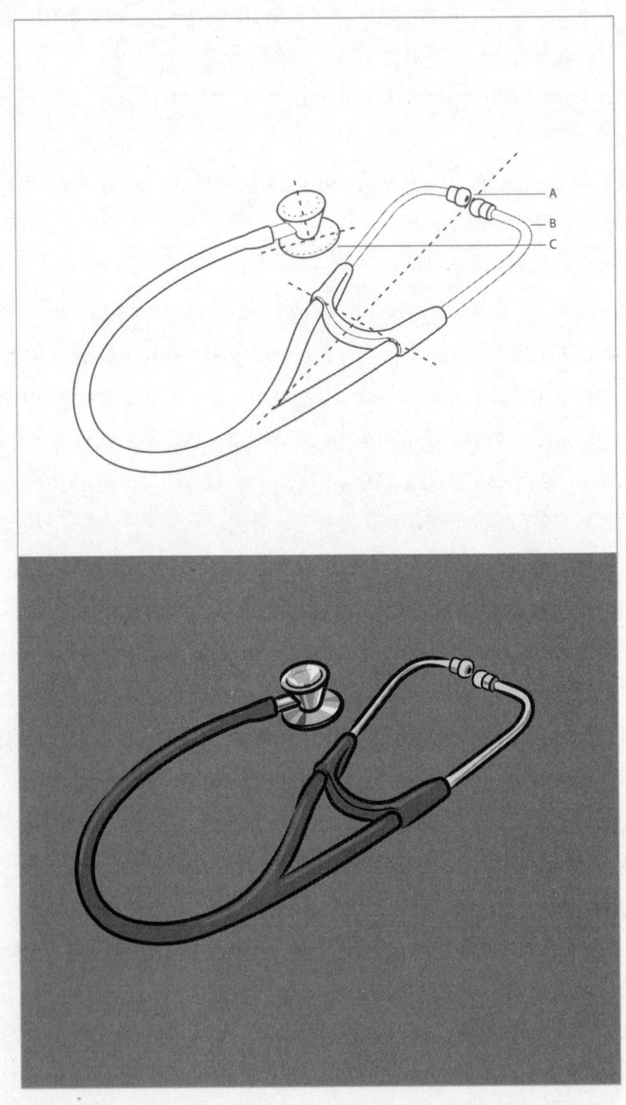

When I say that I haven't exercised in over nineteen years, what I mean is, I have done absolutely no regular cardiovascular exercise since the day of my final high school track meet in June 1987. For full disclosure, in the intervening years there were approximately four or five more attempts to jog, about a dozen lap swims that lasted no longer than fifteen minutes apiece, and some highly comedic tennis "games" played with a wooden racket I got at the Salvation Army. I have also ridden a bike to the grocery store quite a few times, gone on a handful of hikes with well-meaning relatives, done a good amount of city walking, and twice tried to surf. But as a former high school jock, I know not to classify any of this as real exercise.

It was a crucial time for me to be out of the loop, fitness-wise, a time during which elliptical trainers, burlesquesizing, and the Victoria's Secret yoga line were invented, a time when new meanings were crafted for the terms "body sculpting," "boot camp," and "butt blaster." Even airbrush technology got into the act. Back in the '80s, you might spray a sparkly wizard firing up a bong on the side of your van, but nobody had yet discovered how to simulate six-pack abs on a pop star.

Having suffered some serious knee injuries as a teenager, I found most strenuous physical activity quite painful, even just going down a flight of stairs on a bad day. And without anyone pushing me, like my sturdy blond track coach wearing tight shorts and a whistle around his neck, whatever could be the point? To be *healthy*? To strengthen your heart and lungs and bones so you'd be grateful a million years from now when you were old? Face it. If you're a skinny kid with an overdriven metabolism who grows into a skinny adult who'd rather read books, see bands, and drink a ton of beer than participate in your community's charity Fun Run, when you're the kind of teenager and young adult who is so skeptical, who thinks the concept of "the gym" is some sort of unholy assault on the natural world, some capitalist and sociocultural racket to take people's money in exchange for tormenting them about how dumpy they might possibly look in their dumb jeans, there is no conceivable reason you could ever convince yourself to break a sweat, except for having sex and possibly chasing the bus.

But how was I going to go about getting this exercise I now knew I needed? Running was obviously out, and I refuse to participate in physical activities that require the purchase of equipment. The most pervasive options, especially for my demographic—the middle-aged urban white lady in California—were the twin lions of yoga and Pilates. Not a day goes by that I'm not confronted with supertoned bodies parading through the grocery store or pedaling down Berkeley's bike paths (in the nuclear-free zone) with brightly colored exercise mats slung over their shoulders, their strength-filled cores mocking me from every direction.

It has gotten to the point where it is entirely feasible that in my lifetime a hit musical about the life and times of core-strength guru Joseph Pilates could be the talk of Broadway. I mean, the man worked at Scotland Yard, was interned as an enemy during World War I, emigrated to America, developed a devoted following for his exercise program, and left no will when he died, resulting in a bunch of lawsuits, mainly located in Manhattan and Beverly Hills. It'd be perfect. In no time, *American Idol* contestants could be belting out tunes like "Squeeze My Magic Circle," "It's All About Resistance," and "Too Much Pressure (in My Inflatable Ball)."

Back in 2001, when I got pregnant, I bit the bullet and signed up for a weekly prenatal yoga class. Mostly it involved a lot of visualization and some Kegel isometrics, two exercises during which, thankfully, no casual observer could determine the degree of my participation. Honestly, it was my pure fear of childbirth that made me do it; I had a gnawing concern that I needed to somehow prepare for this event, but I knew my preparation certainly wasn't going to involve decorating a nursery, knitting a beanie, or even remounting the smoke detectors that had run out of batteries sometime during the summer of 1999.

After I had Gus, that's when I really felt the need to exercise again. I was already the proprietor of some awfully loud knees, knees that would pop and crunch and literally *wake my baby up* as I tried to sneak out of his room, tiptoeing across the wood floor in slo-mo, casting nefarious shadows on the wall. I looked like a fucking Butoh dancer. Add in the lack of sleep, the sore neck and boobs from breast-feeding, the sheer exhaustion of it all, and for the first time in my life I felt desperate to do *something about my body*.

There had been this one moment, about three days after he was born, when I was whomped by this revelation. I had been doing the dishes. I remember exactly what I was wearing, how I was standing, how the blossoms on the plum tree scattered from their branches outside the kitchen window, when I was entirely overcome by this ludicrous and mighty power. My body, this body I was standing in, the one my eyes were looking out of, had given life to another human being. I was woman. I was invincible. Unfortunately, by the time the water drained out of the sink, that moment was gone and I felt more than worn out—I felt like I'd been *worn*, like in a movie where the alien just needs a warm shell to inhabit before stealing its power and casting it aside.

You know how certain smells, like rancid walnuts or Silly Putty, can bring you back to an exact time and place? Well, that fleeting sensory overload of superhuman power brought me back to a feeling from nineteen years ago, on a warm northern California spring morning, when I sprinted down the long jump runway of the De Anza Junior College track, hit my mark, and soared up into the sky. I immediately knew, as I began my long hang in the air, that something about this jump was different. I felt like I was flying, like I would never come down. When gravity finally took hold, I piked my legs straight out in front of me, reached my fingers out to my toes, and landed ape-style in the sandpit. Seventeen feet ten inches. That's how far I went. Longer than the Hyundai Elantra station wagon I drive now, and about a foot and a half longer than I had ever jumped before. My illustrious school-record-breaking jump, memorialized by a hand-painted wooden plank nailed to the wall in the Saratoga High School gymnasium, marked the end of my physical fitness career. Could I ever get that feeling back?

And which guru to turn to for guidance in the realm of American physical fitness? Because back when I was still wearing the regulation striped Dolphin shorts . . . Wait a minute. Striped Dolphin shorts? Was there not one extremely charismatic man who had been in the fitness game this whole time, ever since I was a kid, an irrepressible spirit with an exceedingly friendly face and, yes, a tight pair of striped Dolphin shorts that were perpetually jam-packed with good vibes? Ladies and gentlemen, I needed to track down Mr. Richard Simmons.

How are you going to deal with being on a cruise ship with a bunch of fat people from middle America?"

My countrypeople, those on the coasts at least, have no problem saying this to me when I tell them that I want to go on a weeklong Richard Simmons "Cruise to Lose." It's not that I'm trying to protect anyone's feelings, really, but my first thought is: *Will there ever be a day when people stop using the phrase "middle America" as code for "unattractive, fat, white, conservative people with bad clothes"?* Did I leave anything out? Sheeplike. Trashy. Dumb. Christian. And why are they so sure that's who's going to be there? Part of me wants to sign up for the cruise just to prove everyone wrong.

It's true that from Richard's website the "Cruise to Lose" looks like it could possibly be the most terrifying thing that ever happened to many people. Mostly because it is an actual weeklong cruise aboard an actual cruise ship. The ones that have outbreaks of norovirus and are constantly featured on television newsmagazines for their rapes and assaults and murders with provocative titles like "Open Season on the High Seas."

Plus, it's a Carnival Cruise ship, the line highly favored by the economically savvy cruiser. Or as David Foster Wallace immortalized it in his mind-blowingly comprehensive essay about a seven-night Celebrity Cruise (a luxury line), "A Supposedly Fun Thing I'll Never Do Again," Carnival is the "Wal-Mart of cruise ships."

From what I can tell over at RichardSimmons.com, the "Cruise to Lose" crowd will constitute about 225 of the nearly 2,000 travelers aboard a ship called the *Triumph.* It'll be a regular Carnival Caribbean cruise to Cozumel, the Cayman Islands, and Jamaica, but Richard's group will convene daily for aerobics classes and pep talks about how to steer clear of the buffet tables and keep your mouth out from under the Softee machine.

Richard Simmons is best known to me, and I figure most Americans, for his effervescent talk show appearances. He bounces in with that soft 'fro in those teeny nylon shorts that showcase those orange, greased-up legs and starts squeaking out double entendres with the voice of a head cheerleader. A caricature, for sure, but a funny one with a big heart, I think. A more entertaining talk show guest than most.

I knew from these shows that he used to be overweight, but I had no idea that his specialty was reaching out to fat women. I guess I missed that part. So the other thing people keep saying is, "Aren't you going to feel weird because you're not fat?"

Not really. If anyone asked me why I was there, I'd say I was trying to start exercising again and this seemed like a fun way to do it. My journalist friends suggest that I publish a story about the cruise in a magazine, noting that I might get a big old discount on the pricey ticket. I'd have the "gonzo journalist" excuse. Unfortunately for my so-called writing career, I don't make a habit of pitching stories (though once, on a lark, I entered the *New Yorker* cartoon caption contest). Perhaps it's a deep-seated fear of rejection, but I think of it differently. I am simply not a fan of talking people into things, having quit that in fourth grade after systematically convincing all the younger kids in the neighborhood to let me "faint them" by prodding them to hyperventilate and then pinning them up against a wall while they held in lungfuls of air.

When Deerhoof wrote that e-mail to Radiohead, they really, really wanted to be on that bill. Me, I'd rather just put on the banana suit to make extra money instead of spending valuable time trying to get published in magazines I don't even read. Considering all I've learned so far this year, that may sound like a cop-out, but it feels honest. However, in the interest of experimentation, I decide to test the waters by mentioning to Richard's travel agent that I am a writer.

The charming voice on the end of the phone, graced by a genial Southern lilt, says I can ask Richard's manager about writing an article, but he will probably say no. Apparently, there had once been a newspaper story about the "Cruise to Lose," and some of the cruisers felt like their privacy had been violated. So that settles it. If I ask, and they reject the idea, there's no way I'd go undercover against their wishes. I decide to pay full fare and skip asking for permission.

When I tell my friend Jan about my upcoming fitness vacation, expecting to receive the same confounding response that most people have given me, she offers to come along.

"I'll be your fat friend," she says. Kind of like a beard.

So now I have the perfect excuse if I need one, plus the added bonus of appearing somewhat noble. What a pal I would be, supporting my fat friend on her Richard Simmons cruise.

One of the smartest, most acerbic people I know, Jan is the first real friend I ever made as an adult. Someone once described her as looking like "Myrna Loy if she never missed a meal," which is pretty right on. She's got black hair with little baby-doll bangs, an alabaster complexion, perpetually immaculate eyebrows, and a sweet bow of a mouth that's always topped with the perfect lipstick. It's that iconic look of a retro pinup girl who's possibly a little too dangerous or clever. Best of all, and this is the ultimate case in point, Jan is usually game for just about anything. Pinochle. Bodysurfing. Cocktails. Dancing with senior citizens at the Irish Hall. Giving her ex-boyfriend's daughter parallel parking lessons on the hills of San Francisco. She's the first one down the slide at a pool party and the only one who ever thinks to bring Rice Krispies treats.

With our plan in place, I call to make reservations. I hope Linda the travel agent, operating out of her office in Kansas, doesn't recognize my voice from the other day. She pauses for a second after I give her my credit card number.

"Um," she says, making me nervous that my card has been declined. "I have to ask."

I don't have another card, and I definitely don't have the cash to pay for it.

But then a magical sequin-spangled rainbow takes over her voice and she says, "Have you ever met Richard?"

"No. I haven't," I say.

"You are in for a treat!" she enthuses and lets out a deep sigh. "You are in for a treat!"

I like the way she makes it sound like, absolutely, I will be meeting him. While trying to figure out if I even own any clothes or shoes to exercise in, Linda forwards me an e-mail. From Richard!

> Hi everyone,
>
> Are you getting excited about the cruise? I certainly am! I'm putting together all my music for the classes—and I'm bringing suitcases of motivation and good cheer. On some cruises, we've had pajama parties. When cruises fell in October, we've had costume parties.
>
> Well, you know we were supposed to leave from New Orleans in 2006, but God had different plans. So as a tribute to my hometown, we are having a Mask Contest! Yes, you have to make it! Your mask can be made of cloth or papier-mâché, or whatever comes to mind.
>
> Oh, I see you're thinking already. That's a good sign. We'll all be wearing our masks to dinner, and, yes, there will be a contest . . . and yes, there will be prizes. So get busy!
>
> Love, Richard

I forward the e-mail to Jan the second I get it, though I'm sure she has also just received it. A second later, I receive the forwarded e-mail from her. Maybe we could print out photos of Richard and cut slits in the eyes? Surely, someone else will think of doing a Richard mask. What to do? I become obsessed with creating a mask that Richard will notice and enjoy.

About two weeks before we leave, I get an e-mail from Richard's publicist. At first I think it has something to do with the cruise, but it turns out to be a generic press release for his new workout video *Supertonin' Totally Tonin'*. (Because I used to write a column, I get e-mails in my junk box about everything from the opening of a California Closets showroom to the latest developments in Ziploc containers.) I convince myself that it wouldn't be entirely unethical to write back and ask them to send me a complimentary video.

The package arrives a few days later. After I pick Gus up from school, I decide to give it a test drive, clearing the Legos from the floor with a wide sweep of my arm. *Supertonin'* is set in a fake mall, complete with a food court, and electronics store, and a shop with a neon sign called Attitudes. I can barely keep up with the steps, but I'm comforted by the different-sized bodies on display. There's one of just about everything. As I sashay and pivot and clap, Gus sits on the couch tonguing a fruit leather and looking annoyed. At one point during endurance training by the "kite store," Richard yells, "I love my rotator cuff!" and Gus gets up and turns off the TV in the middle of my bow-and-arrow move.

Even though I feel kind of lame about my mediocre dancing skills, watching Richard makes me more excited about the cruise than ever. Laughing out loud while you're exercising has to be the best possible way to do it. The video stays in rotation up until the day before I leave, and it definitely becomes easier. I'm no longer cramping up when we glide into the "Greatest American Hero" cooldown. *Believe it or not! I'm walking on air!*

Day One Jan and I take the red-eye into Fort Lauderdale, enlisting the aid of a few Tylenol PMs so we can get some sleep. We're clobbered by the humid Florida air as soon as we step off the plane, even though it's eight in the morning.

We're four hours early at the cruise terminal, and the only other people in the waiting area are a posse of six overweight white ladies, probably around fifty, having a ball, talking about someone's family back home in Akron. So here are the much-maligned, much-speculated-about, fat middle Americans.

They have their name tags on already. I know I've made a lot of progress in the name-tag area recently, but like a jerk, I am not ready to pin mine on yet. It sits in my bag like a foam nose at a clown convention, waiting for me to don it and reveal myself. Wouldn't any open, friendly, kindhearted, effective, successful person also pull out her name tag at this juncture in order to identify herself as part of the group? I know my mom would. This self-improvement stuff seems to require a measure of giving yourself over to the cause, joining up. It's a difficult thing for me to do.

We check in and each receive a personalized plastic card that will serve as a combination room key and charge card for whatever additional costs we incur. My neighbors Pee Wee and Nay Nay, big Carnival fans, warned me about this. All the food on the cruise is free, but apparently you can rack up quite a bill on drinks, gambling, and souvenirs. We decide to bail for a while and find some breakfast and a place where we can heed another piece of Nay Nay's frequent-cruiser advice.

"It's against the rules, but go get a bottle of something beforehand. Save yourself some money. You go on, slip back up in your room, make yourself a margarita."

I also learn, as we sit at a sidewalk café in South Beach drinking coffee, that Donatella Versace is not the complete freak of nature I assumed she was. Her signature look is actually a look shared by an alarmingly large number of women in the South Beach area between the ages of twenty and seventy.

As our cabdriver brings us back to the ship, he helps us with our bags and says, "Okay, ladies! Do all the cruising and boozing you can!"

And this is when the tyranny of fun begins. The Carnival Cruise motto happens to be "Where Too Much Fun Is Barely Enough," and it is something, over the next seven days, that we will hear repeatedly—from the cruise director, from the assistant cruise director, from our fellow passengers, and from each other as we debate whether to take in the hairy chest contest or witness the ice-carving demonstration.

When we are finally allowed on board the ship, we are encouraged to head up to the Lido Deck until our cabin has been made up. "Groove Is in the Heart," the early '90s party anthem, blasts over crackly speakers as waiters amble by with umbrella drinks on trays. I say "umbrella drinks" because I will soon learn that the Carnival Cruise approach to tropical beverages is astonishingly vague. "Drinks of the Day" include concoctions called a Mexican Mama, the Ultimate Suntan, and the Funship Special, but nobody drinking them or serving them is too specific about what's inside them. "It's, um, fruit," one waiter says, "and some rum and maybe vodka." One drink was described to Jan as being "yellow." It's just after noon, the sun-scorched deck is arid, we're already sleep-deprived and groggy from the sleeping pills. Alcohol sounds terrible. We order virgin drinks, hand over our cards, and are each charged $5.50 for what are essentially Slurpees in small plastic cups. So that's the way it's going to be. Glad we bought the large plastic bottle of vodka.

The cabin is small, but nicer than I expected it to be, with fluffy pillows and bright white comforters. Splurging a little extra for the balcony was definitely a good idea. Otherwise, it would feel like being trapped in a linoleum-paneled oil drum. I pull closed the blackout curtains, and we crash out, only to be awakened by the clarion call of an unmistakably Australian accent, which exacerbates its offense by beginning each caffeinated announcement with a hearty "G'day, everybody!"

It's already time for the lifeboat drill, which means we have somehow slept through the preliminary meeting with Richard. How am I blowing it already? We file down the hall to our muster station, noticing how the drill brings out everyone's inner class clown. It also allows me my first prolonged interaction with other passengers, many of whom don't appear to be fat, white, trashy middle Americans. And many who do.

There is something inherently humiliating about being dressed in brightly colored vests as you stand elbow to elbow with strangers, facing out to sea, while being given a safety lecture by a twenty-three-year-old wearing knee-high tube socks. Jan and I are the only ones in our vicinity who have put our vests on incorrectly, as a crew member is quick to point out.

We go back to the cabin and fall asleep deeply again, waking just in time to make it to our 5:45 dinner seating, an hour of day that makes me feel uncomfortably geriatric. I might as well start calling dinner "supper." We reach the dining room before the doors have opened and stand in a holding pattern, backed up a flight of stairs into a hallway.

And then I see him. Actually, it's that voice I hear first. One flight below us, amid the rather pasty, confused mob, he absolutely glows. His skin doesn't look as orange in person, not as sprayed on. He simply exudes a healthy and natural-seeming bronzeness and is wearing his signature red-and-white-striped shorts with a red crystal-studded tank top. The best word for his hair is probably "round."

We make eye contact. I see him spot our "Cruise to Lose" name tags and then he rushes up the stairs. He's coming right for us. Thank God I pinned that thing on! He bounds straight to Jan, wrapping his arms around her, and plants a kiss on her cheek. A big, long kiss. An extended kiss with an exaggerated smooch-and-release-smooch-and-release, complete with sound effects that go *mwah mwah mwah mwah mwah mwah MWAH!*

And then it's my turn. He comes at me with his arms extended, wraps them around my shoulders, and affixes his lips to my cheek. *Mwah mwah mwah mwah mwah mwah MWAH!*

"I'm so glad you guys are here!" he exclaims, as if he's been scouring the ship for the two of us all afternoon. He bends in the knees a little and claps a few times. It feels pretty great.

"*We're so glad to be here!*" I yell excitedly into his face. My smile is huge. Uncontrollable.

He releases his grip and swivels his head around theatrically, before moving on to another pod of ladies, while Jan and I make our way to our table, exhilarated.

"I can't believe that just happened," Jan says as we head into the enormous carpeted dining room looking for our table. "Getting kissed on the first night."

If I understand correctly, we will be eating dinner at the same time, with the same group, for the next seven nights. We're about to get to know some strangers pretty well. I shouldn't tell them I write, I think. Announcing yourself as a writer always makes you seem suspect. I've decided to say I'm a teacher, which is true sometimes, and maybe I can use the banana job for a laugh if I feel comfortable.

Everyone is already seated when we arrive at the table, and I do a quick assessment as I scan the name tags. To my left, from a town in Pennsylvania I haven't heard of, is a lesbian couple, one younger and a bit larger than her partner, a blond outdoorsy type who reminds me of my mother-in-law's ex-girlfriend. I can tell the other four women are family before I even look at their names. The youngest one, Trisha, is adorable, very fit, and in the middle of telling her mom, "Ma! Ma! You know I don't like tadda sass on my fish." It's got to be Boston. Her mother, Denise, probably in her early forties, is blond, with feathered hair and round glasses. The other two women, Edie and Carol, are obviously sisters, in their sixties.

We quickly find out that Edie, who has been on six previous "Cruises to Lose," is Denise's mother-in-law and Trisha's grandmother. The woman to her left, Carol, is indeed her sister. They're all from the Boston suburbs, though Edie has recently moved to Florida. And I was dead wrong about the lesbian couple.

"Well," the husky younger one goes, digging her elbows into the table and chucking her head to the side, "Mom here thought Bill and I were absolutely bonkers to go to Mexico on our honeymoon." I spot the wedding ring.

Huh. Well, obviously her mom's the lesbian.

"She and Dad travel all around the country in their mobile home."

Okay, so nobody's gay. Well, except Richard. And except for the fact that Richard has never officially come out as being gay. Fine. Richard Simmons is not gay.

Edie tells us that the workouts get very hard, and by the end of the week we will have done thousands of leg lifts.

"Oh, there he is!" she says. "Making the rounds!"

I see him a few tables away, with his hands on the backs of two chairs, leaning down into a table, his hip cocked a little.

Conversations halt midsentence, and all heads turn to watch him as he moves about the room.

"Hi, ladies!" he says as he approaches. "I'm just coming through to see if everything's all right." He looks like he doesn't have time to stay and chat, but all of our eyes are begging him to. It must be that way at every table he visits.

As he strolls around, he pauses next to me and Jan, leans in between us, and says slyly, and only to us, "Is this the hooker table?" Then he abruptly turns and walks away. Jan and I burst into laughter, and knowing we're still watching him, he flips up the flaps of his little shorts, flashing his butt cheeks without turning his head. The man is a genius.

The rest of the dinner goes okay. No one asks us any personal questions, but we do learn a lot about our tablemates. Within minutes, we find out that Trisha's boyfriend's name is Dylan, Denise misses her husband already, and Terry and Barb are dirt farmers who live on the same family farm with their husbands. Also, everyone at the table either hates Indian food or has never tried it, but knows they hate it because the smell of curry is so gross. This warrants a kick under the table to Jan and brings us to the one topic that everyone at the table can talk about for hours: food.

Each of the Losers' tables comes well appointed with diet spreads, sugar substitutes, and low-calorie salad dressings, including but not limited to products like I Can't Believe It's Not Butter, Molly McButter, Butter Buds, Equal, Splenda, Sweet'N Low, and, making its premiere, Wish-Bone Salad Spritzers, a spray-on salad dressing that promises just one measly calorie per squirt. The whole dining table could easily be one big lazy Susan for the condiments. Just like smokers, people have their favorite brands and would rather fight than switch.

"It's Butter Buds or nothing," Carol says.

Ordering dinner turns out to be a chore because even though there is a spa menu on top of the regular menu, most of our tablemates, and one in particular, are painfully picky about their food. An order might go like this:

"I want the pasta that comes as a side with the prime rib, but without any onions in the sauce because I hate onions. Then I'll have a baked potato on the side, with no butter because I'm using my Butter Buds, and then I'll just have some steamed vegetables when you bring them, but not if the vegetables tonight are zucchini and peppers. Bell peppers give me gas."

This kind of thing leads into a conversation that would go, "Oh, me too! I hate bell peppers. Even the different-colored ones are disgusting."

"Oh, really? I love peppers, especially grilled in a fajita. I could really go for some fajitas right now. I wonder if we're going to have any Mexican food."

"Well, you can get Mexican upstairs at the buffet sometimes, but I don't know if that's a specially themed night, like a fiesta night, or if it's all the time."

After dinner, Jan and I excuse ourselves and go back to our

cabin for a cocktail and a cigarette. Though I quit smoking years ago, it seems like a perfectly appropriate thing to do on the private balcony of your cruise ship's cabin as you watch the sun set into the Atlantic. Not so great for health and fitness, though. When we open the door to our cabin, we both scream, noticing that our cabin steward, Reynaldo, has dimmed the lights very low, creating a spotlight effect with one of the track lights. Sitting there on the foot of my bed is an animal sculpted out of a bath towel. I think it's a cobra. Jan thinks it's a swan.

Day Two I roll out of bed at 7:15, lace up my new exercise shoes, fill up my official water bottle emblazoned with a silhouette of Richard, and pin on my name tag. Jan has already made it clear that she won't be attending any of the 7:30 A.M. "Rise and Shine with Richard" classes because she's on vacation. I'm one of the last ones to arrive in the Rome Lounge, the ship's main showroom, and for the first time I see the whole group assembled. Two hundred and twenty-four people, nearly all white women between the ages of thirty-five and sixty, wearing colorful exercise clothing and carrying the black Richard Simmons tote bag we received last night. The tote also boasts Richard's uncanny silhouette and contains an alarming number of products for dry mouth, including lozenges, spray, toothpaste, and some sort of special "dry mouth gel." And a tablet of preprinted permission slips to use for your children at school.

The layout of the room makes it an awkward space in which to exercise, with rows of upholstered benches and immobile cocktail tables, but the group makes do, spreading across the theater's aisles and balconies, arm's distance apart, taking up the entire room.

For the very prompt, there are spaces on the stage with Richard. This is obviously a hot commodity and probably fills up before daybreak. At first, I didn't understand it when I read in my binder that Richard would show up a half hour before every class for autographs and pictures. I could imagine him doing this for the first couple of days, or perhaps once during the first class and once during the last class, but I had underestimated his power. Severely. This morning the line to talk to Richard, who is perched on the edge of the stage in black shorts and a black crystal-studded tank top, stretches down the aisle, about fifty people deep. I overhear someone say that a woman in upstate New York does all of his tank-top bejeweling.

I take a seat on a bench and keep my eyes fixed on Richard. He seems genuinely happy, taking time with each person, wrapping his arms (and sometimes legs) around them for pictures, or placing a hand on their arm as they speak. People bring him gifts. I watch him unfold an afghan, gush over it, hold up a framed photo, kiss someone. Jan and I were not alone with the kissing. Nearly everyone gets a kiss upon arriving at his side, and then again when leaving. Richard Simmons has probably kissed more women than Gene Simmons.

When he has finally spoken and posed with, squeezed, and smooched the last person in line, he grabs the microphone and walks out onto the apron of the stage.

"*Good morning, everybody!!*" he yells, feet planted firmly in ballet's first position, heels together, toes pointing out, bending at the waist.

The group answers back, automatically adopting a goofy schoolgirl lilt to our voices, "Good *morn*ing, Rich-ard!" It just seems like the obvious way. But it's not enough for Richard. He gets a little more shrill.

"I said, GOOD MORNING, EVERYBODY!!!!!"

We crank it up a notch. "*Good MORNing, Rich-ard!*"

Appeased, and without saying another word, Richard cues the sound booth and the classical music swells. Richard leads us in a series of flowing, low-impact stretches. It feels really good to be doing this, to be up early and moving.

This is when I have my first of many "arms over the head" revelations. I realize, in this moment, as I move in unison with over two hundred people in the showroom of a discount cruise ship, that I sometimes go for days without even simply reaching my arms up over my head. I'm sure a lot of these people do too. I think of John Gray's assertion, made during that wild, shaking, globe-hopping "exercise" session he did in Atlanta, that symphony conductors have the longest life spans because their arms are always over their heads.

The man in front of me sits down halfway through the stretches, winded, and continues them from a seated position. He is one of the few men here, and it looks like he's with his wife. He's also one of the largest people. At about six feet tall, he must weigh nearly 450 pounds. (Later I find out that he is in the military and will soon be heading to Iraq.)

After the stretches, Richard tells us to take a seat and get out our binders. He sits cross-legged on the edge of the stage and holds the microphone low on his chest by gently pressing it between flat palms, back very straight.

"Sit up straight, everybody," he says. "Now we are about to begin a very exciting and challenging week. I'll be giving you a word of the day every day, and today's word is *respect*. Write it down! You need to learn to respect yourself before you can dream of giving respect to others."

He explains the challenges of the cruise, including the cocktails, the food, the infamous chocolate buffet.

"They dip everything in chocolate on this cruise!" he says. "They dip newborn babies in chocolate!" Beat. "And they're delicious!"

Suddenly, he pops up onto his little white shoes and says, "Okay, everybody. Now let's get on the scale!" There is an audible gasp throughout the room.

"I'm just kidding!" he says. "Boy, you should have seen your faces when I said that. You were all thinking, 'But, Richard, I haven't pooped yet!'"

People laugh at the potty humor, but I can't. The way my mind works, I immediately force myself to envision every single one of these people sitting on their toilets, purposefully trying to get the poop out before they weigh in.

On a dime, Richard turns serious, silently scanning the room. "You know these cruises are very hard for me. Physically and emotionally. I see some of you who are in chairs who didn't have to be in chairs last year. I want you to know that I take this very personally." He's talking about a few people sitting in the aisles in their motorized power chairs.

"It's hard for me to say this, but I just want to let you all know that I'm thinking . . ." (sniffle) ". . . about ending it this year." Gasps and cries of "No!" and "Richard!" go up around the room. People start chattering with their neighbors.

"Yes." He nods solemnly. "This is the twenty-fifth cruise, and I think I should just quit."

The room becomes a morgue.

"But," he continues, "*if* we have a great week, and *if* everybody works hard, I might be able to pull off another year." We erupt into cheers for this possibility, but Richard stops us cold.

"*But* I really don't think so."

Dead silence again.

I can't believe how easily he has everyone, myself included, in his palm. It's visceral, as if he captured the energy we created during the morning stretch and pulled it like taffy with his threat.

I go up to the dining room for breakfast, which is always open seating. I desperately want to eat by myself but am trying not to stand out. I also want to experiment with feeling like part of the group. Terry and Barb, the mother-daughter nonlesbians from my dinner seating, have an empty spot at their table, so I pull up a chair. I meet Roberta, a frosted blonde with flushed cheeks who ends about 40 percent of her sentences with the statement "Well, I'm from New York, so . . ." (for example, "I had to pull on the ponytail of a cabdriver, a man by the way, with a ponytail, because he was driving too fast. Well, I'm from New York, so . . ."). Most of the talk is about losing weight, and that's when Gina, an attractive blond woman of about forty-five, asks me, "Have you lost a lot of weight, Beth?" I tell her no, that I came with a friend, but I'm a big fan of Richard's and the cruise sounded like fun. I realize as it's coming out of my mouth that this is the perfect answer. If you tell a fan of someone that you're also a fan of that person, they probably won't doubt you. They may try to demonstrate that they are a *bigger* fan than you, but they won't think you're lying. Plus, I quickly was becoming a fan.

When my cereal and fruit arrive, Gina leans over and says, "So have you ever had a weight problem, Beth?" I tell her no, and she looks a little disappointed. Then I realize it's just concern.

"You must be so bored with all of this talk about calorie-counting and fat-burning."

She tells me that a few years ago there was a recovering anorexic on board. Supposedly, a few of the women made her feel unwelcome and Richard went nuts, laying into them and pointing out that the cruise was for anyone with a desire to be healthy. I worry that Gina thinks I have a special problem. The part of me that needs to be lobotomized wants to smile earnestly and say, "If I could just lose these stubborn last fifteen pounds, I'd feel perfect!"

Terry and Barb are talking about life on their farm, explaining that a "dirt farmer" is someone who does all the work on their own land. I feel like such a rube. I thought it meant that they "grew" some special kind of highly fertile super-soil. Why didn't I ask last night instead of pretending I knew what it meant? I definitely wasn't using my empathic listening skills.

When there's a moment of silence, Roberta breaks something to us.

"Well, I say I'm from New York, but I moved to Jersey in '96. I used to go back and visit, but forget it. I haven't been back since 1999 because of what happened to me."

"What?" Terry asks. "What happened?"

Roberta gives a look of simultaneous disgust and amusement. A real comedian's look. It's amazing to me how many comedians are on board this ship.

"Get this," she says, and kind of hunkers down and leans in. "I was walking down the street, just walking right down the street in Midtown, and some guy comes up and *takes a picture of my crotch.* Just puts the camera right in front of me down there and snaps a picture! And I told my husband, 'Forget it, Vince! I'm never going back to New York ever again.' And I haven't been back."

There's a fragile moment we all plunge into together as the full impact of the story registers. Everyone looks distraught.

"That is so weird," Gina finally says. "Why would someone do something like that?"

Slowly, I shake my head as backup, but I'm pretty sure I know exactly why someone would do something like that. I am fairly certain that somewhere out there on a website called the Cameltoe Report or Cameltoe Watch are candid shots of what could be referred to as Roberta's "other cleavage."

My parents raised me right, so I keep my mouth shut. Before I get up to leave, Gina has another question.

"So where's your friend? You said you're here supporting a friend?" she says.

"Yeah, where's Jan?" Barb wants to know.

"She's not really a morning person," I explain. It's the truth.

"We got to get her out to 'Rise and Shine' tomorrow," Terry says.

"Oh, you can bet we're gonna give her a hard time later!" Barb laughs and elbows her mom.

I go back to the cabin and crawl into bed to sleep some more. Jan is a champion sleeper, still conked out when I get there, and still conked out when I wake up after my two-hour nap. I am paying back years of sleep debt. About an hour before our 1:30 P.M. "Sweatin' and Tonin'" class, we finally wake up and get some lunch. I'm finding it pretty easy to eat healthy so far, which is not so much a testament to my willpower as a gut reaction to the piles upon piles of food everywhere.

When we arrive in the Rome Lounge, there is again a line down the aisle of people wanting to talk with Richard or get their picture taken with him. The ship also employs a number of roving photographers, and there is always at least one present at our classes. Later in the day the photos get posted in the ship's gallery for purchase, starting at $10 a pop. I see Richard open a gift bag containing homemade pot holders and wonder what he does with all this stuff.

Today's sound track is a country-disco mix, with hits such as "Rhinestone Cowboy" redone with an aerobics-friendly beat. Richard explains that he pays licensing fees for all the music he wants to use for his classes and videos and then auditions and hires specific singers for the appropriate songs. It's obvious that he is very hands-on with his exercise empire. He also still maintains and teaches at his exercise studio, Slimmons, in Beverly Hills.

The workout is fun, and I can keep up okay, but what I love the most is watching the whole room dance together. It really brings out my schmaltzy side, seeing all these people who are pouring sweat and smiling, trying to keep it together, cheering one another on. Richard, as you might imagine, goes full tilt the entire time, yelling out words of encouragement as he pulls people up to flank him.

"You're beautiful!" he squeals, launching into an Angel, his signature move, the one depicted on the water bottles and bags. He blows kisses and mouths *I love you.*

After the workout, we sit down for our pep talk.

"Okay, everyone," he says calmly. "Breathe in."

We all take a deep breath in and hold it.

"Now breathe out!"

We let out our breath in a giant *pahhhhh!* and Richard plugs his nose and says in a baby voice, "P.U.! I smell fried shrimp!"

"I'm like your Tinkerbell. Your class clown. Your court jester," he says. "I believe I was put on Earth to make people laugh."

Jan heads to the gym to work out some more, while I collapse on my bed and check out today's *Carnival Capers*, the ship's daily entertainment bulletin. Tonight is something called "Formal Night," though neither Jan nor I brought anything remotely formal to wear. Jan points out that the gift shop will rent tuxedos to men, and for women, a "gold crepe blouse" is available on loan for a small fee, but we wing it. Jan wears a black dress with flip-flops, and I wear one of my ancient thrift-store finds, a colorful cotton dress with geometric patterns, surely something a housewife would have worn to do errands in 1966.

Walking across the ship to the dining room is a special people-watching treat. Women of all ages and shapes wear floor-length gowns—backless, strapless, cleavage-enhancing. There are rhinestones, crystals, diamonds, a handful of tiaras. The ship's photographers are out in full force, posing couples all over the place, against giant backdrops of tropical sunsets or English gardens. Complete strangers compliment one another on their looks as they pass in the halls. We arrive last for dinner and find that our outfits fall squarely in the middle of the road for our table. The Massachusetts ladies are all decked out. Sequins reign supreme, and Trisha, having straightened her hair, looks striking in a sexy black strapless cocktail dress. Barb and Terry, on the other hand, are wearing slacks and conservative blouses instead of T-shirts.

In between courses, Richard's travel agent, Linda, appears and ushers us to our exclusive photo session with Richard. She's about fifty and is positively svelte, with the demeanor of a beauty pageant contestant—gracious and composed—and impeccable hair and makeup.

"Keep things moving," she says, all business. "Richard has a lot of photos to take tonight, and he needs to eat his dinner, too."

We are led to the nearby Oxford Bar, a British-style smoking lounge with royal portraits and built-in bookcases, where Richard is waiting for us in a tuxedo, long-stemmed red rose in hand. It's shocking not to see him in shorts.

Watching him pose for pictures while this close up is pretty miraculous. Consummately professional, he creates for himself these perfect, relaxed smiles, shot after shot, all while being funny and charming. When it's Jan's and my turn, we step into the lights, taking our places on either side of him against the backdrop, a scrolled-down poster of a grand wooden staircase.

Richard notices Jan's new tattoo, which so far is just a quarter-sleeve outline of foliage on her upper left arm, and says, "Oooh, this is cool. Are you going to get it colored in?"

"Yeah," she says. "It's not done yet."

Though there are quite a few people waiting, and we were told to make it quick, Richard doesn't appear to be the least bit rushed. It's like Jan is the only person on earth.

"What colors are you thinking of?" he says, running his hand along the lines. There is no trace of his campy side at all.

"I'm thinking green for the leaves, and then maybe some red here. Maybe pink."

"That would be pretty. Or maybe some purple." He turns her arm a bit to get a better look. "What do you think about purple?" He looks into her eyes and then back at the lines. So intent is he that I step away to give them privacy.

Though the word *guru* means "teacher" in Sanskrit, one Hindu etymology also interprets it as "slayer of darkness." I love this because, to me, the histrionics and shtick of these gurus is darkness. To see him turn that off, to slay *that* darkness and instead be real, is revelatory.

Back at the table, our rock lobster, a compact and tough version of the arthropod, has arrived. The northeasterners have every right to be talking smack about it. Suddenly, Jan goes, "Oh, no. Oh, shit."

I look over and she's holding her hand in front of her mouth, moving her tongue around. She chipped the crown off her front tooth on part of a lobster shell. Unable to face our tablemates with half a front tooth, she heads back to the cabin, and I fend for myself for the remainder of the meal. It's actually pretty easy because no one asks me anything. They don't even inquire why Jan has left in the middle of dinner with half of her food still on her plate. When I bring up the big news from this morning's "Rise and Shine"—that Richard may not do a cruise again next year—Edie shrugs it off.

"He says that every year."

So there's definitely some emotional manipulation at work, but even so, before going to bed I say to Jan, "I know this is kind of weird, but I'm really looking forward to seeing Richard tomorrow. I'm really excited to see him."

"I know," she says. "I feel the same way."

Day Three Docked in Cozumel, our first order of business is to find a dentist to fix Jan's tooth. It's pretty easy to do because we promptly discover that when a couple thousand people disembark a mammoth cruise ship, everyone in the port is anxiously awaiting your dollar. I mean, your arrival. After declining to get in line to have our photo snapped with one of the official costumed "Aztecs" stationed on the gangway, we are directed across the road to a small concrete building where Jan is charged only sixty bucks for a crown. We're snorkeling within the hour. After a couple of hours on the beach, it's time to head back to the ship. Such a bummer to have to get back on that thing so soon. We are, however, looking forward to our afternoon workout.

When we walk into the lounge, we are hit with the fog of moist bodies. The room is the biggest meeting place on this ship and is constantly in use. By 3:30 it has already seen "Rise and Shine with Richard," a "Cozumel Shopping Talk" by Stuart the Australian cruise director, and something called "Balloon Bingo." On the heels of our exercise class is "Bargain Bingo Madness."

"My whole goal is to get your panties wet, and I think I achieved that!" Richard says after the workout, to squeals of delight. "Now sit up straight and press your back into the seat cushion!" he orders. "Get it all sweaty! Let those bingo people know you were here!"

Dinner is underwhelming again, but picks up afterward when Terry has her first-ever cappuccino. She's diplomatic.

"If this is what it really is, I don't get it at all."

I order one, and it is truly terrible. It tastes like the regular bad coffee with a watery white froth on top. We also learn something interesting from Edie the vet.

"Richard had about four thousand plugs put in his head. And they took, so now it grows on its own."

Interesting.

We also learn that he is fifty-seven years old and got his start on TV with an appearance on *General Hospital*. Jan and I note that a variety of Richard-related topics come up, but not one person speculates about his romantic life. He's flirty with them and they enjoy it. Why taint the magic?

There's a meeting tonight called "Meet the Pros," where people are encouraged to stand up and give inspirational testimonials. Terry has lost 110 pounds, and Barb has lost 75, but when asked if they are going to take the stage, they both demur, saying that they've "cheated." Terry has had gastric bypass surgery, and Barb has had Lap-Band, the laparoscopic surgery in which your stomach is clamped off to create a minuscule pouch for food. Richard doesn't approve.

"And I'm not supposed to eat bread," Barb says, taking a bite of a roll and laughing. She lifts up her T-shirt and shows us her scar.

We file into the lounge and take a seat in a circular booth for "Meet the Pros." For over an hour and a half, people get up and tell their stories. Most talk about their crippling self-esteem problems and abusive relationships. Gigantic pairs of jeans are held up and applauded. Gina, my tablemate at breakfast the other day, reveals that she turned to food for comfort when her young son tragically died. It's moving. Nearly every testimonial ends in tears and hugs, and Richard often cries along. Jan says it's a lot like Overeaters Anonymous meetings.

When the event is over, there are yet more opportunities to get your picture taken with Richard. We look over at the spectacle. Women are lined up, clutching the eight-by-ten photos of themselves that were taken at that morning's exercise class. So now they've purchased that photo from the ship's gallery and they are getting it autographed by Richard while the ship's photographer is taking another photo of them *holding the newly autographed photo*. Which they will probably purchase tomorrow. A veritable and metatastic Russian nesting doll of postmodern super-fandom.

Jan shakes her head and says, "I swear to God, in my whole life I have never seen so many fat people who were so excited to get their picture taken."

That night we go to the piano bar and drink a few $5 cans of beer. The piano jockey is a skinny Australian dude with a shag hairdo. He does a mean Elton John, which is mandatory in this sort of situation, what with everyone calling out to sing "Rocket Man," "Crocodile Rock," and "Candle in the Wind" all the time.

As the piano slowly rotates around on a platform, he belts out "Daniel," probably for the hundredth time that month, and everyone sings along.

"Hey!" a spiral-permed blonde yells out after the song. "Does everybody know that we're cruising with Richard Simmons?"

A few people go "woooo!" in a way that indicates celebrity name recognition but not necessarily enthusiasm specific to Richard. Suzanne Somers or the Verizon Guy probably would have gotten the same response. But then one ruddy mustachioed guy in a tank top with his arm around his lady chimes in, "All you guys better watch your ass! Don't bend over!"

This is a pretty big hit with everyone except for me, Jan, and the piano player. It's depressing. Mostly because it's exactly what everyone told me to expect from people on such a cruise.

We go up to something called "Deck Party" on the Lido Deck, which promises the biggest Mexican buffet of the cruise, beginning at 11:30 P.M. The music is pumping, and a few people are out on the floor. We find a good spot on the balcony to take in the action. We're amazed by how many people have not applied even a lick of sunscreen since they got on the ship. Noses, bald spots, necks, feet, and décolletage are lobster-red everywhere we turn. Jan can't take it anymore. She's getting too depressed. I decide not to go back to the cabin with her but wait it out until the people-watching kicks into overdrive. I pull out a cigarette from Jan's pack, and a hand reaches over to light it for me. As I turn my head, I see that it is attached to a skinny, slumped boy in a brown Garbage Pail Kids T-shirt. His dark hair is a little greasy, and his skin is shiny. Sticky-looking.

"Thanks," I say.

He nods his head and takes a drag from his cigarette. His misery is overwhelming, especially juxtaposed with this cracked-out tropical party atmosphere. I can't help but ask him what brings him aboard the *Carnival Triumph*.

"I'm actually feeling homicidal," he says, all droll, without looking over at me. I'm hoping that the bartender has not received any special training by the Department of Homeland Security, or he's headed for the brig.

He looks into my eyes for the first time. "My family is worried about me."

He says his mom is a fan of cruises; she's been on a few with some co-workers and lady friends and saved for years to bring all her kids on one. He's here with his brother, his sister, their spouses, and his four nieces and nephews. He's sharing a room with his mom.

I want to ask him what he does, but I hate how that question always comes off like you want to know what somebody's job is.

"So what do you do?" I say anyway. I can't think of anything else.

"Nothing, really."

"Oh. Cool," I say and look away.

"I play music, and I have a recording studio in Denver. I'm also a pot dealer."

"Do you smoke a lot of pot?" I ask. Like I couldn't tell.

He perks up a little. "Yeah. Do you? Do you have any on you?"

I tell him no, I don't smoke pot, it makes me hyper, but the friend I'm with does sometimes.

His big brown eyes go off like flares. "Does she have any?"

I tell him no, sorry, we didn't pack any weed for our cross-country flight and subsequent cruise into international waters. He sizes me up for a sec and goes, "Well, do you have a Valium or anything?"

His name is Tim, and he is clearly suffering from severe THC withdrawal, which, according to marijuana experts, includes restlessness, irritability, mild agitation, insomnia, and sleep EEG disturbance. It should be pointed out that this largely describes how we've been feeling the last few days aboard the *Triumph* as well. At least during the times we're not with Richard. So Tim and I are bonding in that special way that the dissatisfied often do.

We talk for a while about music. His band recently opened up for Sonic Youth, and after we bat a few band names around, we realize we know a few people in common. I hate when this happens. In this crazy modern age with decreasing opportunities to remain anonymous, I'd rather not find out someone's MySpace handle within the first five seconds of meeting them. I'm old-fashioned that way. I like to think back to days gone by when my parents would receive a surprise phone call at the house. It would turn out to be some old high school buddy or someone my dad had known in the Navy, someone they hadn't talked to in years, who was calling simply because they had a layover at the San Francisco airport and wanted to take advantage of local calling rates on the pay phone while they waited. I barely remember what it was like to meet an interesting person and then not feel compelled to Google the shit out of them the next day.

He says that all he's been doing since we set sail is chain-smoking and drinking like a fish in a so-far-unattainable attempt to self-medicate. It's challenging to get drunk at sea level when you're from the Mile High City.

"Deck Party" has finally seen enough alcohol that it's starting to look dangerous out here. Two roving yahoos, so sunburned they look like they could be body-painted in the stands at a Cleveland Indians game, are roving around with a video camera, panning up and down all the sexy babes, trying to interview them. Except they're too hammered to enunciate clearly. It's funny for a second, but we decide to find somewhere less sensibility-offending to talk. We go to the fake English bar and pull up a leatherette settee.

It's true that I have a soft spot for moody, borderline depressed, somewhat obsessive, vaguely alcoholic men. And Jews. I'm smart enough not to have married one, except the Jew part. I always enjoy talking to these people, listening to their problems, discovering how their self-hatred dovetails so nicely with their misanthropy. Almost like another species, it's their boldness (or perhaps illness) to go where the evil, cynical parts of me only dream about going that I appreciate. They'll snarl at people they don't like, ignore them completely, or tell them to fuck off. There's a part of me, probably one filled with the sweet jelly of optimism or the creamy swirl of narcissism, that wants desperately to understand them. Sure, they hate everybody, I think, but maybe they will like me. They're sort of like a club with a velvet rope. If I figuratively have big enough boobs or slip them a twenty, I could get in.

Tim slides his little plastic card across the bar to the bartender to buy me a beer. We sit there silently for a few minutes. Then he says, "I saw you before."

"You did?" I say, surprised. He says this matter-of-factly, not flirtatious at all. I can't even imagine what form flirtation would take in a personality so marked by indifference.

"Yeah. I saw you walking on the deck earlier and thought, *Oh, there's someone who doesn't look completely unintelligent.*"

Okay, so he's kind of a snob, a little immature, but I choose to chalk it up to chemical withdrawal and the extreme duress of vacationing with your entire family on a funship. I also have to admit that he is the most exciting person I've met so far (besides Richard, of course). And definitely the only one on board this ship who looks like a cross between Greta Garbo and Stephen Malkmus.

He walks me back to my cabin, and I try hard not to think about any single episode of *The Love Boat* that involved late-night walks back to someone's cabin. At least I wasn't barefoot, wearing his dinner jacket, with a pair of heels slung over my shoulder. We make a loose plan to hang out the next day ("I'll be around." "Yeah, me too.") and as I say good-bye he catches me off guard by swooping in for an enthusiastic, back-cracking hug. Literally, those skinny arms manage to lift me off the ground, he draws my body into his, and he starts pressing the palms of his hands methodically down the length of my spine, popping at least a half dozen vertebrae along the way, before stopping at my waist. Then he releases me gently back down to the ground, turns abruptly, and slinks down the long narrow hall without saying good night. I watch him the whole way, and he doesn't turn around once. I am overcome with a feeling I now know is oxytocin-related.

Day Four I oversleep and miss "Rise and Shine with Richard." Part of me knows that it's no big deal, that I can just ask someone later what the word of the day is, but I also feel guilty. I signed up for a program, and by missing one of its components, I am not fully "with the program" anymore. Slightly hungover, I'm disappointed with myself. Time crawls aboard this ship, and I wait fitfully for the afternoon so I can absolve myself at "Sweatin' and Tonin'." I want the adrenaline rush, as well as another dose of Richard, another hit of whatever mysterious agent occurs during synchronized aerobics with a large group of optimists.

Finally the time comes, and I suit up in my T-shirt and sweatpants. Richard is demonstrating a few moves that will be introduced in today's workout, and everyone has spread out over the floor, filling up the aisles. Jan and I head up to the balcony, where there's more room to fully execute our Angels. At some point, while we are "sparkling up" with our hands, Richard spots Jan and me and smiles. He waves big and blows us kisses.

The dinner table conversation tonight is some of the best ever, mostly provided by Trisha, who is heard fretting to her mom, "Uh-oh. My alcohol is wearing off!"

"Hey," I say to her. "What about when Richard made you take a sip from his water bottle this afternoon? You looked horrified."

"I hate germs," she says. "I need to take a Klonopin just to ride the subway. I can't even eat an apple because it's too much like eating my own mouth."

Quotes such as these renew my faith about prolonged exposure to total strangers. Something really good is going to come along if you just wait it out.

When we step into the lounge for the mask party, we realize that we had a different idea than the other cruisers, most of whom created elaborate Mardi Gras–style masks. Jan's co-worker somehow knew that Richard collects dolls, so Jan printed out gigantic porcelain doll faces and cut holes in their eyes. Creepy. Everyone is instructed to parade onto the stage, give the panel of judges a look, and then pose with Richard for a photograph that will be sold to you later.

While waiting in line, Jan and I decide to choreograph a dance as we take the stage. It's not so much a dance as a kind of robotic, broken-doll-parts shuffle, and it's created with the explicit desire to delight our host.

Richard puts on a look of mock horror as we approach. We look so much weirder than everyone else, and we're just making it worse. As the photographer lines us up, Richard looks at me, looks at Jan, and then sticks his thumb in his mouth like a baby. Later, when the judges announce the winner, a woman with an elaborate butterfly-themed mask, Richard sheds tears.

"I feel like I am an ugly bug on my journey toward becoming a butterfly," she chokes into the microphone.

Day Five After our stretch this morning, Richard tells us he hopes that we're going on to Grand Cayman to see the butterflies. The symbolism of the butterfly is extremely important to him, and I'm sure the winner of last night's mask contest played right into that.

"They're just such special creatures," he says earnestly. "God hand-painted each and every butterfly with His own palette of love-colors."

I pick a flake of synthetic snow out of my ear. During the last song of the workout, the production crew fired up the snow machine used for the evening stage shows and sent a shower of tiny plastic chips fluttering down on our heads. Even though it is so thick and moist in here, and it was difficult not to inhale them as we huffed and puffed, it was kind of a perfect moment. Everyone looking around in wonder and amusement as it fell upon us, lifting our arms to the sky as if it were real and this was some kind of miracle.

We were also still energized from Elijah's appearance onstage. During a routine to the song "Love Will Keep Us Together," Richard called him up to big applause. Elijah is a Simmons staff member, and I've noticed him because he is one of the few men around, and also one of the few black people.

"This is our song. Isn't it, Elijah?" Richard says. "We've been together so many years!"

I'm sure he means as friends and co-workers, but I can't help but wonder if there's more to the story. As they dance, Richard flanks him and hugs him, or steps in front of him and grinds away, a hilarious expression on his face like, *Whoops! What am I doing now? This isn't okay, is it?*

Richard later tells us that one of the most important lessons in life he learned from his dear father: "Everyone you meet is a blessing." I remember the similar words of Jack Canfield: "What opportunity does this [person] present to me?" I guess Jack's lesson is a bit more mercenary.

I think about Tim from the other night. Is he a blessing? An opportunity? Because, honestly, I've been trying to keep my distance from him. His extreme pulchritude (see Garbo-Malkmus reference) combined with the disorienting weirdness of being on this ship is making me wish for an opportunity that I would probably regret.

I decide not to even get off the ship in Grand Cayman. My

cruising malaise has officially arrived. I just read and nap all day and am somehow not entirely satisfied with even that.

The big news at dinner is that Richard has been spotted wearing pants for the second time.

"Doesn't Richard look handsome tonight?" Edie says, barely moving her mouth, fanning herself with her hand to signify the hotness. He's got on crisp white trousers and a pink shirt, buttoned halfway up. The outfit accentuates his tan, but his hair is not the crowning glory it was when we set sail. It is starting to deflate, moving into damp Jheri curl territory. At home I imagine he has a standing weekly hair appointment, like a grandma. Someone to set and spray it into a perfect confection of gravity-defiance. He obviously didn't bring his stylist on board, which endears him to me even more. His eyes, however, still sparkle like a cosmic elf's. And his energy seems to have evened out, become more relaxed.

Denise is homesick and not feeling up to dinner this evening, so when Richard comes around to our table he sits in her empty chair. I ask him what he did today, and he says that every time he comes on the cruise he asks all the maids and stewards in his cabin's section if they want him to bring them something back from the port.

"Usually, they say, 'Oh, no. We don't want anything!' but this morning when I got up at 4:00 A.M., there were two lists waiting for me. Earrings, stuff like that. So I went out and got it all and brought it back for them."

He says this sweetly, not bragging about what a hero he is. On our way to dinner, Jan and I realize that none of our dinner companions, with whom we have spent nearly a total of eight hours, has yet asked us anything about ourselves. During a conversation about pets, Jan did reveal that she owns a cat. We speculate that maybe they think we're gay, being from San Francisco and all, and they don't want to have to think about that. Maybe it's the same thing with Richard. No one wants to bring it up because no one wants to know.

Trisha says, "We had to take the nugget into port."

"The what?" Deb says.

"The boat thing. The nugget?" She pauses for a second. "That's not right, is it?"

"The tender?" someone says.

"Right!" She laughs. "I knew it was some chicken thing."

Day Six We're in Jamaica. After "Rise and Shine with Richard," I go back to the cabin and wake Jan. We've decided to hike up Dunn's River Falls, a natural waterfall high in the tropical mountains, filled with cool plunge pools that empty out onto the beach. It's something my parents did here on their honeymoon forty-one years ago, and the pictures of them, giddy and in love as they splash through the trail of water, are absolutely halcyonic. Jan and I also have a chance to make a memory with pictures. As we exit the ship, we discover that today's photo opportunity is appropriately Rasta-themed. Decked out in green, red, and gold with a voluminous head of dreadlocks, a tall native stands at the end of the plank with the ship's photographers.

"Get your picture taken with a real live Rastaman!" the photographer barks, gesturing to his accomplice.

"Hey, mon," the Rastaman says, baked.

The falls are gorgeous, but being hustled through them en masse by overaccommodating guides is a total bummer. Hundreds of us from the cruise leave the Dunn's River Falls like a pack of wet and slightly shell-shocked animals, if animals had cellulite and the desire to capture every third moment on their digital cameras. I hear the wife of a New Jersey couple tell the guide, with a huge smile on her face, "Thank you so much for saving my husband's life." Then, as soon as he's out of earshot, she turns to her husband and through clenched teeth, with a nasty expression on her face, says, "That's it! You are going on a *diet*! That was humiliating! I'm surprised you didn't have a heart attack!"

We're slow to dry in the humidity, so we pass drippingly through the gauntlet of hair braiders, wood-carvers, and bead sellers on our way back to the bus. A man thrusts a pipe in my hand and asks if I like to party. I say, "No, thanks," even though I could be such a hero if I scored something for Tim. Nah. He's an addict. He'll surely find something on his own.

We try to go to the beach with our final two hours in port, but all we can find is one where we have to pay to step foot on the sand. One of the many indignities of traveling by cruise ship is that you are not given a lot of time to get off the main tourist track. We peek into the one crowded and overpriced jerk chicken place, near the patio at Margaritaville, where plenty of cruisers are continuing their weeklong benders, and leave. Dejected, we get on the ship an hour early and submit to the buffet.

The afternoon workout is the hardest yet. Jan does the whole thing, sweats a lot, and doesn't find it that difficult. She even goes to the gym afterward. During dinner the waiters get up and do a dance. Diners at other tables are all hopping up to dance with their waiters, but no one at our table moves a muscle.

"I didn't get my dessert yet," Barb says.

I feel bad that no one wants to dance with our waiter, maybe because he fouled up a few of the trickier orders, so I get up and cut a rug with him, as well as with the special-needs lady at the table next to us. She is wearing a tie-dyed Bob Marley shirt that she must have picked up in Jamaica today.

I go to check my e-mail, for seventy-five cents a minute, and get a message from Eli. The subject line reads: NEUROMA! He says he is now the proud owner of a pair of orthopedic shoes. He signs his note "Love, Grandpa."

When I get back to the cabin, Tim is in there with Jan.

"He brought us presents," Jan says as Tim sits somewhat shyly on the couch. He raises up a scrawny arm and holds out a tiny origami turtle, crafted from the pages of the *Carnival Capers.* I am touched.

"Look what he brought me," Jan says, holding up a fat joint.

"Whoa! How did you get that?" I say, putting the turtle on my open palm and petting its back with my finger.

Turns out he got off the ship, went into the main shopping market, and bought it off of the first guy who asked what he was looking for. Then he says he saw the dealer tap another guy and point Tim out in the crowd, freaking him out enough that he went directly back to the ship to stash his drugs. Then he got off the ship again, walked around for a bit, and when he returned, just before the ship's departure, he was taken out of line and thoroughly searched. By then he had nothing on him. It was juvenile, but I couldn't help but be impressed by his street smarts.

Jan goes to the showroom to take in the Carnival Triumph Dancers, and Tim and I hit the balcony to smoke. Something has to be amiss in my brain box if I am now voluntarily smoking pot. Tim's already heard what a novice I am, but after I take two or three hits off the joint, it soon becomes clear that I may as well have snorted a foot-long rail of speed.

I am flying, entirely unable to contain my amazement and wonder at the peculiarities of the universe. I keep having to stifle these little screams, telling myself, no, it would not be super-funny if I decided to jump over the railing onto the balcony below.

I can tell my behavior is a little disconcerting to my new friend, the professional stoner. Tim is the kind of cool and mellow stoner one is used to seeing portrayed in movies. The kind whose eyes get squinty as he nods slowly with his mouth agape.

Then he speaks.

"My sister is really into shopping at the FranklinCovey store. She's the kind of person who keeps a log of how many trick-or-treaters visit her house each year so that she can be prepared for the following year."

It's astonishing, and I want to say something, but I can't. Someone has stuffed my mouth full of this morning's synthetic snow. I snap my beak open and shut like a baby bird.

Then I remember the contents of the Richard Simmons gift bag. The arsenal of dry mouth products! I go inside and gather them up, which seems to take about ten times longer than it should. I get distracted with the presentation. Which would be funnier? To display them all on the bed or to pull them out one by one from behind my back? As I'm debating this, while chugging water from a pitcher, Tim comes in and mumbles something about leaving.

"Oh, okay. See ya!" I say, but then something trembly underneath my skin changes my mind. I lean in to kiss him, and not like a pal would. No, not like that at all. Instead, I transform into some impassioned dragon-slayer who is bidding a final adieu to the lover I will never see again as I slip under cover of the night. I reach my hand behind his head and attach my mouth to his, entirely inappropriately. And then he leaves.

I collapse onto my bed, remaining there, facedown, my mind racing. My hands are icy, balled up into tight fists, tucked under my chest. The hallucinations commence. Who hallucinates on pot? Apparently, a mom on vacation aboard a cruise ship who's just kissed an avant-garde guitar player/drug dealer from Denver.

What happens is that I'll see something like the Liberty Bell in my mind. Then I watch as another object, such as an umbrella, slowly moves closer to it in a jumpy series of still frames, until it strikes the bell, and I hear a loud noise. But instead of the ringing of a bell, the noise it makes will be a cymbal crash or the blare of a big-rig horn with the Doppler effect. This continues for the next two or three hours. A plant stand floats toward a fire hydrant. Sound of applause. A set of antlers meanders in the direction of a bathtub. A rooster crows. When I finally fall into something resembling sleep, I awake with a start every fifteen minutes thinking I have missed "Rise and Shine with Richard." When 7:00 A.M. finally comes, I am sweaty and disheveled, but grateful. Another day, another chance to feel healthy. Thank you, Evian advertising copywriters, for providing me with my first clear thought of the day.

Day Seven On my way to "Rise and Shine," I run into our next-door neighbor, a gloomy, heavyset woman in workout wear whose name tag indicates that she is part of Richard's group, though I don't recognize her from class or the events. We have seen her and her husband a few times going in and out of their cabin, each time looking positively miserable. Sad zombies in sweatpants, never talking or making eye contact with each other. I once saw them heading up to the "Big Gala Buffet," the monster of all cruise ship buffets, which begins at 12:30 A.M. They had clearly gone to bed earlier and set an alarm to wake up for the buffet. In fact, a lot of people had done that. Interrupted their blissful sleep to pile plates full of prime rib and stuffing. It was depressing. I think about the stories from the other night at "Meet the Pros," so many people leaving bad or abusive relationships, and I decide this is probably what's going on with this couple. He is mad at her for dragging him on this cruise, and she is trying to lose weight to gain the confidence to leave him.

The mood at "Rise and Shine" is somber. Richard begins the routine wordlessly, leading us through stretches that seem extra soulful. His hands are especially graceful today, and he doesn't smile, infusing the stretch with a sense of longing and loss. When the song is over, he takes his seat on the stage's apron and slowly scans the room. Then he begins to cry.

"Today's word is"—he chokes on it—"today's word is *silly,*" he says, smiling through the tears. "I have based my whole life on being silly. As a child, I loved the circus, but most especially I loved the clowns because they made people laugh." He goes on. "When I die, and they write the new dictionary . . ." he looks around and laughs, "all it will say under the word *silly* is 'Richard.'"

He reveals something special about the words of the day. If you take the first letter of each one—Respect, Energy, Vitality, Love, Independence, and Silly—and reverse them, it spells SILVER, in honor of the twenty-fifth anniversary of the cruise. Upon hearing this, everyone bursts into applause at the ingenuity. It was there all along, slowly unfolding, and not one of us had noticed it.

At the final party that night, there is a huge ice sculpture of Richard doing an Angel. Richard's image is also carved into the occasional watermelon. We nibble on plates of fruit as diet soda is passed around on trays. An awards ceremony is held, with Richard handing out titles such as Best Smile, Most Inspirational, and Most Infectious Laugh.

I hate to say it, but Richard's tears seem fake. Forced. I don't think he's pushing himself to cry because he's a phony, though. He clearly loves his followers and thinks of them as extended family. Plus, it has to take a lot out of him to not only conduct all the exercise classes and meetings but to also be so emotionally available to everyone all week. He looks exhausted.

Still. The rate at which he recovers in between presenting each award is peculiar. At one tear-filled juncture, he sobs, "I live for you guys . . . and I would die for you." Like the most famous Jewish carpenter. And then, bam, he's back to aerobics instructor mode. "Okay, Brenda! Time to get off the stage! I've got a lot of awards to give out here!"

It seems more like he's taking an emotional shortcut. He wants to convey the message that he is indeed vulnerable and moved, but he's not quite up to fully "going there" at the moment.

Jan and I say good-bye to our tablemates and wander over to the piano bar one last time.

"It was fun in a way," Jan says as the crowd around us launches into "Candle in the Wind." "But I kind of wish we just went by ourselves to Hawaii or something."

Yeah.

Physically, I am stronger than I was a week ago, but mentally I feel a bit addled. As inspiring as it was to see Richard in action, to see him giving of himself so thoroughly, to experience true joy as I sweated and toned to loud disco beats, I don't think I'm cut out to be a Richard Simmons lifer. I definitely need the cardiovascular exercise, but his hugs and kisses are a valuable resource, and there are plenty of others out there who need them more. His butt cheeks, however, are another matter. He's free to flash those at me anytime.

May

A PLACE FOR EVERYTHING (IS NOT THE BASEMENT)

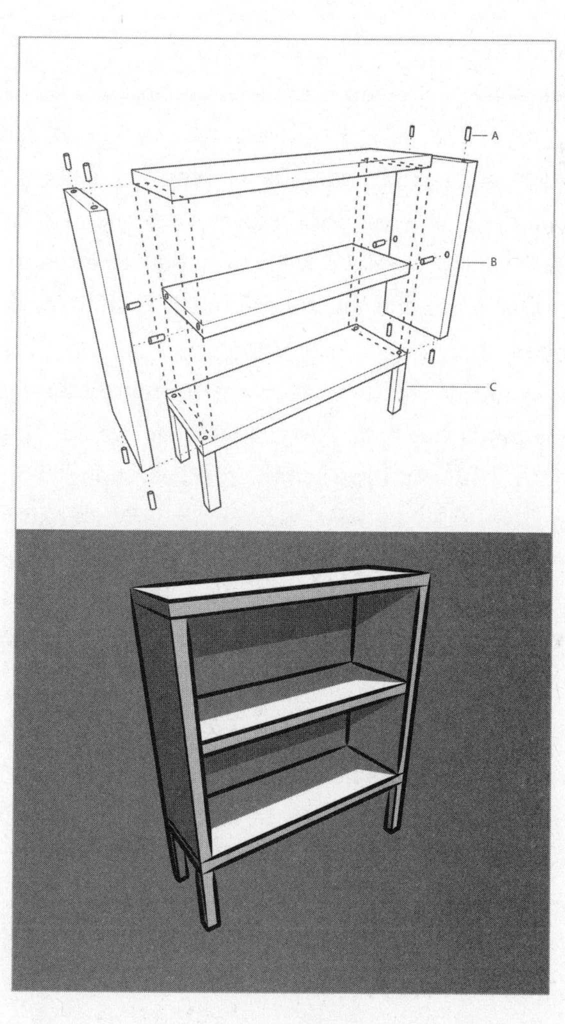

Eli arrives at the airport in his new doctor-prescribed orthopedic shoes.

"They don't look so bad," I say, giving him a big old squeeze in the middle of the pickup lane. And they really don't. The best I can describe them is probably "brown leather shoes with laces." They would make a great illustration in the dictionary next to the phrase "men's shoes."

"Yeah, the guy at the shoe store was trying to talk me into getting these weird, marshmallowy, space-age tennis shoes, but I couldn't do it. Wait until you see the sandals, though."

The sandals? I don't know why, but whether it's a hairy-toed hippie in a Teva or a metrosexual in a suede flip-flop, I have never liked the way a man-foot looks in a sandal. Mandals. For Jesus only.

The traffic cop pierces the air with her whistle, grimacing at us as she blows and blows.

"And I'm not allowed to go barefoot. Ever," Eli says incredulously, ignoring the cop as he loads our bags in the back. "So I have to wear the sandals in the house at all times. They're kind of like Birkenstocks." He frowns. "But uglier."

"Mommy!" Gus is yelling, straining at the seat belt. "Mommy-MommyMommy!" I jump in the backseat and give him a bunch of kisses all over his sweet little face. He's got dried yogurt down the front of his insect T-shirt and a train clutched in each fist. It's possible that he's never looked happier, and it makes me completely melty. He kisses me back wherever his mouth can reach, including each of my eyelids and a nostril.

Eli looks worried, his forehead producing an Egyptian cartouche of wrinkles.

"Something's wrong with the car." He turns off the hazards and pulls into traffic. "It made a clunking sound when I got on the freeway and now listen . . ."

Ugh. We just spent a couple hundred bucks on it a few months ago. I contemplate for a moment if we could ever become one of those Berkeley bicycling families, those dew-faced sprites who pedal all over town, even when it's pouring rain, orange flags jutting up from their seats like fluorescent non-prehensile tails. I am such a product of California car culture. I like to drive. I know I'm supposed to say, "I can be different," but the truth is, "I am like that." I am really like that. If a paradigmatic shift feels too big to make, it's possible it shouldn't be attempted at all.

We drop Jan at the BART station so she can head back to her apartment in the city, and the car makes it into the driveway. Barely. I yank my duffel bag out of the hatchback.

"Close your eyes, Mommy!" Gus says, grabbing my hand. "We've got a surprise for you."

He leads me up the walkway.

"Okay! Open them!"

I look up and see that the treacherous rotted-out front step has been fixed! It hasn't been painted yet, and the other steps around it are splintered and about to go, but still. It makes me unbelievably pleased.

"You fixed the step!" I say, giving them both a hug. I wonder if I'll throw open the front door and discover that Eli has also painted the living room, had the bedroom walls repaired, hired a deep-cleaning crew, and let a home makeover show with really good taste come in. This is how I used to think when I was a kid. I could convince myself that while I was at school my mom was redoing my entire bedroom to look like the inside of *I Dream of Jeannie*'s bottle. Instead, I pull the plug on my rich fantasy life and slather Eli with John Gray's "knight in shining armor" treatment.

"Honey, this is amazing. You have made me so happy with this demonstration of your Martian physical prowess. You are a very capable and competent man, and I am acknowledging that I appreciate you."

"Yeah," he says, grinning a bit. "I, uh, hired George to come over and do it. I paid him fifty bucks."

Our friend George occasionally works construction.

The old me might have said, "Fifty bucks! That's a couple bags of groceries!" but instead, I keep my mouth shut. I focus on the fact that the step is fixed and I am happy about it. And the postman will be pleased, too. And my dad can stop haranguing me about potential lawsuits. His recovery from the heart surgery went well, though he's having trouble exercising because his knee needs replacing. He's also just been diagnosed with something called "frozen shoulder syndrome," which causes him a lot of pain and limits his range of motion so severely he kind of looks like a *T. rex* when he's reaching for a cup of coffee.

I climb up the stairs, stepping firmly on the spot that I've spent over a year avoiding. I stand there beaming, reenergized, a total *Rocky* moment. I am ready to be the slayer of tiny nuisances, the reaper of petty annoyance. This month I am going to make my home a better place to live.

Our house was built in 1912, but the previous owners had done a lot of remodeling sometime in the late '80s or early '90s, if that was the time period that the Sizzler decided to go with the Miami color scheme. The kitchen especially, with its mint and salmon concrete countertops and black appliances, particularly seems to have been inspired by the decor of the steak, seafood, and salad chain. The only improvement we had done, besides taking out a loan to have Joel's in-law apartment built downstairs, was a little painting. And actually, we hadn't even done that ourselves. For my birthday a few years ago, Jan showed up with some cans of paint and spent hours desalmonizing the walls. I think it was because she hated it as much as we did. Eli and I have never really been "nesters."

But this month won't be about interior decorating. It can't.

Habit 3: put first things first.

First, I must tackle a storage cabinet jammed full of old postcards, half-burned candles, plastic cups, board games, puzzles, serving bowls, a fountain pen, and strings of broken Christmas lights, and then maybe I'll be ready to remove the flannel sheet from the bedroom window and buy a curtain.

When I moved in seven years ago, I thought I had a system. Most of my belongings had been sitting in a storage locker, and I figured if I had been able to go without them for six months, they probably weren't very important. I decided to shuttle all of the boxes into my new basement, without opening them, and would only move things upstairs on an as-needed basis. The system kept the house clutter-free for a while, except that I never once attempted to organize the contents of those boxes. Because of this, whenever I needed a three-hole punch or a travel mug or wanted to look up that one Sesshu Foster poem, I would scavenge through an exploded maze of half-filled cardboard boxes and jumbled garbage bags, now mostly smelling of mold. When I couldn't find whatever I was looking for, I would go out and buy a new one.

"You have two of everything," my dad grumbled one day, looking around the basement at three broken Weedwackers and four mangled Styrofoam coolers. It was nice of him to downplay it. The basement had since become home for the extra junk of four more people. First, Eli moved in, bringing with him instruments, recording gear, oversized photographic portraits of families that were not his own, and other things we might need someday like plastic robot dolls and a rusty mini-refrigerator that smelled like liquefied lettuce. Then Gus was born. Lumpy bags of old clothing and heaps of primary-colored plastic thingamajigs quickly accumulated. When Eli's grandpa Gus died, we inherited enough tools for an entire carpentry shop, in addition to some family heirlooms, including the many prototypes for his inventions. One of these was a battery-operated lever with a clip to which you attach your tea bag, so it will automatically dunk it in and out of your teacup while it's brewing. (I don't think he ever got a patent on that one.) On top of that, we rented out our closetless in-law apartment and needed to give our very tidy tenant, Joel, some extra storage. Joel took one look at our basement and summed up our problem like this:

"It's like you guys never threw out anything that you thought was funny when you were twenty."

Ouch.

So after we have dinner, Eli goes off to work and I get Gus asleep. Then I plunge into my new book, *Organizing from the Inside Out* by Julie Morgenstern. I had never heard of Julie, or any organization expert for that matter, but her name was the only one that came up when I asked around. Apparently she and her company, the New York–based Julie Morgenstern Enterprises, are Oprah's go-to people for this kind of thing. Amazing how much more capable you can feel by simply associating yourself with a known associate of Oprah Winfrey's who's not Dr. Phil. Julie's credits also include being on *Good Morning America*, organizing the offices of American Express, and scoring a back cover blurb from Mandy "the Patink" Patinkin. ("The only thing I don't understand is how Julie looks so young. . . . I'm certain God hired her to organize the first six days of creation!")

Julie's introduction is inspiring. She's conversational, to the point, and doesn't try too hard to be clever. Plus, like any good guru, she is living proof that her system works. She says she used to be horribly unorganized, living in a constant state of disorder and chaos. When she mentions that she once spent four hours scouring the parking lot at O'Hare airport because she paid no attention to where she had parked her friend's car, I felt like we were kindred spirits. Her whole goal is to help you understand how simple it can be to get organized so that you can enjoy your life more fully. I love how easy it sounds.

Julie summarizes her method, which is easy as one-two-three: analyze, strategize, and attack.

Analyze I'm beginning to learn that I really loathe analyzing myself and my behavior, but here Julie is asking me to figure out what's holding me back from being organized. In her list of "psychological obstacles," one pops out: "fear of success/fear of failure." She writes, "If being organized allows you to accomplish anything that you want, and you have a deep-seated fear either of success or failure, then you may be using disorganization as a convenient way of holding yourself back."

It reminds me of Jack Canfield's discussion of the comfort zone. I'm pretty comfortable having my house and files unorganized because when I'm procrastinating, it's convenient to be able to say I have to "clean the house" or "organize the desk." It sounds lame, but I like having an ongoing project that can never be completed. Sort of like in college how there was always that thirty-year-old dude in your astronomy class who'd been working on a single bachelor's degree for twelve consecutive years. *I started out as a psych major in '77 and did some comp lit for a while, and now I'm thinking about going into physics. I'm on the twelve-year plan. Ha-ha. Oh well. Want to go to happy hour at the Crow's Nest? Oh, right. You're only nineteen.*

Framing it in that light makes it less attractive already. I don't want to be that guy.

This system is more than just going to the Container Store and sealing up all your junk in a bin. Julie knows it's uncomfortable, but you need to take the time to figure out what is working, what is not working, which items are essential, and what's causing the problems. She says you need to do this even if you are organizing "a sock drawer." I try not to imagine what kind of person is so organized that, having completed the spice cabinet and the linen closet, the final frontier comes in the form of the sock drawer.

For the record, my sock drawer currently has blank taxi receipts, hard candies, and stray coffee beans in it.

Julie recommends keeping a "problems log" for seven days to fully understand all the frustrations you are feeling in your living space. There are also statements to complete, such as:

> I can never find my keys, wallet, cell phone, lipstick, library card, shoes, paring knife, wine opener.
> There's no room for books, records, CDs, clothes, dishes, shoes, sheets, the spare futon for guests, blankets.
> When people visit, I am surprised because I have probably not invited them over.

Common answers that Julie lists for "Why I Want to Get Organized" are:

> Stop spending so much time looking for things
> Reduce the feeling of being overwhelmed
> Set a good example for my kids

I would add to that: so I can stop complaining about being unorganized. It's like that friend you have who's always stressed out.

After a while you don't want to ask her how she's doing anymore because you can't hear another monologue about how overwhelmed and busy and tired she is. There used to be a time when I thought people were being more "real" when they would go into detail about what was happening with them. More and more, I wish people would go back to the old standby "I'm fine. How are you?"

Strategize: Creating a Plan of Action Julie says that even if you have the desire, time, and determination to get organized, you won't be able to do it if you don't have a clearly thought out plan.

One of her "secret weapons" is something that occurred to me one morning as I dropped Gus off at school. She calls it "the kindergarten model" because classrooms for little kids always have designated zones for certain activities, like the dress-up area or the building block area. The items that you need to do each activity are always stored in the same place when you use them, and when it's time to clean up, it's easy to put things away because everything has a home. Why is our entry hall a perpetual Junk Mail Zone? How did the floor under the desk become the designated Broken Electronics Zone? Would I miss not having a Cardboard Boxes That Need to Be Broken Down Zone?

Her other big tip is to estimate realistically how long it is going to take you to get the job done right. For instance, a typical overhaul on a living room could take twelve hours to do correctly. Obviously, I have no idea what I'm in for.

Attack: Getting the Job Done The five steps to getting organized are:

1. *Sort*: To see the big picture, you have to look at every single scrap of paper or item of clothing and say, "Do I use this? Do I love this? Does this make me or cost me money? What

category does it belong in?" Start with what's visible. This is the stuff you use often, and you will be more encouraged when you start seeing a difference immediately. I guess this means that I don't have to deal with the collection of stray buttons, ticket stubs, foreign coins, business cards, and ancient netted bags of Jordan almonds that are commingled in a shoe box and shoved underneath the dresser in my closet. Yet.

2. *Purge*: Toss no-brainers like tattered clothes or bedding. I skip this one or I'd be left with about three pairs of underwear, four T-shirts, and one set of sheets. Give away or sell things you haven't worn or used in two years. If you have five black sweaters, like I do, try them all on. It will be obvious which are the two to keep. Feel bad about getting rid of the blue glass dolphin figurine your mother-in-law's neighbor gave you for a wedding present? Don't. Set it free.
3. *Assign a home*: A genius once said, "A place for everything and everything in its place." I realize most of the clutter in my house is stuff I never found a place for. The camera, Gus's extra car seat, the stepladder, my asthma inhaler, a foldout futon for guests, the biannually used juicer, bills that need to be paid. Drifters, all of them.
4. *Containerize*: This exciting new verb means that you get to spend a lot of money on plastic bins with lids.
5. *Equalize*: This is when you periodically evaluate your system, making "tune-ups" when necessary. You don't set your radio dial to NPR and just leave it there even when pledge drives or Garrison Keillor come on. Be prepared to make adjustments.

Now that I'm feeling sufficiently gung-ho, I call the offices of Julie Morgenstern Enterprises. Receptionist with a British accent! Nice touch. A lovely associate named Ellen Kosloff comes on the line, becoming lovelier by the minute as her enthusiasm spills over.

She listens in a way I imagine a top-notch therapist would, not even perceptively cringing when I say that Eli parks his bike in the living room or that we need a place to store mustaches and wigs. Ellen immediately makes me want to surrender to her, to do everything she says.

But then comes the terrifying part. I am instructed to provide a floor plan of my house and take 360-degree photos of every room, with all drawers and closet doors open.

"Just so we know what we're dealing with," Ellen says.

That afternoon I get out the camera and start in Gus's room. The top of his chest of drawers is not even visible because it is so loaded up with cars, drawings, rocks, coins, toilet paper rolls, plastic animals, and rubber bands. Some of these are "containerized" in drinking glasses or shoes.

Even though Ellen said that I'm supposed to leave everything as it is, there is no way I can go through with it. I put down the camera and start throwing stuff in garbage bags.

"It'll be funnier if you just leave it as it is," Eli says.

"I don't want it to be funny. I don't want to live in a funny house. I want to be seminormal at least. We have the power to achieve that."

He looks at me sideways and leaves the room. My ever-expanding self-help vocabulary is kind of a turnoff, I know.

Good thing they don't make digital cameras with smellovision yet because something is brewing in Gus's closet. I have always feared that my house would end up smelling the way that people's houses smell when they have little kids. Now I know for sure that it actually does. It's as if someone burned a stick of butter in a sauté pan and then decided to make a roux with a few cupfuls of baby powder. Sweet and rancid. There are board games, Legos, a never-used crystal punch bowl set, suitcases, and the SpongeBob piñata still stuffed with candy and toys from Gus's birthday party when it rained. It also doesn't help that we have shoved his closet full of thirty-year-old polyester clothes and secondhand shoes. A pair of chocolate brown panty hose hangs from the nose of a jester doll. A sticky ooze of Desitin, which he hasn't needed in over a year, has emancipated itself into an old container of Oil of Olay facial cleansing pads that now contains plastic animals, old credit cards, and beads.

I find an electric breast pump that a friend had given to me. She used it daily for years, and though I had planned on cleaning it up and regifting it, when I zip it open and look at the plastic tubes, I gag. I remember sitting at the kitchen table, with the suction cups over my boobs, trying to eke out some milk to put in a bottle for the babysitter. Squeezing and freezing, pumping and dumping. *Thank God that's over,* I think, as the leatherette-encased contraption sinks deep into the trash bag with a thud. Oh, that feels good. I start piling clothes into a separate trash bag. Everything in here smells like a baby who eats only Twinkies and was born in a thrift store. Three hours later, I haul three suitcases, a fax machine, and two bags of baby toys down to the basement, the oversized trash bag out to the curb, and four bags of clothing to the green donation bin on the corner.

Then I pick up the camera again and take the picture.

I subsequently move through all the rooms in the house, straightening up before I shoot each angle, in a futile attempt at turd-polishing.

I e-mail the pictures to Ellen, who suggests that perhaps I would like to speak with Julie herself. Ellen seemed so capable that I never would have suggested this, but then it occurs to me that perhaps it's an indication of how much help I need. Logically, I know my house is not horrible in a "daytime talk show" way, but I worry that the type of person who usually hires a professional organizer is an anal-retentive obsessive-compulsive who wants approval on the sock drawer. Like those gym bunnies who work out a few hours each day but buckle and get lipo for that last two pounds anyway.

Just like that, a phone date with the master is set up for the following week.

In the meantime, I painfully continue my analysis step, exploring why my clothes closet looks much like it did when I was thirteen. Socks hanging out of drawers, sweaters balled up and tossed to the highest shelf, inside-out dresses sharing hangers with wrinkled blouses that are missing buttons. I actually like most of my clothes, but I treat them with no respect whatsoever. I keep my housecleaning supplies, *which I hardly ever use*, in better shape. Oh why, pop psychology gods, why would I do this?

I have a breakthrough. It's probably because I have always been ambivalent about fashion. Part of me enjoys interesting clothes, and another part of me thinks they're a big waste of time. I've long had this idea, a mostly misguided one, that there is something virtuous about dressing down, about not calling attention to yourself, not wasting time cultivating a "look." I thought this even as I scavenged for floor-length hostess gowns at rummage sales and handed over hard-earned pocket change for amateur crocheted sweater vests at garage sales. Clearly, my closet is that ambivalence writ large. A similar analysis probably explains the way I "file" the household bills. When you never have enough money to pay them, why bother trying to organize them? Why go to the trouble of elucidating how broke you are?

The day of my phone meeting with Julie, I decide that it would be a good idea to record the conversation so I can refer to it later. A method that many of my friends who go to psychics use. Eli says we have some kind of RadioShack device that will do the trick, but guess where it is? The basement. Cue Penderecki horror movie score. Having spent a half hour down there the other day spelunking for my awful long-waisted leather pants for Carole Murphy (the lesbian comedienne character) to wear, I have doubts about reconnaissance. I submit to buying a new one.

I get Gus in the car to bring him to school, but by the time I've parked he's not looking too well. His cheeks are all red and his forehead is hot.

"Okay," I say, stroking his hair. "Mommy just has to go to Radio-Shack and buy a thing, and then we'll go home."

"What thing?" he says. "What thing do you have to buy?"

"It's a thing so we can record a phone conversation I'm going to have."

"I wish you were only a banana," he pouts. "A banana never has to buy a thing when I'm sick."

The trip to RadioShack is painless, though. A miracle, a first. Unless you count the psychic pain of spending $15 on something we already own but are too disorganized to locate. (By the way, Julie acknowledges that this is an ongoing problem of the highly unorganized and contributes deeply to financial problems.)

When we get back home, Gus is clinging onto me monkeylike, and Eli is on the phone. His voice has an unusually polite quality, like how I imagine he probably spoke to his step-grandmother Midge when she was alive. Midge was a Fairchild Aviation heiress who married Eli's dad's father. Even though Eli never knew his dad, which is sad, we get a lot of laughs knowing that he is somehow related to East Coast blue-blood millionaires. Especially when we are paying our electric bill in installments.

"One moment please," Eli says, handing me the phone. Then he whispers, "It's that lady. You had an appointment at ten!"

"What?!" My hand is over the mouthpiece, which I logically know makes matters worse. The sound of muted distress burns through the lines.

"Julie!" I pick up the phone breathlessly. "I'm so sorry!" I shout, letting loose with a string of overly emotional apologies more appropriate for running over someone's pet. "Wasn't our appointment for 1:00 P.M.?"

My clock says 10:15 A.M., which I'm simultaneously realizing is 1:15 P.M. New York time.

What an amateur I am. Getting the time zone wrong.

"Oh! Your time! Your time!" Like there could be any other.

I start talking too fast about the dumb time zone. She seems a little annoyed. I can just picture her sitting there in her perfectly organized Manhattan office, wondering where her one o'clock appointment was, before deciding to get proactive and pick up the phone herself, even though I was supposed to be calling her. There is a brief silence.

"Do you need another few minutes to get it together?" she asks calmly.

"That would be great!" I say. "I am so, so sorry. I'll call you back in five minutes!"

I hang up the phone, ripping the new recording device out of its packaging.

"Mommy, I do want to go to school," Gus says. "I feel better now."

Eli tries to set up the recording gadget on our cordless phone, but it doesn't work. He says it might be compatible with our old fax machine phone, the one I just brought down to the basement last week. Thanks to the geologic layer effect, I'm able to scurry down into the rubble and locate it semi-immediately. The only problem is, I can't find the receiver for the phone. The connection was always loose, and when I transported it, I didn't remember seeing it in Gus's closet.

So Julie Morgenstern, America's number one organizing expert, is presently sitting in her office waiting for one Beth Lisick of Berkeley, California, to call her back. This overwhelming feeling of naked lameness is becoming more and more familiar. In no single year of my life, including seventh grade when I got the Olivia Newton-John "Physical" haircut, have I ever felt lamer.

Eli is late for work now, but I need him to help me set this up.

"Don't worry about it," he says. "We don't really need the receiver because I can run the line through the other phone, but we have to keep the hang-up button down."

I rummage through one of our three junk drawers, looking for tape, as Eli grabs a peanut butter–covered knife that's sitting on the counter and shoves it into the receiver cradle. Works like a charm.

I take a deep breath and call her back. It's been almost fifteen minutes.

"I only have about fifteen minutes to talk," she says curtly.

I'm tempted to remind her about a certain story of hers involving the O'Hare Airport and see if she still has a body memory of what that was like, but thankfully, she warms up right away as I explain my organizing needs. She starts looking through the photos.

"So this is Gus's closet I'm looking at with the SpongeBob piñata?"

"Right."

"And this is a picture of it having been cleaned out?" She says it gingerly, not insinuating how laughable it is that I consider this "clean."

She asks me about the fact that we have one desk in the living room and one in the dining room. What is the difference between them? I realize that I open up my bills and put them on the desk in the dining room, but try to keep them filed in the desk in the living room.

"That is what we call 'inconvenient storage,'" Julie says, chuckling a little. I think of Richard and what a kick he got out of his rotator cuff. Specialists.

Realizing we have only a few minutes, I ask her for recommendations on containers, an area I'm discovering I'm very uptight about. I don't want to spend a bunch of money on containers. The Container Store wasn't founded until 1978, and people somehow got along just fine before that. Julie sets me straight.

"Your impulse is to go right to containers. It won't work. It won't last. You really want to do it *from the inside out*. I think with proper marching orders, you could implement a program yourself, but it's okay if you can't. There is no judgment in that. It's a matter of what you have talent and patience for, and what you don't have talent and patience for."

I appreciate her professionalism. Talent. Patience. I could use another helping of both, please. But here she is looking at pictures of our ripped couches and bedsheet curtain and three separate junk drawers, and she is telling me I can do it. She is not trying to sell me on more services; she's acting like she believes in me.

The next step, she says, is the "needs assessment" consultation with her most senior associate. This is where I will get my "marching orders."

We bid farewell, and an appointment with Deb is scheduled for the following week. The two-hour phone consultation will cost me $350, which for some reason doesn't sound outrageous, even to a cheapskate like me. This must have something to do with how far beyond my skill set these talents are.

The morning of my needs assessment, I decide to go running for the first time in about five years. I thought with my newly refound physical fitness I would be able to jump back on the horse, but after the first five minutes I just feel old and creaky. My hips seem all out of whack. The car exhaust is annoying me. The roving gang of thirteen-year-old boys who smoke pot all day and never go to school makes me depressed. I putter along, ankles popping, knees crackling. When I reach the stoplight, I double over and let my knuckles graze the sidewalk. Being limp like that feels good. It feels really good. How I wish I weren't standing on the corner of Alcatraz and Sacramento in front of a sketchy liquor store, so I could let my defenses down and just swing here for a while.

Strangely, the listless hanging fires up my powers of positive thinking. I know it's a good thing to boost my heart rate. It's nice to be outside instead of sitting in front of a computer. Look at all the flowers blooming. I keep jogging along. My neighbor the big rig driver is heading off on a run. I wave. My neighbor the free-lance mechanic is working on a car in the street in front of his apartment. We smile at each other. When I get back home, my next-door neighbor Cliff is off to visit his wife in the hospital, something he has done every single day, twice a day, for the past six and a half years since her massive stroke. I stop to chat.

"All right now, Beth!" This is Cliff's totally cool way of saying hi. I wish I could appropriate it, but no matter how hard I try, I will never be a sixty-year-old black man.

"You know, yesterday when I went into her room, I got a little smile," he says. "I told her, 'Betty, you just made my whole day. I don't care what else happens today. Just because you gave me that smile, I know I'm going to have a good day today.' And you know what she did? She reached up like she was going to tug on my beard. She tried to pull on my beard! I tell you, it's things like that that can really keep you going."

Clearly, a certain banana needs to work on her gratitude.

When Deb calls, the first thing she does is line up all the pictures of my house. A smattering of shame coats me as I imagine the photos getting forwarded around the office, from Ellen to Julie to Deb, like the JPEG of a starlet's hairless vulva.

"Tell me your frustrations," she says. Deb sounds like an empathic listener already. These organizing ladies have serious skills.

I tell her about the clothes and the toys and the bills, hating the timbre of my voice as I do. I wonder if she's thinking, *Another day, another stressed-out mom who can't find her keys.*

She gets me to focus first on the positives and tell her what *is* working in my life.

"Do you have problems getting out of the house in the morning?"

"No," I say proudly. "I don't. I can totally get out of the house and get Gus to school on time."

"Great! And what is it about that routine that works?"

Of course, like a pro, she's just given me the answer. It's because it's a routine. A habit that I've cultivated. I tell her she's doing a fine job of boosting my self-esteem.

"I find that almost everybody has somewhere that they're organized."

We start the tour, looking at the pictures I've sent. Here's the highlight reel:

Dining Room

"What works in here?"

"Um . . . well, we eat at the table. Does that count?"

"And it's usually pretty clear of stuff?"

"Yes, because we pile everything on the desk over there."

"I see. So the desk is where things get dumped."

"Yes."

"And it's just piled there."

"Yes."

"And there's no system for this stuff."

"Right."

TV Room

"I think I'm seeing a toolbox on the floor next to the chair."

"Yeah, not that there's tools in there or anything."

I remember receiving that toolbox as a corporate thank-you from the Levi's Corporation in 1999 for some spoken-word thing I did. It was covered with a custom-made magnetic poetry set that had words like "hip" and "edgy" in it. Now it is filled with rocks Gus has collected from the playground at school that he calls his "African bubble-gum rocks." A phrase that sounds like it could have been made with a magnetic poetry kit itself.

Gus's Room

"Is that a couch against the wall?"

"Yeah, it was my grandfather's. It's an antique psychiatrist couch, but the springs need to be replaced, and it should be reupholstered. Maybe we could put it in the basement?"

"Do I have pictures of the basement?"

"No."

Our Room

"I see in this photo, over there next to the window . . ." (she's referring to the window with the bedsheet on it) ". . . what looks like a . . . is it a mattress?"

"Yes, it's a futon for when we have guests. Maybe I could put it in the basement?"

Throughout the call, I keep suggesting that we put things in the basement. I am such a scamp, but she's onto me.

"Okay, but is the basement dry?"

"Um, no. Well, parts of it are. Yeah, I guess that's not a good idea. If I put the futon in the basement, then I could never, ever make anybody sleep on it again."

I wonder if she can tell in the pictures there is a trash bag taped to the wall to seal off a mold outbreak.

"I'm seeing two dressers. One with a lot of boxes underneath it. Tell me about this."

"Um."

"And what about this sofa in the bedroom."

"Well, again, it's one of those family heirloom things."

"So does that mean you'll always keep it?" She says it gently, but the point is clear. Just because it's a family heirloom does not mean I have to keep it forever and ever.

When we get to the closet, I make a confession. Something I have never told anyone.

"Our shoes are in a wine rack." I say it breathlessly. Confessing, yes, but also hoping she'll ignore it.

"I'm sorry. Your what?"

"We keep most of our shoes in this wire wine rack thing that we got at a garage sale."

"Oh." She sounds amused. "And is that working for you?"

"Well, no."

"Okay . . ."

I feel reflective.

"I think it's because a shoe and a bottle of wine are not really the same shape."

"Good."

Kitchen

"What's in the big plastic bag?"

"I've been collecting wine corks for my uncle who makes fishing lures."

She's silent for a second, and suddenly I get embarrassed by the sheer volume of wine corks, corks that must correspond to finished bottles of wine. I add, "I've been collecting them for a long, long time."

Silence.

"Maybe I will mail them off!"

She's looking at another photo.

"Are those your cleaning products up there?" she asks, referring to one of the pictures.

"Yeah, we moved them up there to be safe."

"But that is a cabinet above the stovetop, isn't it?"

"Yeah. That way Gus can't reach them because we never got around to putting all those safety latches on the cabinets."

"So it probably gets pretty warm up there."

She is like a skilled piano teacher. Letting me hit a clam over and over until I finally figure out it's the wrong note.

Why, yes. Come to think of it, it is warm up there where we store all of our highly flammable chemicals.

Thanks, Deb!

After two straight hours on the phone, yet another junior high flashback for me, we hang up. I for one am exhausted and can only imagine what Deb must be going through. Or maybe after a career of this stuff, she's seen too many doozies to be affected. Does seeing a plastic garbage bag duct-taped to the wall in someone's bedroom ever roll right off your back?

Later in the afternoon, as part of our "taking care of business" agenda, Eli has a doctor's appointment to get a big lump removed from his chest. He confesses to having a giant crush on our doctor, which reminds me of my "Cruise to Lose" dalliance. I still haven't gotten around to telling him yet. As more time passes, it seems so much easier to keep ignoring it. During a break at one of my banana jobs last month, one of my Fruit Guys pals, Erin, got it out of me that I met a cute guy on the ship.

"Did you make out with him?" She grinned. She's a married lady, like me, with a couple of kids.

"No!" I lied, acting shocked.

"Really?" she said. Was I that transparent? "'Cause that's what people do, you know, in those types of situations. You're on a cruise. . . ." Her voice trailed off, and thankfully, we went on to another topic. But something about the way she had said it made me think that maybe it wasn't such a big deal. A lapse in judgment. Sleeping dogs and all that.

I think of this as we drive to the doctor's office.

"It's sweet that you have a crush on Dr. Kawai," I say.

"Yeah," he says, "my crushes are always on older ladies."

"That's awesome. I'm just going to keep getting more attractive to you as I enter menopause."

Eli makes his eyebrows dance up and down real fast and goes, *"Hot flash!"* This thing he's getting removed he first noticed growing smack dab in the middle of his sternum about four years ago. Dr. Kawai checked it out and told him not to worry about it, but if it got bigger and he wanted to get it removed, he could. It has definitely grown bigger, into a disclike shape, resembling a stack of three or four Necco wafers. Hard to ignore. Because he's working every day and night this week, we decide to multitask and merge "couple time" with "minor surgery." Then afterward, instead of lunch or coffee, we're going to stop by the orthopedic shoe emporium to get his shoes adjusted.

"Just imagine how many weird appointments like this we're going to have as we keep getting older and older," he says as a man named Cyrus inspects his middle metatarsals.

"I know," I say, grabbing his hand, thinking of my mom and dad. "We get to slowly fall apart together."

The next evening I receive an e-mail from Deb. She has already written up my marching orders! I'm pleased to see that I can implement most of them straight away.

I create a "baking zone." Baking is something I like to do, the closest thing I have to a hobby, and she instructs me to devote an area to all my baking stuff. A cabinet that used to have a cheese grater, the bag of corks, disposable chopsticks, an ancient can of shortening, and a citrus juicer now is home to measuring cups, cookie cutters, pie dishes, muffin cups, and the rolling pin, as well as flour, sugars, and vanilla.

Another one of her suggestions is that I remove a glass door from a cabinet in my kitchen. The bottom of the door is at countertop level, so if anything is on the counter in front of it (usually the chopping board, but also Gus's lunch box, the fruit bowl, a stack of unopened mail or papers), the door cannot be opened. By removing it and rearranging what's on the shelves, I'm able to take a bunch of stuff off the countertop and move it into the cabinet, now easily accessible, and create more surface area. (The only problem with this is what to do with the glass door after you take it off. If you're us, you put it on the front porch, where it still remains.)

I purchase my first Morgenstern Enterprises–sanctioned container, one with wheels that fits under Gus's bed. I put all of his extra sheets and blankets in it, freeing up an entire shelf in the hallway cabinet. Always thinking, Deb knows what to do with the free space. *Consider moving your cleaning supplies from above the stove to this newly open area.*

I begin work on my "transient paper system," creating folders labeled with "action phrases" like TO FILE and TO PAY. Deb suggests setting up one day a week when I process my paper so that I don't feel like I'm doing it "all the time."

Our clothes are going to take a long while, at least an estimated twelve hours for both of us, but I begin my sorting process. Guess who happens to have thirteen socks with no matches? The same no-longer-lactating individual with three ugly nursing bras in her underwear drawer.

My parents take Gus for the night so we can go out to dinner with some friends and see a band. By midnight, we're exhausted. We duck out before the set is even over. Though tired, I'm feeling pretty good. Having the house organized has made me noticeably less stressed out.

For instance, usually on a weekend like this when I'm faced with single-momming it, when Eli is working ten-hour shifts on both Saturday and Sunday, there is a small component of dread involved. I want to plan fun stuff to do with Gus, but I'm always trying to fold laundry, pay bills, and clean out the refrigerator in between games of Sorry! (That's classic Venus behavior, by the way. According to John Gray, men are much better able to turn off their brains and chill out. It's that age-old scenario of the man coming home from work and flipping on the TV, while the woman endlessly putters around the house folding towels and wiping down the windowsills with a damp sponge. Gray says women don't turn off their brains until they pass out at the end of the day.) Without as much to worry about in the house, I can enjoy hanging out with Gus more. It's been a lot more fun playing cards or doing watercolors when I know right where to find the things we're looking for. I never thought I could get satisfaction from snapping a lid onto a plastic container that houses Hot Wheels and Hot Wheels *only*.

Making the turn onto our cross street after our date, we see four cop cars lined up at the end of our block, siren lights spinning. Yellow police tape is cordoning off the entrance to our street. Eli rolls down the window, and an officer comes over and says someone was shot and killed tonight. Three doors down from our house. There's a cluster of neighbors gathered on the sidewalk, and Pee Wee tells us it was Dre, a father of two who was holding house parties to help pay his rent. Dre was collecting money at the door, and when he confronted a teenager about not bringing a gun into the party, the kid shot him point-blank.

The next day there are news crews outside for most of the morning and afternoon. Dre's wife and family are out in front weeping, retelling the story to friends who stream in hour after hour. There are candles burning and photos out on the stoop.

Our neighborhood is a dangerous place to be sometimes. I think about my conversion to organization, about having a semblance of control over what is happening inside your house when you feel like you can't do anything about what happens outside.

It's why Americans love gated communities and build safe rooms.

I come home one afternoon a few days later and find someone has graffitied a big R.I.P. DRE in Sharpie on our fence. I respectfully let it sit there for a few days before going out at night with a brush and a can of paint.

June

THE HAMMER THAT ROCKS THE CRADLE

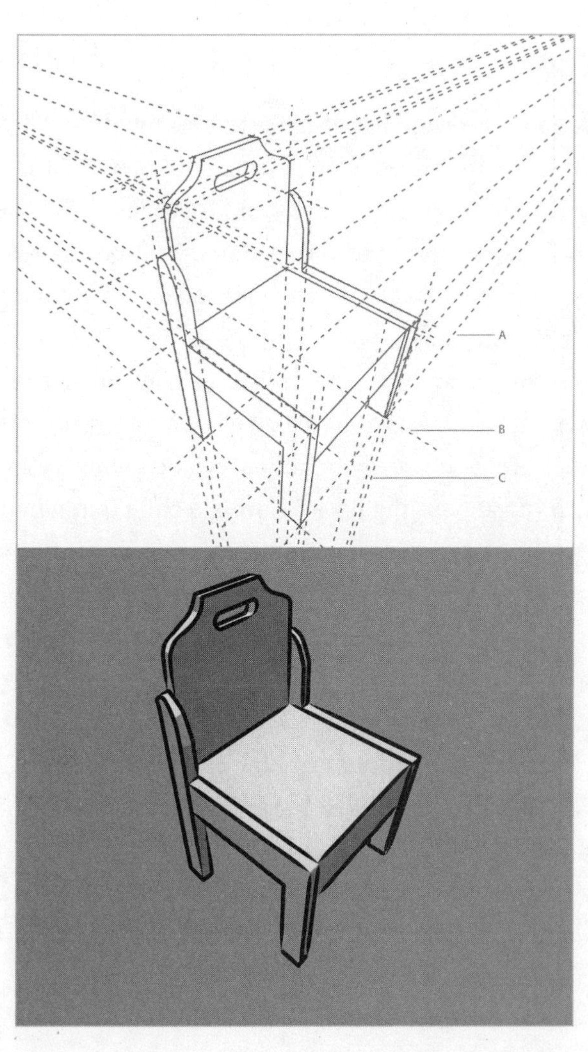

"Okay, sweetie! It's time to get dressed for school!"

That's me in the morning, trying to pretend that getting dressed is a super-fun activity for a four-year-old. Why sit around eating cinnamon toast in your pajamas all morning when you could tug on a pair of jeans with an elastic waistband and get strapped into a car seat?

Gus, of course, can hear it in my voice. The lame adult tones of fake enthusiasm and anxiety. We've been having issues about getting dressed lately, so I really might as well be saying, "Please don't start screaming and crying now. I have a feeling that what I'm saying is going to trigger some screaming and crying, but if you look deeply into my eyes, you'll understand that the only thing I want for you is eternal happiness, and let's not fight about it, and also, could you just please calmly walk to your bedroom and get your clothes on, please? Without screaming."

He ignores me. He's busy right now anyway, building miniature garages for his cars out of blocks and Legos. It's possible he didn't even hear a thing.

I walk into the living room and squat down next to him.

"Hey, honey. It's time to get dressed now. We want to make sure we get to school for Circle Time!"

"No!" he whines, not looking up. "I'm not done building my houses yet!" His lower lip starts trembling.

I keep up the chipper mom-voice, the one that sounds a lot like I'm talking to a dog. "We can finish it after school. Come on, it's time to go. Mommy has to go to work."

"No! I'm not doing it!"

"Gus." And now stern. "You need to get dressed."

"I don't want to get dressed. I'm not going to school today!"

"Um, actually. Yes. Yes, you are going to school today." My voice takes a hike into mildly sarcastic territory, something I try to keep a lid on.

It's clear I'm not getting anywhere. I let out a big sigh while folding my arms across my chest. That looks good. Way to stall. Thinking . . . thinking . . . and . . . got it.

"Gus, if you don't get dressed now, you're not going to have any cars to play with when you come home. Now I'm going to count to three."

Nice one. Counting to three!

Except he just keeps playing and doesn't look up. I go to his room, pick out some clothes, and bring them back in the living room.

"Look! Here's your shirt right here."

That's it. Trot out the chipper mom-voice for an encore.

"Your Lightning McQueen shirt! I'll help you!"

"No!"

"I don't think Elliott has seen your Lightning McQueen shirt yet. He loves Lightning McQueen!"

Nothing.

"Okay. One . . ."

He stacks a block.

"Two . . ."

He drives two cars into the garage.

"Three. Okay, that's it. I'm putting your cars away."

"Waaaaaa! No! No!"

Earsplitting screaming and shrieking ensue. He tries to jump up and grab the cars from me as I make a big huffy production about putting them on the top shelf in our closet, which, thanks to Julie Morgenstern, is now home to stacks of neatly folded sweaters. He's grabbing at my pants, jumping and hollering. I pick him up and try to hug the anger out of him.

"Come on, honey. Let's get dressed now."

I sound so defeated, like a lady in a Lifetime movie who finally buckles under and decides to take her husband back even though he slept with the nanny.

"No! Noooooooooo!"

Now I'm pissed. I put him down. "Okay. Go to your room. Come out when you are ready to get dressed."

Ready to get dressed? A difficult concept for him to grasp, I'm sure, as he takes off in the opposite direction, headed straight for a recently constructed pillow fort. I take his arm, lead him back to his room, and shut the door.

He opens the door.

"You must be ready to get dressed because you're opening the door."

"No! No! No!"

I lift his hand off the doorknob and shut the door. He opens the door. I shut the door. He opens the door.

"Are you ready to get dressed?"

"No!"

"Then you're staying in here. I'm setting the timer for five minutes."

I shut the door and hear him heading for his other door, the one that connects to the bathroom. His little feet tear across the tiles, into our bedroom, and then he appears in the living room with a huge grin on his face. I want to laugh, but I can't. And honestly, I don't really feel like it.

"Fine." I say, taking him by the hand again. "I'll set the timer for another minute. Every time you come out, you get another minute."

"You can't make me!"

"Actually, I can make you."

I say it all smug and shit. It's seriously getting like *Three Faces of Eve* around here. Somewhere deep inside, it hits me that this whole thing would probably make a pretty choice YouTube clip. My sad, frustrated mom-face scrambling for a solution while getting taunted by someone who wasn't born until 2002. I can imagine forwarding the video to my parent friends, typing in a little message ("Look familiar? Ha-ha!"). And it would be funny if I found it on YouTube, as opposed to its way-too-frequent rotation on MeTube.

I go around to the bathroom, lock the door so he can't escape that way again, put him in his room, and shut the other door. I hold on to the doorknob and pull so he physically can't come out. He's pulling back.

We are now having a tug-of-war. There is no way this can be the right thing to do.

He tugs and yells for another minute or so. Then he gives up. Through the keyhole, I see him open his closet door, get out a puzzle, and plop down on his blue amoeba-shaped rug. Thank God.

Now it's time to play beat the clock. Can I gather up all our stuff before the timer goes off? Lunch box, computer bag, library books, jackets, envelopes to mail. I lump them in a heap by the door.

Just before the timer goes off, he calls out to me, sweet as pie.

"Mommy, can I come out yet?"

"Thirty more seconds, honey."

I feel like such a jerk, but I know that you're supposed to follow through with the punishment. Studying the collage of debris on the kitchen floor, I lean against the counter and wait. Parsley leaf. Crunched-up peanut. Tomato sauce splatter. There has to be a better way to get him to do what he's supposed to.

Finally, his door clicks open, and he nearly takes my breath away. All adorable in his jams and bedhead, his cheeks still wet with tears. I give him a big hug.

"Are you ready to get dressed now, honey?"

"Yes," he says, defeated.

Parenting was the first endeavor I'd undertaken in my life for which I actively sought out advice on how to proceed, for which I bought a book to consult when I was confused. My pride had to be swallowed whole, even as I gagged. There were so many of the alpha-parenting things I had relished rejecting, like moms' groups and infant music classes and neurotic message boards. We hadn't bought too much unnecessary shit or done over-the-top research on car seats and strollers. Desperately, I just wanted to be a natural parent. Like my parents were. I wanted to be one of those people who are all, *What's the big deal? People have been having babies forever! My parents didn't need a book to raise me!*

Consider my mom. This is her recollection of raising three kids who were born within four years of each other.

"You guys were great," she'll say, shaking her head at all the fun memories. "Really good kids."

"But, Mom. How did you do it? Didn't we fight? Wasn't even one of us a problem?"

"No! You guys were so cute. I mean, Chris had a couple ear infections that would make him cranky, but I guess we were just lucky. Do you remember having lunch on Cape Cod that one time? In 1976? At the Coonamessett Inn? You guys said you were going to start a hotel together! And then that man came up as we were leaving and said he had such a good time watching us because we were all having so much fun!"

We never called her names? Never ran out of our rooms when we weren't supposed to? Never went to bed and then stayed up demanding a glass of water, more light in the room, another story, just one more song, and then whimpered that we were hungry after not eating the dinner she cooked for us?

"I just remember all the good stuff!"

That's a tactic, I suppose.

So the particular issue we're dealing with now is this discipline stuff. We've tried counting to three. We've tried time-outs. We've tried taking toys away. Embarrassingly, we even tried spanking him on a few extreme occasions early on when we were at our wit's end. None of it works very well. We still end up going through the same struggles almost every day, and Gus appears to rather enjoy arguing.

"Hi, Daddy!" he'll say to me, smiling.

"Hi!" I'll say back, going along with his game.

"No, you're Mommy!" He'll laugh.

"Okay, I'm Mommy."

"No, you're supposed to say you're Daddy!"

"Oh, sorry. I'm Daddy!"

"No, you're not doing it right," he whines. "Say you're Mommy!"

"I'm Mommy. Wait, I said I was Mommy the first time, but you didn't like it."

"*No!*" he screams. "Say you're Daddy! Say you're Daddy!"

"Okay. Hi! I'm Daddy!"

"*No!* Don't say hi."

A familiar series of frustrated emotions and actions follows. He probably just wants me to be wrong, which I can understand. Still, even when I try being wrong, I don't do it the right way. I get as annoyed with him as he gets with me.

"I wish I could put him in a can," I'd mumble to Eli as Gus

writhes and screams like he is being dipped in a vat of boiling oil because I won't let him have candy before bedtime. I can't even bear to type what I've thought on other occasions, but the word "can" eventually became our code word when he was driving us nuts.

"We need the can," Eli would say to me as he walked away from one of Gus's tantrums, exasperated.

"Maybe he has some sort of food allergy," a friend with two very calm daughters suggested after observing one of his meltdowns.

I even tried to capture some low points on my digital camera, like one book recommended. Upon replaying them, with all the wobbly framing while he angrily tried to grab the camera from my hands as his screams overloaded the tiny microphone, I found myself sinking deeper into despair. It was terrifying to see my little guy so upset. I wanted to help him.

I don't mean to paint a picture of Gus as a big bag of tantrums. He's an awesome kid—smart and funny and compassionate. He behaves at school and is generally well liked by his teachers and other kids. Our problem is that he's also a couple of those other classic toddler adjectives like "strong-willed" and "vocal." Just not really a mellow, roll-with-the-punches kind of guy. He is a lover *and* a fighter, stubborn in a way that will probably turn out to be a good quality when he's older. According to Eli's mom, he's a lot like her son as a child. (Not to blame anyone's genes or anything. ELI.)

We are on the hunt for an effective discipline plan, something that feels like it is simple enough to explain to him. Even though my biggest fear is being one of those newfangled parents who overthink everything, I also understand that it is ridiculous to concern myself with becoming "one of those people." It reminds me of some of my alcoholic friends who couldn't face AA, even after years of unsavory blackout drinking, for fear of being "one of those recovery people." At some point, you need to get over it and get some freaking help.

At the Smart Marriages conference in Atlanta, while wandering that evangelical convention floor, I saw a book called *1-2-3 Magic: Effective Discipline for Children 2–12* by Thomas W. Phelan, PhD. I picked up a pamphlet but was initially disappointed because the method sounded like what we were already doing. We would count to three, and if Gus didn't do what we wanted, he would get a time-out. Maybe it worked with other kids, but there was nothing magical about how it worked with Gus. A lot of the time we couldn't even get him to stay in his room for the time-out.

The second day of the conference, on my way to voyeuristically enjoy that seminar on porn addiction in the church, I saw Dr. Phelan and his wife chatting up passersby. He gave off a distinctly Mr. Rogers vibe, if only Mr. Rogers had a substantial salt-and-pepper mustache and a set of Martin Scorsese eyebrows.

I introduced myself and told them I had a tantrum-prone four-year-old at home, immediately wondering if it was more acceptable to say "strong-willed and vocal." I explained that we already counted to three and gave time-outs, but it wasn't working. They looked upon me kindly, like perhaps they were about to invite me to a jamboree, and Dr. Phelan said, "Yes, well. It will work if you follow it exactly as it's written in the book." His eyes sparkled behind his eyeglass frames, which were the size of playing cards.

As if being pushed onstage from the wings, a nondescript woman walked up and interrupted us.

"Dr. Phelan, I just want to say thank you. Your book changed our lives."

"Wow," I said to her, glancing over at Dr. Phelan. "It really works, huh?"

He looked pleased enough, yet not impressed in the least, nodding politely, as if to say, *Yes, well, there is a reason I put the word* magic *in the title.*

"With our oldest child, we didn't know about it, and we had a really hard time," she continued. "When our second came along, we started using it, and it absolutely works."

With that, she walked away. A shill couldn't have done it better.

Dr. Phelan handed me a free copy of the book with these words of wisdom: "Good luck, and remember to do it just as it's written. It really will work if you do it right."

I vowed to follow the program to the letter.

The convention floor, in between seminar sessions, was a caffeinated babel of techniques, methods, and schemes meant to improve all manner of relationships. If you tried to follow all that advice at once, surely, like the tower, you would collapse. It was a feeling that was becoming increasingly familiar to me this year. Over in a quiet corner, near a girl in a flowered dress silently handing out biblical bookmarks, I phoned Eli.

"Everything's going to be okay!" I gushed to his voice mail. "I just met this nice Mr. Rogers man who has a discipline book, and it's going to change our lives!"

I wanted so badly for this to be true.

I grabbed a cup of coffee and started reading. The beauty of the "1-2-3 Magic" method is its simplicity, girding my intuition that children's discipline should not be a complicated affair. The book is slim, with cartoony clip art representing both white people and brown people. Graphics also include outsized question marks in a 1970s sitcom font and a few chubby fingers with strings tied around them when there is an "important reminder"! "Quick" is even spelled "Quik." This was my kind of child-rearing book.

The three main components of the book are:

Controlling obnoxious behavior
Encouraging good behavior
Strengthening your relationship with your child

Dr. Phelan states up front, "You will be able to do it when you are anxious, agitated, or otherwise upset (which for many of us parents is every day!). You will be able to be a kind but effective parent when you are busy, in a hurry, or otherwise preoccupied. You'll get them to follow the rules with no arguing, testing, or hitting."

One of the first things to acknowledge is that there are two types of behaviors, "stop behavior" and "start behavior." Whining, yelling, teasing, and hitting are examples of stop behavior, while things like getting dressed and cleaning one's room are start behaviors. There are different tactics for dealing with each one.

The two biggest mistakes that parents make, Phelan says, are too much talking and too much emotion. Guilty as charged. He says that too much talking irritates and distracts kids, and by assuming your kid is a "little adult," you spend way too much time trying to reason with him.

"Hey, Gus. Can you stop slamming the kitchen cupboards open and closed?"

"But I'm trying to see if I can squish this spider."

Slamming continues.

"Well, it's really loud and it's not good for the cabinets."

More slamming.

"But I don't want this spider to bite me," he'll say, slamming it again.

"I'll come over and kill it if you want. Or we could capture it and put it outside."

Slam. Slam. Slam.

"Gus, it's annoying and it's giving me a headache."

Slam.

The problem is that because I am constantly astounded by how smart kids are, it seems like it would occur to them to stop being obnoxious if it were just brought to their attention. Alas, you can't really turn to a four-year-old and say, "Hey, man. Can you chill out? You're being really lame right now."

Embarrassing to admit, but I've tried that, too.

Speaking of this little adult phenomenon, last Saturday afternoon I decided to take Gus to go see a band called the Sippy Cups. My friend Alison, who's a great singer and songwriter, started this group with some of her other parent-musician friends. They were all in bands before they had kids, so they decided to create a show for families, something kids would like with music that wouldn't be a bummer for the parents. They do original compositions as well as cover songs by David Bowie, Syd Barrett, the Beatles, and the Ramones. It was so nice to be able to have something to bring Gus to in the middle of a weekend afternoon, and also kind of a relief to see so many parents at once, doing the familiar public dances of beaming pride and stress management.

At one point in the show, Alison saw a little girl in the audience, probably around three, wearing a Rolling Stones T-shirt and a denim miniskirt. The band was about to play a Stones song, so she asked the girl if she wanted to come onstage. Reluctantly, the girl got up and stood there, stiff as a board, looking out at her parents, so very confused. She had no idea that the big red mouth with the protruding tongue on her shirt was directly responsible for the uncomfortable position she was now in. Tears started to roll down her face. Silently, and with some enjoyment, I began to judge the parents, shaming them for trying to dress their daughter in something they thought was cool. An outfit for a little adult.

Ever since I've had Gus, it's been hard to ignore the media frenzy over something referred to as the "hipster parenting movement," which seems to focus mostly on fashion and falsely conveys the idea that it's an organized entity determined to put a pair of Converse on every kid while instilling them with an appreciation for the songs of Nick Drake. I've found myself reading these articles, slightly agitated, passing judgment on other people's name choices ("The couple's kids, Rodeo Starr Parish, 2, and her six-month-old brother, Tupelo Rocket . . .") or entertainment ideas ("We take

Comet and Agnes to happy hour at our neighborhood bar before going to the Roller Derby"). Maybe it's a result of all the self-help this year, the quest to be more aware of my thoughts and feelings and the reasons I think and feel them, but I'm trying harder than ever to be more discerning in my negativity. I look at this poor girl and stop myself quicker than it takes a temporary tattoo to dry. Being a parent is hard enough. Not everybody in this room has a tantrum-thrower, but all the adults in here, no matter what their kids' names, are currently dealing with bed-wetting or whining or learning disabilities and that weird grip of inevitability, and yes, it's all part of the great circle of life that is natural and normal, but it's also exhausting and frustrating. I'm not going to stoop to bagging on someone because they decided it would be cool to cut their son's hair into a Mohawk or an ironic mullet. In the end, it's not important. The agenbite of inwit is gnawing at me again, because sometimes I secretly enjoy being a jerk.

I read on and see that when introduced to "1-2-3 Magic," some kids will be immediate cooperators and some will be immediate testers. I'm pretty sure I know which one Gus is going to be, but here's a look at how the program works:

If your kid is having a tantrum, look down at him flailing on the floor, hold up one finger, and say, "That's one." Do this very calmly.

Important reminder! Wait five full seconds before doing anything else. That's another thing we were doing wrong. We were probably only giving it about a second or two. Phelan says this pause gives your little shorty time to think. Not talking or being emotional forces the kid to take responsibility for his own behavior.

Then, as he continues spazzing, look at him calmly, hold up two fingers, and say, "That's two." As the tantrum continues, wait five more seconds, and say, "That's three. Take five."

That's when you send them off for a time-out for five minutes. Like other parenting manual writers, Phelan agrees that one minute per year of the child's life is sufficient. You are to say nothing at all as he goes to his time-out, and absolutely nothing when the time-out is over.

This is a huge deviation for us, who more or less badger Gus all the way to his room. I always thought of it more like explaining, but it's not.

"Five minutes!" I'd say. "You are going to go to your room for five minutes, and after you get out I expect you to clean up your toys without arguing or throwing them."

Then, after his time-out was over, instead of starting fresh, I'd say, "Okay. Now are you going to behave for the rest of the afternoon? Because I really don't want to give you another time-out," or whatever. Yuck.

By not discussing the behavior after the time-out, you give the kid an opportunity to start with a clean slate. He'll look forward to being released and getting on with his day if he knows you're going to shut up when he comes out.

Your authority is not negotiable, Phelan writes.

I love this one, as I imagine how annoying it would be constantly negotiating bedtimes, baths, cleaning up, and going to school. I agree that the sooner you establish parental authority, the easier it's going to be for everyone. Plus, all that yammering I was doing now seems like a failed attempt to assert my authority. If I assume it's there all along, hopefully Gus will start to, too.

There are also alternatives to the time-out, like loss of toys, allowance, or privileges, as long as the punishment fits the crime. He says that the woman he once met who poured Drano down her daughter's throat for talking back did not have the right idea.

Exceptions to these rules include giving your child an "automatic three" for hitting instead of letting him have two more swings. Also, if he's called you a new word you haven't heard him say before, and it bothers you, you can later explain to him what the word means and why he can't use it in the house or at school.

We wait for an evening when Eli is going to be home for dinner, and then we have what is referred to as the "kickoff conversation."

"Hey, Gussy. We're going to have a little talk, okay?"

He looks skeptical, but complies immediately, leaving his Popsicle sticks and Elmer's for later. We all sit down on the couch.

"What?" he says, looking back and forth between us like a low-level mobster about to get fingered.

God, I remember that feeling. Scrolling through your brain to figure out what your parents were going to pin on you.

"You know how sometimes when we ask you to stop doing something, you don't want to? And we end up yelling and sometimes you have to have a time-out?" I say.

He's looking a little stunned. The formality of the whole thing is throwing him off, I think, because the last time we did this we had to tell him that my parents' dog died.

"What we're going to do from now on is count to three. If you haven't done what we're asking you, you will have a time-out."

"You already count to three."

"I know." I debate whether to explain the whole five-second rule to him, which is what I normally would do. It seems like that would be falling into the little adult trap. ("Gus, the difference now is that we are going to take five seconds in between numbers so that your developing brain has the opportunity to process the information and eventually you will learn to take responsibility for your behavior.")

Eli chimes in. "And after the time-out is over, we won't talk about it anymore and everything will go back to normal. Okay?"

"Okay."

He's an angel. For a moment, I believe he will never test us again.

Dinner goes well that night until Gus decides it would be funny to put the cap of a pen into my mashed potatoes while I'm still eating them. Phelan stresses curbing any undesirable behavior by counting, and Gus knows not to play with food at the table.

"That's one," I say.

He pulls the cap out and tosses it. Not hard, in an aggro way, but enough so that it lands on the floor behind Eli.

"That's two," Eli says.

"I didn't do anything!" he whines. "I was getting it out of the potatoes!"

Eli and I look at each other across the table, making dumb, clueless faces. We can't decide what to do. Whining is technically a stop behavior, so should we count him? He was just trying to explain. But he obviously knew that throwing the cap wasn't okay, so making excuses to back out of it shouldn't be okay, either. Should it? Are we going to give him a time-out for this?

We let the whining slide, which is quickly followed by a surefire offense.

"Gus, please pick up the cap and put it on the counter," Eli says.

"No!" he counters.

"That's three," I say. "Five-minute time-out."

Well, we didn't do it perfectly, but it feels like an improvement. Until we try to get him to stay in his room for the time-out.

"What does the book say?" Eli asks as he picks Gus up and puts him in his room, only to watch him run out the door. He picks him up again while I grab the book.

"It says if he doesn't go automatically, you can move toward him, and if he doesn't start walking, I can gently escort him by the hand. Or he may need to be carried. Either way, remember to keep your mouth shut."

I practically clap my hand over my mouth. We maintain our silence, but I can't help but feel like I'm acting, following my script, which tells me to remain calm and stay quiet.

The book also says, though I refrain from reading this out loud, that if your kid is older and bigger, don't get into a wrestling match with him. You may give him a choice of punishments, including docking allowance, losing electronic games, or having an earlier bedtime.

Phelan says that you should start the time-out over if the kid comes out prematurely. Some kids, he notes, will keep coming out over and over again until they have accumulated a ridiculous amount of minutes. This appears to be happening as Gus keeps popping out like some kind of vaudevillian. Phelan suggests child-proof doorknob covers or even locks on the outside of the door, which seems extreme. It's possible that the door can remain unlocked or even open, but the first time the kid comes out, the door gets shut or locked.

"Gus," I say. "I will not start the timer for your five minutes until you stay in your room."

It works! After we pick him up and replace him about four more times, he stays in. When the timer goes off, we pretend like nothing even happened.

"Hey, cutie!" I say, opening the door to his room. "Let's show Daddy that cool paper airplane you made at school, and then we'll go get in the bath."

He seems as relieved as I am that the whole thing is over.

We continue this way for another week or so, and it's working incredibly well. He gets a few time-outs a day but will now often stop doing something obnoxious at the count of one. We experiment with letting him keep the door open, which doesn't fly. He stands at the door and screams, so we go back to shutting the door. Eventually, we place a chair in the hallway.

I like "1-2-3 Magic," and the house feels calmer, but it also feels a little strict. I think it's important for Gus to feel like he can reason and bargain with us sometimes, that we want to hear his side. Can you ever ignore anything using this system?

Yes, eventually, Phelan says. But in the beginning, when in

doubt, count. You and your kid can even work together to make a list of countable behaviors. Here are what Phelan calls the "six basic testing" tactics:

Badgering: "Can I? Can I? Can I? Can I? Please, please, please."
Temper: "I hate you!"
Threat: "If you don't let me watch *Dragon Tales,* you can't come to my birthday party."
Martyrdom: "Nobody loves me, and I never get to do anything."
Buttering up: "You look pretty, Mommy. You always look pretty!"
Physical tactics: The incredibly painful nose flicking.

So after almost two weeks, with things going great, we decide to loosen up a little. This is what happens: Eli picks Gus up from school, and they successfully negotiate how long they will stay on the playground afterward.

"Five more minutes!" Eli says.

"Ten minutes!" counters Gus.

"How about seven?"

"Eight minutes!" Gus cries.

"Okay, seven and a half minutes," Eli says, feeling good about how it went.

After they come home, we go with our tenant, Joel, to a nursery to buy plants for the backyard. Joel has recently become obsessed with gardening, which is exciting, because our backyard has been a bounty of weeds and dirt clods since we moved in. (I actually caught Joel pouring a pan of boiling-hot salt water onto the weeds in the cracks of the cement on the driveway, a DIY tactic he stumbled upon on the Internet.) At the nursery, I only count Gus once for purposely pulling the petals off a flower after I had told him not to. Dinner goes great. Gus eats a huge bowl of salad and some sweet potatoes. Then it's time for his bath. It's a hair-washing night.

"First you have to do the Shark Show, then we can wash my hair," he whines.

"Okay," I say. The Shark Show is a musical theater review we do with some plastic sharks on the side of the tub. Technically, I could have counted him for this, but I don't.

I put on a fair to middling Shark Show, about five minutes long with some business involving an evil shark who tries to scare the other sharks, a couple songs, and then I'm ready to get on with the hair washing. Gus, however, isn't. He hates getting water near his face, so rinsing his hair is always a huge deal that involves a dry towel to cover his face and a washcloth that is gently wrung out on top of his head to get the shampoo out. He won't let us even pour a small container of water over his head, or gently spray him with the shower nozzle, even if his face is covered with a towel and his head is tilted up.

It comes down to this: he refuses to move closer to me so I can rinse his hair out because, as he puts it, "I need to stay over here so that the big bubbles don't go over to the other side." He was making a game of keeping all the bubbles on the right side of his body and having only bubble-free water on his left.

"Okay, you can stay there, but it's going to take me a little bit longer to rinse your hair because I can't reach you very well."

I should have counted him.

I wring out some water on his head a couple times, but apparently I'm doing it incorrectly.

"You aren't supposed to rinse the washcloth on the side without bubbles. You are messing my water up!"

At this point, I'm annoyed, and instead of counting him, I take advantage of the fact that Eli is home. I walk out into the kitchen where he's doing dishes and say, "Can you help me out in there? I can't take it anymore. He needs his hair rinsed out."

Eli goes in, and within three minutes Gus is screaming his head off. After trying to negotiate with him, Eli got impatient and told him if he didn't move closer, he was going to pour the water over his head. When he refused to move after Eli counted to three, Eli rinsed his hair with water and Gus went ballistic.

The next forty-five minutes is an ordeal I'd rather not relive. Trying to dry off a wriggling, naked, screaming four-year-old and get him into pajamas. And then we feel like we can't give him a time-out while he's naked. Him especially. He doesn't like being naked. He doesn't even like being barefoot. I'm thinking he'll calm down once he has some pajamas on, once we're getting on with the bedtime routine, because leaving him seething and naked in his room seems cruel.

After he finally calms down—which involves giving him some kind of control via unlimited toilet paper to wipe his nose on, letting him waste sheets and sheets of it sitting on my lap while I sit on the toilet seat—I go to get him a glass of water and bring him the jar of straws so he can pick one out like he likes to.

"Do you want to pick a straw, honey?"

Softly. "I want two."

"You can't have two. Why don't you just pick one? Do you want a blue one?"

"I want two straws, please."

I don't know how to proceed. He's had such a hard night that I want to give him two fucking straws. But what about staying consistent? When we let him take more than one straw, he takes four or five and then throws them out and the waste makes me pissed off. He asked for two straws because he knows he's not allowed to have two straws.

"Just one straw."

"I want two!" He starts getting mad again.

"You have a choice. You can have one straw or no straws."

"Two!"

"I'm going to count to three. If you don't choose a straw, I will pick one for you or you can drink your water without a straw."

I count to three, he folds his arms over his chest, and I put the straws back on the counter. He starts to scream again, though a little halfheartedly. He doesn't have much more left in him.

"Come on, sweetie," Eli says, hugging him. "Let's read a book."

"I want three books," he sniffles. If we're running on schedule, we usually read three books, but all the tantrums have already made it an hour past his bedtime.

"Just one tonight," Eli says. "It's really late."

Again, they go through the one-two-three thing with the books (choose one book or we'll just turn out the light and have no books). Gus won't choose, Eli turns out the light, and Gus cries.

I go in and tell him I'll help him pick out a book. He is so exhausted he can barely keep his eyes open, but he is dead set on reading a book. He sits in front of his bookshelf, overwhelmed.

"I can't decide. I can't decide," he moans.

"Let me just help you. Why don't we read *Go, Dog, Go!* We haven't read that in a long time."

"No."

"How about *Curious George*?"

"No."

"*Clifford*?"

"No."

Cat in the Hat, Hop on Pop, Actual Size, Twelve Little Race Cars.

I desperately try to vary the choices. Animal books, rhyming books, funny books, books about kids who go on adventures without their parents. Nothing. I am being so patient, trying to leave my body and maintain calm.

Finally, he sees a Thomas the Tank Engine book and can barely lift his finger up to point to it.

We get into bed and he leans back, so relieved not to have to fight anymore. When I finish the book, he asks me to tell him a story.

I stroke his hair. "Once upon a time there was a little boy

named Gus who was totally magic. One day he decided that he wanted to fly. . . ." And he's finally out. Two hours after getting into the bathtub.

I go out into the dark house. Eli is gone, off seeing a band whose new record he helped make at his studio. I get a beer out of the fridge, open up the Netflix envelope, and watch the Enron documentary *The Smartest Guys in the Room*. All of my frustration melts away, or is transferred, as I watch the footage of the fabricated California energy crisis, remembering all the times we couldn't pay our gas and electric bill in full because it had doubled in price. Those are the guys who need to be put in a can.

Looking back on it, it's easy to see where we went wrong tonight. I'm sure it was confusing for him that we weren't counting him the way we said we were going to. Eli and I decide to stick with the program a little longer.

I remember something that Stephen Covey wrote in *The Seven Habits* while discussing personality versus character ethic in regards to his and his wife's relationship with one of their many, many sons. Granted, his son wasn't a testing toddler at the time, but it seems like good advice to remember when trying to raise a little person.

"We decided to relax and get out of his way and let his own personality emerge. We saw our natural role as being to affirm, joy, and value him. We also conscientiously worked on our motives and cultivated internal sources of security so that our own feelings of worth were not dependent on our children's 'acceptable' behavior."

So of course you want your kid to be liked, and you want him to be "good," but by putting too much emphasis on the details of how he manifests his personality (thinking of him as "dramatic" or "emotional"), you are valuing that more than his true character.

And personality-driven, quick-fix self-help programs are what Covey finds problematic.

"There are people we trust absolutely because we know their character. Whether they're eloquent or not, whether they have the human relations techniques or not, we trust them. . . ."

A few days later, we're riding in the car.

"Hey, look at the dog on the guy's lap," I say to Gus, pointing to a lab sitting on his owner's lap behind the wheel of the truck next to us. "It kind of looks like the dog is driving the car."

"It *does* look like the dog is driving," he says, laughing.

I look at him in the rearview, cracking up.

"Here's something better, though, Mommy," he says. "What if the dog was driving the truck, but instead of paws the dog had big man-arms?"

This strikes me as the funniest thing I've heard in weeks. A dog with man-arms. Just the phrase "man-arms" alone is amazing. This feeling I get as I'm laughing, and as I'm watching him laugh, is the closest I've ever been yet to experiencing a miracle. In moments like these, the strangest thing happens. All of the frustration and anger and confusion I feel about anything gets completely annihilated. Not just negative feelings related to parenting, but every negative emotion I'm capable of gets wiped completely away for a few seconds. After all we've been through, I'm sitting at that stoplight honestly thinking: *This is the easiest job in the whole world. I am so lucky.*

July

PARTY OVER HERE

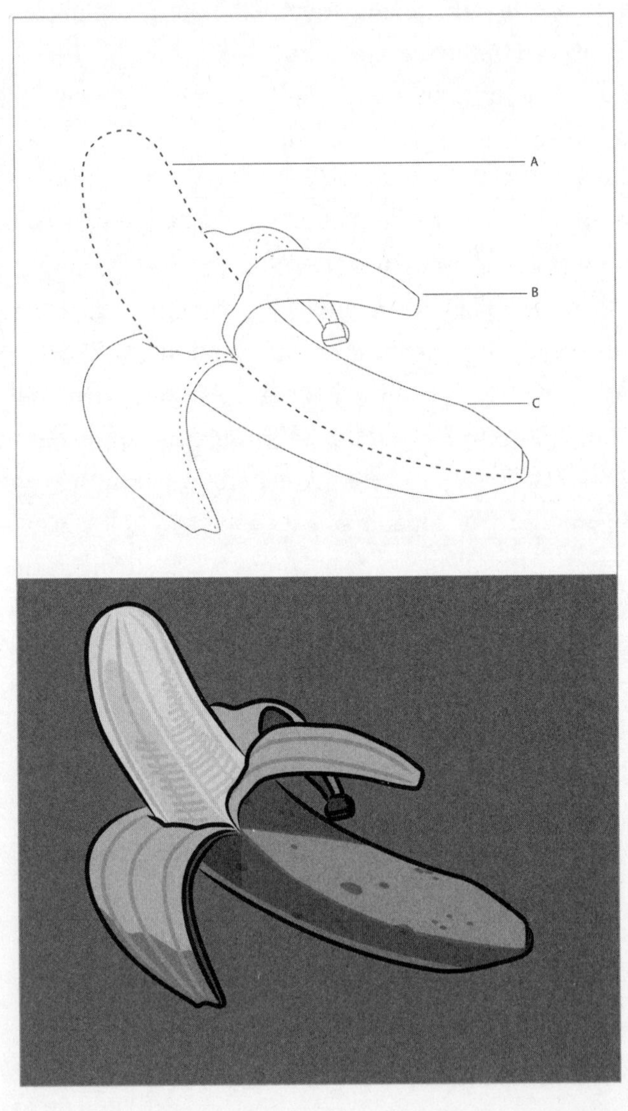

Improving my sex life seemed like such a good idea back in January. Now I realize that I have already read plenty of magazine articles about couples who get a little wild and decide to go to a tantric sex workshop or a role-playing seminar. My mother-in-law even recommended a class called "Sex for One," about the joys of self-loving. Not that we're experts or anything, but Eli and I don't feel like we need to get schooled on new sexual techniques. We've identified our problem: we need to have sex more often. So that's what we're going to do.

August

STALLED OUT

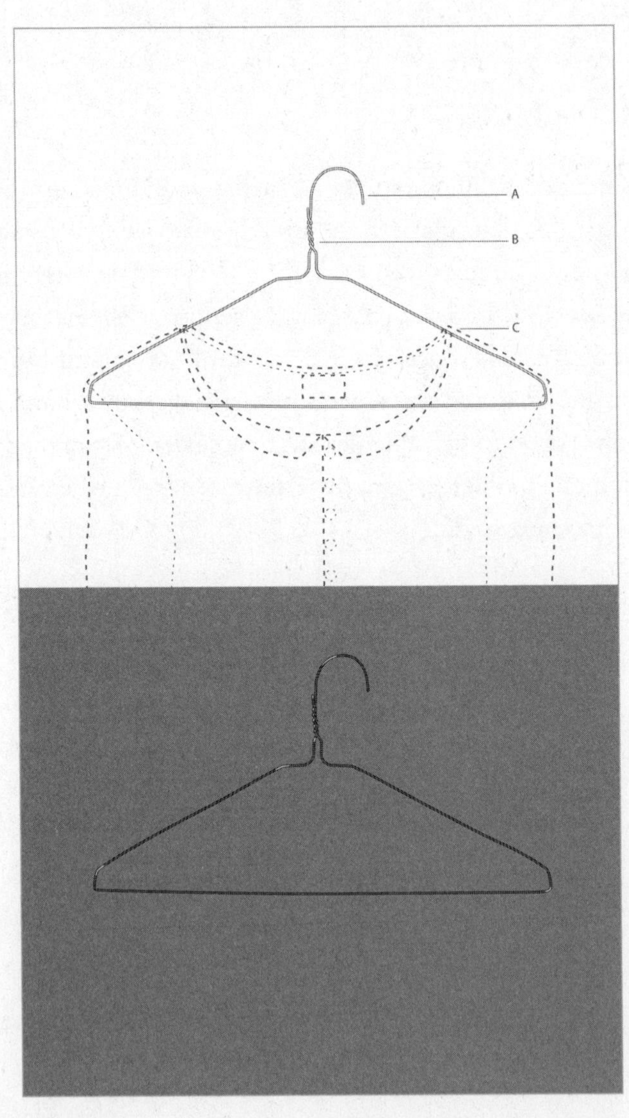

For the first time all year, I am feeling extremely relaxed. Coincidentally, I'm also slipping on my self-improvement project. At some point, I thought it would be helpful to hire one of those wardrobe consultants, those fashion-forward bitches who come in and tell you that your favorite jeans make your butt look terrible, or whatever, but I can't bring myself to do it. Financially or emotionally. The thought of it makes me extremely unmotivated.

The truth is, what I've been wearing a lot is the banana suit. I've done five banana jobs this month, including one at an outdoor mall in San Francisco where I was approached by a life coach from the Dale Carnegie Training Center. I guess he could tell by looking at me that I might need some help. We met later for coffee, but after that he wouldn't leave me alone. I kept blowing off his calls and e-mails until he finally stopped, even though I understand that avoidance is neither a success principle nor an effective habit. Or even very nice.

September

CREATION THEORY

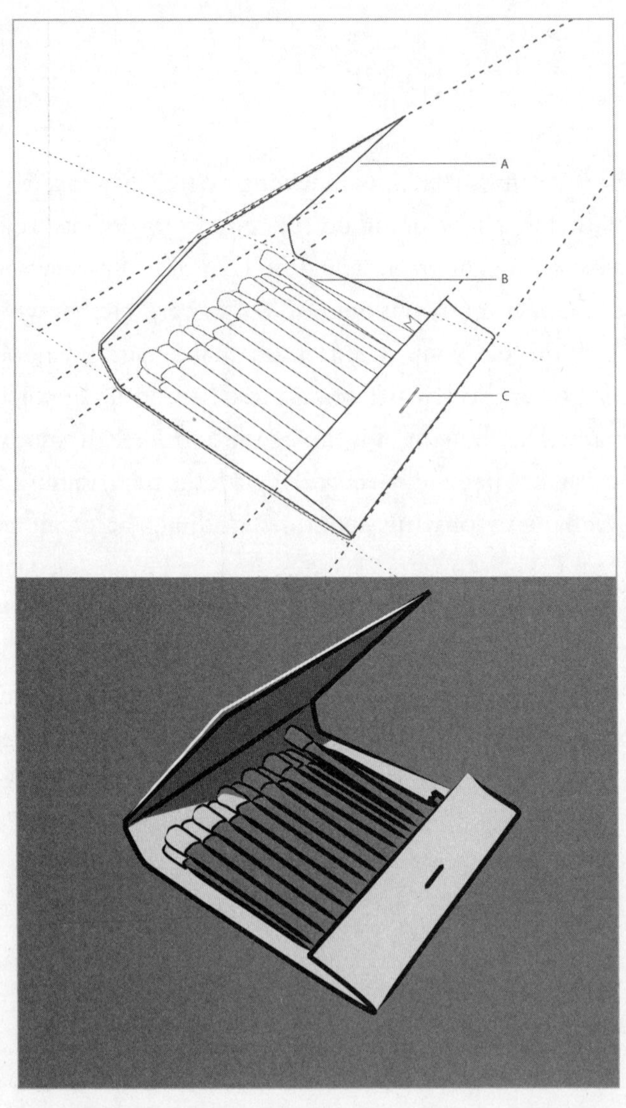

The scene would start with an overhead shot. Just right over the bed as two bodies lie tangled in crisp white sheets, waking up from a ten-hour slumber. As the shot pulls back, we see the beautiful rustic furniture of the bedroom, the ancient wooden beams along the ceiling, the soft, golden light coming through the slats of a shuttered window. It pulls out further to reveal a seventeenth-century stone building, a neat row of cypress trees, a vineyard, a lush green hillside, and a placid blue swimming pool.

It is September 1, and Eli and I are waking up in a villa in Tuscany. We are screwed.

It all started about two years ago when I was visiting my brother Chris in New York.

"What if," he ventured, after taking me out to an insanely expensive sushi dinner at a fancy place called Nobu in Tribeca, "after Lora has the baby, we all go to stay in a villa in Tuscany? Mom and Dad and Paul could come. It will be fabulous."

For the record, he did at least put on one of those blue-blood martini-drinking accents when he said the last part. *Fahbulous*. It's difficult, and not recommended, to say the word *fabulous* in a normal voice, even if you are talking about something truly warranting and/or pertaining to marvel.

Of course, in the heat of a moment that was laced with sake and a certain swelling of filial warmth, I said, "Of course! It will be amazing! Hopefully, we'll have some money by then and we'll be able to afford it. We can start saving now!"

Two years passed. Chris and Lora created a hilarious, adorable son named Theo, and we didn't save a dime.

When Chris called to get our final confirmation, I told him I'd have to call him back.

"What?" he asked incredulously. "Of course you're going."

Eli and I frantically talked it over on the phone during a break in one of his sessions.

"There's no way we *can't* go, right?" I said. "I mean, when in our lives will we ever have the chance to do something like this?"

To put it mildly, we are not very fiscally responsible people. We are so used to the intrinsic domestic havoc of being two married freelancers (*Two Married Freelancers*—sounds like an Alan Alda movie from the '70s) that we are often able to make great leaps of logic like this. It didn't feel all too crazy to write my brother checks for a total of $4,000, in three installments—almost the entire amount in our bank account each time. But then Eli and I started fighting. At first I was the big old wet blanket, aka the "voice of reason."

"We have to back out! There's no way we can do this. We cannot even afford to buy paper towels on a regular basis, and we are about to spend two weeks letting an Italian lady named Maria cook for us and do our laundry?"

By this time, photos of Casa Bacanella, the converted seventeenth-century silk factory, had been whisked across the Internets to us. Replete with a portrait of the *donna locale* who would be tending to us.

"Listen," Eli said. "Either we have to do it and not regret it, or we can't do it at all. It's stupid to pay for it and then complain the whole time about how we can't afford it."

"Okay," I said. "Let's not do it. I'm going to call Chris right now and tell him not to cash the check."

When I called Chris, surely interrupting him from creating a hot new ad campaign for American Express, he gave it to me straight.

"Dude, sorry. It's too late to back out. We can't find anybody else to take two weeks off with this kind of notice. I know it's rough, but I think you guys are locked in."

I crossed my eyes, bit my tongue, set my hair on fire, and managed to summon up an effective habit. If I was going to be languishing about a Tuscan villa for a few weeks, blowing through the entirety of my income, there must be some kind of self-helping I could be doing. Though, as far as I knew, there was no known movement predicated upon spiritual renewal through carbo-loading or increased productivity by way of grappa abuse. Then I remembered something.

Over the years, I had heard a lot of people mention a book about creativity called *The Artist's Way* by Julia Cameron. (Keep in mind that before I lived in Berkeley I lived in Santa Cruz and San Francisco. Kind of a stacked deck, I know.) There's no denying that creativity is a huge part of my life, but strange as it sounds, I'd never given it much thought. Was I taking it for granted? Was it something I needed to explore? Work on? Protect?

After doing some research, I discovered the book has sold a couple million copies and also garnered an impressive cult following. Nearly every single day, somewhere in the world, usually in a location near mountains, water, or an energy vortex, a workshop spawned by the book *The Artist's Way* is taking place. There was no way I could afford to attend one of them at this point, but perhaps I could create my own workshop while on vacation.

Stifling the cringe mechanism was rough. Was I really going to set about reclaiming my creative spirit under the Tuscan sun?

As Julius Caesar might have said, step up to the vomitorium and take a bath in it.

But perhaps I could think of it as my first-ever writing retreat. Recently, I'd unearthed the balls to apply to the MacDowell Colony, the exclusive artists' colony in New Hampshire, only to be rejected, so this could be my chance at having a creative sanctuary. Albeit without any sightings of osprey or Galway Kinnell.

I write this now from Casa Bacanella, where it is quiet enough to hear the towels flapping in the breeze on the clothesline. Twenty-seven hours into it, I have so far only had regrets for about twenty seconds at the airport when Eli wanted to spend four euros on sunscreen and I knew that my parents, and Chris and Lora, had plenty we could use.

"We only have $400 to last us the next two weeks," I reminded him.

He replaced the tube on the shelf, and neither of us mentioned that the $400 was all the money we had, *period*. There were no paychecks coming in the mail. Once we got back home, we'd be starting from scratch.

I begin my morning by grabbing a towel and bringing my book out to the pool to do some reading. It's about seventy-five degrees, not a cloud in this vast cerulean sky, and I spend some time simply holding the book in my lap, pondering the improbability that I would ever relate to something with the subtitle "A Spiritual Path to Higher Creativity." The author, with tousled curls, stage makeup, and a plunging neckline, holds her head in her hand, smiling one of those at-peace-yet-still-a-minx grins. Well, she's not really "holding" her head, is she? It's more like an attractive framing device, like she really wanted her hand to be in the photo because she has divined after years of informal research that you can learn so much about a person by studying her hands. The accompanying bio says Cameron is a novelist, playwright, songwriter, and poet and divides her time between Manhattan and the "high desert of New Mexico." She does strike me as very "Taos." And I always enjoy hearing about people who divide their time between cities as easily as I divide my time between my bed and my car.

I can't crack it open just yet. My surroundings aren't quite through kissing me as I lie prone on the chaise. The air, my God! It's so damn fresh here. What's the name of that new age practice where they manipulate your chakras by infiltrating your nostrils and ears and ass? Rolfing? I want to lie here and be Rolfed by this air today, letting the book provide a cool and pacifying weight on my lap like a lead apron at the dentist's office. Now that's a good feeling.

Chris comes out with his book, a scathing novel about the solipsism of Hollywood written by an insider with a bone to pick, and scoffs at my reading material.

"Dude. Tell me you are not reading *The Artist's Way*."

I stare out at the rolling green hills and say in a hypnotized zombie voice, "I am not reading *The Artist's Way*."

He keeps staring, so I ask him if he's ever read it.

"No," he says definitively, "but I'll tell you something about that book."

We are momentarily distracted by the sight of Lora, a total babe, wandering out in her bikini with Theo on her hip.

"Waaaaait," she says, drawing the word out for a good long while. "Why are you reading *The Artist's Way*?"

"That book," Chris continues, "appears on the bookshelf of every failed artist I know."

Lora nods in agreement.

"And every successful artist I know?"

"Yeah?"

"Does not have that book on their bookshelf."

"Yeah," Lora says. "One of my bosses gave it to me once. He was all, 'I just think you are so *creative*, but you aren't able to express that as a producer, so I thought this would help.'"

With that, I remove the book from my lap and dive into the pool. And in the pool I remain.

Later that night, after stuffing myself with a truly memorable meal Chris cooked, gnocchi with wild boar and broccoli rabe, I settle in again with Julia.

The first few pages are a challenging swallow. There is so much talk about spirituality, creativity, synchronicity, recovery, growth, commitment, and various journeys, I feel like I am standing in front of the community bulletin board at my neighborhood organic vegan restaurant. (With four Bay Area locations, and one opening soon in Los Angeles, Café Gratitude has items on its menu called I Am Flourishing, I Am Elated, and I Am Honoring, etc., so that every time you order some kind of sprouted nut butter wrap, you are forced to vocalize an affirmation. Your order is then repeated back by the server, who then affirms you by saying, "Okay, You Are Abundant!")

The first part of Cameron's course, one I will start to implement tomorrow, is what she calls "the morning pages," three pages of longhand stream-of-consciousness writing executed first thing in the morning. Nothing, she says, is too silly, petty, stupid, or weird for morning pages. By doing this, you are hopefully able to get over all the garbage that stands between you and your creativity. Just let go of your inner censor and feel free to write something, anything, such as my first no-holds-barred offering:

> I can't believe I'm here. Gus is having the best time ever hanging out with his cousin and playing trains. My handwriting has gotten so bad now that I type all the time. Look at this. It's horrible. That bottle of wine we had last night was so

> amazing and I think it only cost like eight dollars or something. These people know how to live. I forgot almost all the Italian I learned in college and am embarrassed to try saying stuff to Maria. We are going to go to a jousting festival later.

For three pages this persists.

With every word, I feel more and more like an incredibly uncreative person with no real spark or insight. Julia says this is normal.

It's true, however, that when I come down to the kitchen to get my coffee and talk to everyone, I feel somewhat unburdened. It's as if I've already expunged most of the mindless interior chatter from my brain. I wonder if it would be rude to suggest this exercise to my mom, who likes to narrate her own thoughts and actions as she goes about her day.

"I'm going to go look in the fridge and see if we have any half-and-half for the morning," she'll say as she goes over to the fridge to see if we have any half-and-half for the morning.

"Your dad takes half-and-half, and you do. Does Chris? What about Lora, I wonder? Eli does too. Oh, that's right. Chris and Lora do. I think everybody takes half-and-half except for me. Well, we should certainly get some more half-and-half."

Then my brother will enter the kitchen, and she'll say, "You take half-and-half in your coffee, right, Chris? I thought so. And Lora too. Everybody takes half-and-half in their coffee except for me. I'm going to put it on the grocery list. Get more half-and-half."

The other basic tool Julia says I will need is called "the artist date," a block of time set aside to nurture my inner artist, to take her out and show her a good time. Treat her like a lady. She explains that this may take the form of a long walk or a special visit to a "junk shop" or an "ethnic neighborhood" (ironically, close to my normal life), and I might feel the desire to stand myself up for my date out of a fear of self-intimacy. My biggest hurdle with this book so far is a story that my friend Mark once told me about his mother.

Apparently, his mom, Dorothy, dresses pretty conservatively, but one Saturday morning while he was visiting her in Fresno, she asked if he would like to go to a downtown arts and crafts festival, seeing that he himself was an artist and everything. (I'm not sure she had ever actually seen his photos, which were inspired by the grotesque work of Joel-Peter Witkin and featured, say, a naked 400-pound man with a one-inch penis wearing clown makeup.) When his mother emerged from her bedroom, she was wearing an outfit he had never seen before, a long cowboy duster coat and matching hat, printed with a black-and-white Holstein cow pattern. She said it was her "artsy coat" for when she was going to do something "fun and creative."

This is what pops into my mind when I hear the terms "artist date" and "inner artist." It's a hard image to shake.

Dipping into the well of experience. This is what Julia says happens when we create art, and she says we need to restock this well with focused attention. The artist-brain, she says, can be found in doing everyday tasks like peeling vegetables, driving on the freeway, or showering. Fair enough. Or, she says, it also works to spend five minutes dancing barefoot to drums, which doesn't seem like it will be happening for me anytime soon. I usually scurry past the drum circle at the flea market as fast as I can. But why? Is it because I'm one of the millions of people who will unabashedly claim that hippies freak me out? Or is it something deeper? I am afraid to open up and let go, scared that I will wind up barefoot, hanging around the edge of a parking lot in a haze of pot smoke, chewing on a length of sun-dried banana with my eyes closed. Would that be so wrong?

At the end of the chapter, there is a contract. I, the undersigned, understand that I am embarking on an intensive guided encounter with my own creativity. I will commit myself to excellent self-care, adequate sleep, diet, exercise, and pampering for the duration of the . . . uh-oh . . . *twelve-week* course?

I flip to the back of the book. Indeed there are week-by-week breakdowns for twelve chapters, but I've only given myself four weeks to complete this one.

I immediately flash on the Executive Book Summaries people from Chicago and decide to design a consolidated "Artist's Way" course for myself. I'm sure most people integrate the program into their regular lives, juggling work and family, along with their barefoot dancing. With all the free time I suddenly have, it should be no problem to squeeze in three chapters each week this month.

The sound of a lone dog barking off near the village is heard as I prop myself up on the fluffy cumulus of pillows and begin my study. Instead of feeling a sense of smug satisfaction that I have isolated myself from the group and am quietly improving myself, I am jealous that everyone else is downstairs watching the first season of *Entourage.*

Note to reader: I read every chapter in the book, but I have been informed by the management that the experience is possibly too grueling to recount on a week-to-week basis. What follows are simply the chapter headings and abbreviated notes from my journey through *The Artist's Way.*

Recovering a Sense of Safety This chapter seems to be all about telling yourself that you are not a piece of crap. I am instructed to write down my affirmations, and luckily, because affirmations are part of so many self-help programs, I have a bunch lying around that I can recycle. My affirmations have become as easy to spout as my Social Security number.

Julia encourages me to go back to painful events, listing any enemies of my creative self-worth. I usually find it helpful to block out negative things that people have said or written about me, but there is one incident that never seems to go away no matter how much alcohol I've tried to pour on it.

About seven years ago, I went to my neighborhood bookstore in San Francisco and placed an order for a book. The cashier asked for my name and number so they could call me when it came in.

"Oh, Lisick," he said, looking up at me. "Wasn't your book on our bestseller list last year?"

I hadn't known about that, and he went into a drawer and pulled out the list to show me. Number ten!

"Hey, that's really cool," I said. "Thanks for telling me!"

"Yeah," he said, returning the piece of paper to the drawer. "I just thought I'd tell you because it's probably the only bestseller list you'll ever be on."

My hands went partially numb, and I didn't quite know what to say. I just looked at him for a second, until I realized my mouth was making a strange shape I associate with Donald Trump. The shape just before pronouncing a hard "ch" sound. Then I walked out, praying he wouldn't be there when I returned to pick up the book.

Julia says that it is necessary to acknowledge these enemies of one's creative self-worth and properly grieve them. She suggests an exercise of writing a letter to the editor in your defense using the voice of your wounded artist child. It's hard not to be put off by all her touchy-feely language, but I also strongly feel that I am over any harm done by this incident. I must have "emotionally processed" it in my own way, which was to tell the story to a million people over the years because it was so humiliating and therefore greatly enjoyable to many.

Recovering a Sense of Identity There sure were a lot of men in wigs at the medieval jousting festival in Arezzo today. Some of them were dressed in armor, which has got to be excruciating in this weather, and still others were encased in polyester tights and leotards, no small feat, either, sweating up a storm as they paraded through the cobbled streets with not so much as an anachronistic Pellegrino bottle under their studded belts.

I found the whole thing pretty inspiring. I mean, here are hundreds of accountants or appliance salesmen or general managers of cell phone retail outlets paying homage to the history of their village by dressing up in cumbersome costumes and attempting to jab a lance at a wooden effigy of a Saracen king. Though it's serious historical tradition in Arezzo, it also must feel pretty fun and creative for the guys taking part in it. Preparing and performing in this is probably plenty of a creative outlet for some people. Like those Mummers in Philadelphia who spend eight months out of the year sewing feathers on their costumes for the New Year's Day parade.

Here's one of my big beefs so far with Julia. I believe, as she does, that everyone starts off creative. I also believe that it's a cool idea to reach out to people who are desperately unhappy and unfulfilled because they are not expressing their creative sides, but in trying to disavow the idea of the "tortured artist," advocating that you can be centered and healthy and still create art, she is perpetuating this myth of how precious artists are. Her incessant coddling is making me crazy. Attitudes like this are why I have such a hard time admitting that I am an "artist" of any sort. Making a big deal about being an artist is like bragging that you have lungs. (No offense meant to the lungless.)

It's in a little quote in a sidebar, by Henry Miller, that I finally find something that resonates with me.

> Develop interest in life as you see it; in people, things, literature, music—the world is so rich, simply throbbing with rich treasures, beautiful souls and interesting people. Forget yourself.

A beautiful quote. And here I am, this whole year, remembering myself constantly.

Recovering a Sense of Power Now I understand what it means when certain segments of the population say they are "going on vacation." We have definitely slipped into a rhythm now. It's been almost a week, and we are now capable of easily spending the whole day doing nothing but swimming, reading, eating, and planning dinner.

Julia actually brings up Jung's concept of synchronicity, the "plate o' shrimp" idea from *Repo Man*. She encourages the blocked artist to be open to the possibility of an intelligent and responsive universe. This, she says, is why we have the expression "Be careful what you wish for." She even mentions that you should try thinking of articles of clothing you want because they will "come into your possession at disconcerting speed." I flash on my black hooded sweater hiding in the bushes.

I try to think of something I knew I wanted but never asked for out loud, something that ended up appearing anyway. After my second book came out, Gus was born and I was trying to figure out if I should go get a regular job again. I knew I would never seek out a literary agent because it seemed too humiliating. It would be like admitting I wanted a bigger audience or more money, neither of which I was prepared to do. One day there was a reading for Litquake, a San Francisco literary festival that featured about fifty writers reading all day in the public library. Our good friends were getting married that day out at the Marin Headlands. After a ceremony on the beach, there was a reception in one of the cool old refurbished military buildings, but I was supposed to drive back into the city for my reading. I really didn't want to leave before the reception. Litquake, I decided, would be fine without me. There were so many authors on the bill, no one would miss me. Plus, there was a Blue Angels air show that day, and the traffic on the Golden Gate Bridge would be terrible. In the end, Eli talked me out of it, reminding me that I had made a commitment and the organizers were friends of mine. So we went.

When I got there, the program was running way behind schedule. There were musicians onstage who were supposed to be playing in between the readers but because of the scheduling problems had been sitting there with nothing to do all morning. I got inspired. Instead of reading what I had planned, my scheduled ten minutes, I realized it would probably make everyone happy if I cut my slot short. I asked the band to improvise with me, and I read a short three-minute piece, a fake letter from a disgruntled bridesmaid. Afterward, a woman named Arielle who was in the audience came up and said she'd love to take me out to lunch. She became my agent and sold two books for me, something that might have never happened if I'd followed my own instincts and not gone to the reading. Wait. All my gurus say I *should* trust my instincts. Now I'm confused.

Recovering a Sense of Integrity I have been having really nutball dreams lately. Julia says in this chapter that my dreams will become stronger and clearer, which is interesting because a few days ago my morning pages officially morphed into a dream journal. All the relaxing is having a wondrous effect on my second life.

> I was at an art auction and there was this weird flying car that had tons of exhaust coming out of it and was making these little cloud-shapes in the air. I was trying to figure out if the

> clouds were also art and could I auction them off. Also, John Dwyer [a guy in a bunch of bands in SF] made a tote bag out of an old FedEx envelope with tons of duct tape and old band stickers on it and some guy wanted to pay a bunch of money for it. Later he was sad when Dwyer was being a dick to him, so I reached into my pocket and gave him one of the exhaust clouds that I had saved.

That's the most interesting thing I've written in weeks.

Julia quotes Chekhov as saying, "If you want to work on your art, work on your life." It's starting to occur to me that all of this "recovery" talk might mean that, implicitly, this is a book for artists who were alcoholics and drug addicts and can't create anything without being drunk or high. This would explain the extraordinary energy she puts into making meditation and tea sound really indispensable to making a painting.

Recovering a Sense of Possibility Like Stephen Covey, Julia understands that people need some coaching with the concept of scarcity versus abundance. It's hard not to feel like your luck could run out any minute and you'll be left with nothing. When something good happens, who doesn't imagine that it might be countered by something bad? The way to solve this dilemma, she writes, is to realize that God's gifts are never-ending. We need to understand and incorporate this idea into our lives: there is enough for everyone. It seems a safe enough philosophy to apply to all of my first-world problems and insecurities.

In other news at the villa, Theo, who will be two next month, is finally exhibiting a few signs of the fabled "terrible twos." My brother has taught him how to growl like a monster, and now when he doesn't want to eat his green beans or let go of the Monopoly tokens, he lets out this loud, grunty groan, like a baby who's been raised by trolls at a Robert Bly retreat. It's hilarious to us, but Lora is growing tired of it. I hand her my copy of *1-2-3 Magic*, and Gus takes great joy in seeing Theo get his first time-out.

Recovering a Sense of Abundance This chapter is all about money, which is the last thing I want to be reminded of right now. Tomorrow morning, before the sun rises, we begin our long trip home. Cortona to Rome, Rome to Chicago, Chicago to San Francisco, San Francisco to Berkeley. Nearly twenty-four hours of travel before we arrive back home to that pile of bills we have no way of paying.

"Lack of money is never an authentic block," Julia advises, referring to artist's block, but it's a good reminder as we hunker down and get back on our feet in the coming months.

Recovering a Sense of Connection Back to the grind. Eli disappears into the studio for upwards of seventy hours a week, and I put out the word that I'm back in town and desperately seeking income. I line up three banana jobs. I also get a Sunday afternoon stint helping my friend Arline at one of her open houses, a $5 million mansion in Pacific Heights, where my instructions are to look nice and make sure people don't pocket the silver. Then I have three days of high school teaching scheduled, and the week after that my mother-daughter book club meets.

One of the traps that artists fall into, according to Julia, is perfectionism. The refusal to let yourself move ahead because you are losing sight of the whole and constantly grading the results. To do something well, she says, we must first let ourselves do it badly. I have always been a proponent of bad art. A night of seeing bad art is better than a night spent in front of the TV. But now that we got basic cable a few months ago, because it was such a good deal for our Internet, I'm not so sure.

Julia writes passionately about her jealousy, which she says is merely a mask for fear. She says frustrated artists often feel like it is those who are less talented or original who get all the glory, that those artists succeed simply because they have the balls or the chutzpah to put themselves out there. I think I "put myself out there" because I don't know what else to do with what I make. I don't feel like my books "deserve" a wider audience or that I have stories or ideas that people absolutely *have* to hear, but if I make something and let it go, I can begin working on something else. The strange thing about *The Artist's Way* is that it never gets around to discussing putting on an actual art show or writing an actual book or making an actual record. I'm starting to think this program is not even meant for artists.

There are a few exercises that I have to pass on. I can't "watercolor or crayon or calligraphy" the phrase "Treating myself like a precious object will make me strong" because I have no desire to be a precious object. I like to own things that I can sit on or lose, like cheap sunglasses and promotional umbrellas. It makes me wonder, though. Could I be more successful artistically if I treated myself better?

My friend recently broke down and went to therapy for the first time in his life. In one week his uncle had died of a massive stroke, his father had died by drinking himself to death, and the girlfriend he thought he might marry had broken up with him. ("I know it's bad timing," she said.) He had found a lot of gay porn on his dad's computer and was especially upset about that, wondering if being closeted had led his father to his severe alcoholism. When he went to the therapist, all the guy wanted him to do was talk about his childhood. He didn't want to. He had issues he wanted to deal with now. Finally, my friend gave him a quick synopsis. ("Okay,

okay. My brother used to beat me up every day. My dad made me kill my baby bunnies when they were sick. I found the neighbor girl murdered while walking to school one day.") Pretty horrific stuff, but he felt like he had dealt with it.

"You certainly have a good coping mechanism," the therapist told him. "But you should be seeing me twice a week."

My friend's insurance wouldn't cover the sessions, and he said in jest to the therapist, "I guess I could start selling some shit to pay for it."

"That's a good idea," the therapist told him. "Whatever you have to do."

My point is: most people would look at my friend and think he has severe issues from his childhood to deal with, but if he doesn't think he does, that's all that should matter. Likewise, if I don't want to treat myself like a precious object, if my creative life is going fine without coddling it like a baby, there's absolutely no reason to start, right? Even if a "creativity" expert tells me to. This seems like a linchpin of why so many people get sucked into self-help and empowerment programs. They can't trust that what they're doing is the "right" way to be doing it.

Recovering a Sense of Strength At this point, I am about ready to toss the book into the recycling bin on the corner. Eli and I are both depressed and fighting about money, and here's yet another chapter with a lot of anecdotes about artists who are blocked because people were mean to them. I'm starting to have a Dr. Phil "get over it" reaction. She does make a good case for anyone wanting to take up something creative later in life by saying that "no creative act is ever finished." Meaning, if you complain that you're too old to take up the piano, because "I'll be sixty by the time I learn," well, you're going to be sixty eventually anyway. Why not get started, because you'll never be finished learning.

Recovering a Sense of Compassion Being an artist requires enthusiasm more than discipline, she writes. (This sounds acceptable until she describes art as "a playdate we make with our artist child.") I think it's that, in their comfort zones, some people would rather be a victim of artist's block than actually make something. This is sort of harsh, but it reminds me of people I used to know who were "living in New York" or "living in Tokyo." Just by virtue of being somewhere exciting they felt like they were "doing" something even when they were just drinking a lot and making the scene. I'm starting to think that claiming you have "artist's block" is just a way of wanting to say you're an artist even if you're not doing anything. She says that a successful creative career is always built on successful creative failures. True enough, but to have a creative failure, you at least have to create some work that's going to fail.

I decide to read over my morning pages. Over the last three weeks, I have had more than fifty dreams that I remembered. I have gone flying, played the flute badly, and swum in an ocean filled with nets. I lost Gus in a crowd that was gathered around a car accident, and I baked a giant pink cake made of ground-up rice and flowers. My dreams are so vivid that part of me feels like I really have experienced all these things. I realize how much I enjoy this other life I have. Lately, I wish I could be dreaming all the time.

Recovering a Sense of Self-Protection I haven't done my morning pages in four days now. Eli and I are trying to come up with survival strategies, including moving to Portland or subletting our house and moving in with my parents. I bring up the idea of him leaving his recording studio to get a full-time job because he is the one with all of the marketable skills. We cook a lot of beans and rice. Julia says to look out for falling into toxic patterns that will slow our growth. She lists food, work, and sex abuse. She left out sleep abuse.

Recovering a Sense of Autonomy There is a lot of information about getting exercise and creating an "artist altar" with rocks or shells or incense in this chapter. She suggests I write and mail an encouraging letter to myself, but I can't imagine wasting the thirty-nine cents. My mom called today to say the doctor had found potentially life-threatening blood clots in my dad's lungs. He stays in the hospital on blood thinners, and when they get home my mom has to keep him away from the meat slicer. He likes his ham sliced very thin.

I am supposed to list ten examples of creative synchronicity, but I can't think of a single one. I had a ton earlier, and when I was in Italy, but being stressed out is like having blinders on. I remind myself to look for them as I walk outside to go to the post office. The first thing I notice, I swear, is a pigeon madly pecking away at a pile of vomit. Is it a mystic vision about recycling? About putting waste to good use? About gaining sustenance from someone else's internal heaving? In a plate o' shrimp whammy, the next week I receive a manuscript to blurb that contains the exact same image. A pigeon pecking away at vomit. Weird.

Suddenly all that heightened awareness that was producing magical or unreal moments is gone. I seem to have snuffed it out with the black cloud over my head.

I am more than ready to move on to my money month. The lesson in this last chapter is that creativity requires receptivity and profound trust. It is a mysterious and spiritual thing. I agree, though I skip signing the closing creativity contract. I shut off the light and perform the exercise that Jack Canfield taught me before going to sleep. I think of how my day is going to go tomorrow, from when I get up to when I go to bed. Then I recount the current day's activities, from turning off the light to putting my feet on the floor that morning. It has helped my insomnia tremendously, which is always worse in times like these. I fall asleep before I even get to today's events. Then a strange thing happens.

It's nearly 2:00 A.M. when Eli creeps into the bedroom, exhausted.

"I have something exciting to tell you," he says. "But I don't want to wake you up, so I'll tell you in the morning."

"Are you serious? Of course you have to tell me now."

"I'm sorry, I shouldn't have said anything."

"What is it?"

"The producer who's in the studio right now might have a full-time job for me at the place he works in San Francisco."

"Wow, that's so weird."

"I know. It's some kind of audio job, but it would have benefits." This is a huge deal because we pay about $600 a month for our health insurance. "Plus, a guaranteed paycheck every two weeks."

"Maybe you should interview for it."

"I know. It seems like I should, just because how weird is it that we were just talking about me getting a job? But what would I do with the studio?"

He had spent so much time trying to make it happen, and it feels like it's almost there.

"I can't just drop it, can I?" He buries his face in the pillow and groans.

"It'll work out. I know it will."

I can't think of anything else to say as I pet his head of thick curls and shush him to sleep.

October

ADD IT UP

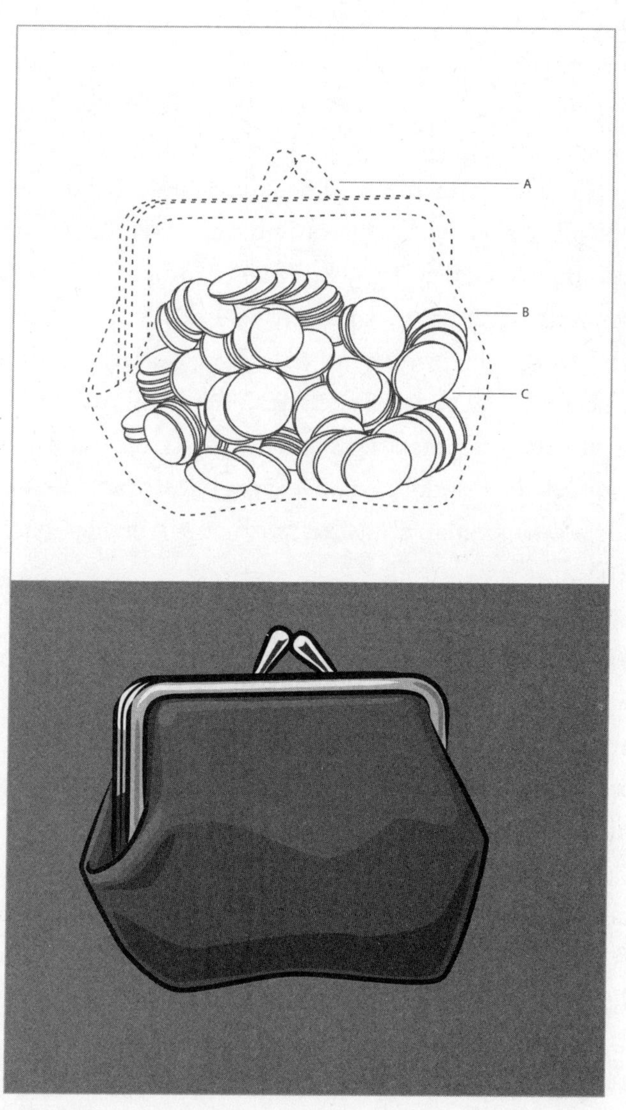

The sheer force of the wind assailing me as I attempt to walk down Mission Street is at once dramatic and comedic, rendering me some sort of gawky Marcel Marceau. Chin buried in my collar, eyes nearly shut, I trudge slowly toward the red carpet and klieg lights, which are entirely out of sync with the bums and the picket line. So are my jeans and sweatshirt. I watch a covey of black-clad blondes with clipboards and headsets do their best to look dead serious while waving guests past the velvet rope. Finally, Bloomingdale's has arrived in San Francisco. Carry on, riffraff!

I am meeting up with my friend Arline, an SF native who was once a real live debutante. Like the kind you see in newspapers bowing deeply in a white dress before a wall of tan stepdads. Her former deb status gets her automatically invited to all kinds of events, from designer trunk shows to restaurant premieres to department store openings. Sometimes, like this afternoon, she'll call and see if I want to tag along. Perhaps I'm up for some champagne and oysters?

"Are none of your fancy friends going?" I ask from the cement quadrangle of the public high school where I am teaching this week. "I want to come, but I look like crap."

"Who cares!" she laughs. "Meet me out front at six."

I get Joel to watch Gus for a couple hours so I don't have to turn down the free food and drinks, thereby messing with my time-honored MO. Call it the mark of a boor, but it's currently impossible for me to imagine a time when I would think, *Free Veuve Clicquot again? What a snore.*

Arline looks pretty, her golden blond hair whipping around with the tails of her blood-red scarf. She's a real estate agent about to close on that $5 million mansion, so she's pretty happy tonight, too.

"I think I may need an invitation," I say, eyeballing the flacks.

"No, no, no," she says. "Just follow me."

"I'll pretend like I'm your assistant."

I let Arline walk in front of me, flashbulbs popping all around us, as I assume a lackey's distance. She glides like a pro. She doesn't bother to stop and show her invitation or give her name, thereby granting me the power to do the same thing. It continually amazes me how far a sense of entitlement can get you. Just as I'm through the second set of doors, I feel a woman tugging gently on the sleeve of my sweatshirt.

"Ticket, please," her frail voice says.

I keep walking. Again I hear it.

"Ticket, please."

If I turn to face her, I will have to look in her eyes and come up with some lame excuse. So I just keep walking, nose in the air like a bona-fide snob with selective hearing. My computer bag slaps my ass as I skitter along. There, on a silver tray by the escalator, are flutes of champagne. My bony fingers grab one by the stem, and I hop on a moving stair, eyes focused straight ahead. I'm in.

Ascending slowly, I finally get the courage to glance down at the swirl on the main floor. I think back to Julia Cameron and *The Artist's Way*. *This is it*, I think. This scalp-tingling adrenaline rush is the stuff that makes me feel alive and creative. Taking risks that could result in humiliation. Being where I'm not supposed to be. I'm not sure that this idea at all jibes with Cameron's sober, holistic approach to tending the spark inside. As Jack Welch said in Chicago, you've got to find out what turns your crank, and what often turns mine is a cheap thrill.

For the rest of the night, in between cocktails and hors d'oeuvres, I marvel at the mind-boggling combination of expensive outfits and cosmetic surgery. It's a different sensation to see these people live instead of on TV. Intertwined with the smiles and air kisses, like a crosshatch, is a near-palpable thread of anxiety. Because the store is open for business for the first time, there seems to be a great deal of "performance shopping" going on. As a flamenco guitarist heats up the "Young Women's Contemporary" floor in front of a carving station laden with fat bloody slabs of prime rib, two male couples coo over sunglasses purchases. A taut matron uncoils a necklace for her enraptured friends with the flourish of a magician. I'd be lying if I said I didn't wish I had money, but most of these people make having money look pretty bad.

Arline and I pull up a leather bench to watch the spectacle, and I give her a recap: We cannot pay our mortgage. We cannot pay Gus's preschool tuition. We cannot pay a single household bill because our final dollars are gone, spent eight thousand miles away on a two-week vacation in a Tuscan villa that is now over. My suntan has faded, and the souvenir bottle of wine is gone. At least there are still the pictures that we will someday, hopefully, be able to download off of our camera. But maybe not, because Gus accidentally dropped it in a plaza in Perugia, and now it doesn't work. I have $6,000 in credit card debt. Eli has $30,000 in outstanding student loans. We have $3,500 of bills due immediately. And the amount of money we have in the bank? $148.73. There are no stocks, bonds, or IRA.

There is not even a savings account.

"It'll work out," she says, putting her arm over my shoulder as a freckled septuagenarian in a backless dress scoots by. "I just know it will."

I believe her, but of course I feel stupid. I wasn't always so dumb about money. As a matter of fact, I spent my teens and early twenties stockpiling the stuff. My first job, as the office assistant in a plastic surgery suite, paid me $5 an hour. I typed up operative reports for ladies getting their eyelids done. I filed Polaroids of liposuction results, including pictures of the pinkish yellow slime sitting in bags on stainless steel tables. I watched as gay men came in with strange bleeding ulcers on their faces that medical science was just beginning to understand. All through college, I worked as much as I could—baking, catering, filing, answering phones. By the time I quit working full-time so I could write more, I had about $12,000 in the bank. A fortune. That was nine years ago, that savings account has long been closed, and in the interim I somehow developed this idea that I didn't care about money. It coincided with becoming a writer. I figured I would never make much anyway, so why sweat it.

The last three weeks have been a mad scramble for cash. I've worked as a banana, a high school teacher, and a stage manager for a food and wine festival. On Monday I'll make a little bit speaking at a high school assembly, and meanwhile, I keep going on voice-over auditions. I have to admit, my offshoot voice-over career isn't going so well. The only reason I started doing it was because I got an e-mail one day asking me to audition for a radio ad. It was a union job, so I had to sign with a talent agency, but after I auditioned (it was for a jeans commercial in which a fairy makes your butt look good—seriously), I didn't get hired. But the agency continues to call me for auditions, though I've only booked one job (as the voice of a sexy talking car that feels neglected now that her owners live in a gated community with restaurants and a movie theater nearby). Showbiz!

The personal finance guru to consult is obvious. It's got to be that lady I always see on PBS when I'm changing channels. She seems very popular. The intense one with the hair. Goes by the name Suze. As ridiculous as it seems, I had no idea what that lady's name was until this year. Now, of course, I see her everywhere. Suze Orman has definitely crossed the plate o' shrimp threshold in my world.

I go online and find a copy of her book *The Nine Steps to Financial Freedom: Practical and Spiritual Advice So You Can Stop Worrying* for less than seven bucks. This book, I find out, was on the *New York Times* bestseller list for eleven months straight and has sold about 3 million copies. Suze has also won two Emmy Awards in the "Outstanding Service Show" category for her PBS specials and has written a bunch of books since this one in 1997, which is now heralded as a "personal finance classic."

After I get home from taking Gus to school, where a note in his cubby reminds me that neither his September nor October tuition has been paid, I get reading. The book begins with a great anecdote about Suze's dad crying whenever someone would win a lot of money on *Wheel of Fortune* because he was so happy for them. She grew up without a lot of money, and in sharing her first "money memory," she suggests that the reader do the same. By doing this exercise, she says, we can learn a lot about how our ideas of money were first shaped and formed.

Suze's first money memory is almost mythical in nature, and it's easy to see why she became money-obsessed as an adult. Her father owned a fast-food restaurant, and one day, during a grease fire, the whole place exploded into flames. She arrived at the scene just in time to see her father emerge from the fire. And then, when he realized that all his cash was still in the cash register, he ran back into the burning building to retrieve it. The drawer had already been sealed by the heat, so he picked the entire thing up and brought it outside, and when he threw the register to the ground, she writes, "the skin on his arms and chest came with it."

My own "money memories," from around the time I was four or five, are hardly as dramatic. The first is of my grandfather Cubby coming out to visit us from Illinois. The big deal was that Grandpa had a $100 bill that he was going to show my brothers and me. For some reason, we were only allowed to see the bill one kid at a time. I'm sure they thought we'd all lunge for it at once. I can remember the anticipation building up as I watched my brother Paul go first to sit on the stairs while Cubby pulled the bill out of his wallet. I knew I was supposed to be excited, that this was a big deal, but when it came my turn to look at the crisp Franklin, I pretended to be more excited than I really was. I was pretty little and had hardly seen any currency at the time, so it didn't strike me as that important. Seeing it now would be a whole different experience. Now I probably would lunge for it.

The other memory is of being upstairs in my bedroom, playing with toys on the floor, and hearing my dad yell at my mom. There wasn't too much yelling in our house, so it made quite an impression. I snuck down to the landing, peeked in the kitchen, and saw my mom crying. The perfect solution dawned on me. I went back upstairs to my bedroom, took the cork out of my piggy bank's nose, and extracted the one and only dollar bill that was inside. I thought what I was doing would help, but when I handed it to her, I could tell she was now trying even harder not to cry in front of me. Later, she came up to my room and gave me the bill back, saying that it was very nice of me to give it to her, but it was mine and I should keep it.

I think of my defining money moments—cuddling up with my grandpa on the carpeted stairs of our tract home to feign enthusiasm over a $100 bill and incorrectly assuming that a dollar would make my mom feel better. No wonder I'm not very motivated by money. I could see it from the comfort of my home, and it wasn't powerful enough to make my mom stop crying. Money: not very exciting, won't make you happy. And this might account for the $148.73 at age thirty-seven.

Orman understands that the thought of taking control of our money can be so overwhelming as to paralyze us. Like Stephen

Covey in *The Seven Habits*, she drives the point home that there is a huge difference between knowing what we are supposed to do and the act of doing something about it. When people give me advice and I sigh and say, "I know, I know," it's clear I obviously don't *truly know* or else I would be taking action.

It's when Suze starts detailing how credit card companies make their money that I want to slit my throat. I always thought my tactic with my one credit card had been "try not to use it, unless you really have no other choice." It isn't the truth, though. The reality is a pretty serious disconnect between my thoughts and my actions. I will use it to reserve airline tickets or rental cars and, out of laziness and ignorance, just keep the charges on the card instead of paying for them with cash. This way I can trick myself into thinking I have more money than I really do.

Once, about ten years ago, a boyfriend complimented me on how low the APR was on my card. We were affectionate like that. I don't even remember what the percentage was because I never, ever paid attention to stuff like that. I did assume, however, that because I'd had the card since 1990 and almost always paid it off in full every month, it made perfect sense that I would have an APR worthy of adoration. I was a great customer. Those offers to switch cards would arrive in my mailbox endlessly, but I never paid attention to them. Surely they were scams. Better to stick with the devil you know.

Suze is all for switching companies. If your card charges an annual fee (mine doesn't) or can't match the percentage you could get elsewhere, ditch it. I grab my latest bill and consciously decide, for the first time ever, to find out what my APR is. It's . . . 21 percent?! Fuck loyalty. Whatever it used to be, I'm certain it wasn't in the double digits! How did I let them do this to me? I rifle through my old bills and see that as I built up more charges on my card, the company kept incrementally raising the rate. Clearly, they figured that was fine by me because I never once brought it to their attention. I even paid an annual fee for a few years in the late '90s. I have been treating my credit card debt like the troubled kid you send off to boarding school. Just keep writing the checks with your eyes closed and pray she will be rehabilitated one day.

I sit there outraged for a couple minutes, loosing a few off-the-meds curses as I slam shut desk drawers. This fucking company that I've been with for sixteen years is screwing me over on purpose because they know I'm a loser who doesn't pay attention. They can tell I'm an imbecile without ever having met me, yukking it up in the break room over another live one actively consenting to her own financial demise, paying thousands of dollars to a stupid multibillion-dollar company that doesn't care about her at all. I get ready to pounce.

Sure enough, when the mail arrives *the very next day* I have two credit card offers for 0 percent APR and no annual fees. I have never actually opened one of these envelopes before in my life, but today I tear at them like they're full of gold doubloons. Instead of patiently filling out the form to transfer my balance to another card, I call my company first.

Rescuing me from the late-era Police track is a customer service rep with an astounding accent, like a Jersey girl by way of Calcutta who just spent a semester abroad being tutored by Madonna. When she answers, I realize I haven't thought out how I'm going to approach this.

"Um, hey," I say, easing my way into some communication skills. "I was wondering. What do they, the bosses or whoever, tell you to say to people when they call and they're angry and they're going to cancel their cards unless you give them a better deal?"

It dawns on me that it would have been easier to just get angry and say I was going to cancel my card.

There's a pause, and then her weird, accented voice says, "Please hold on. I am checking to see what I am authorized to do." After a minute, she's back.

"Yes, it looks like I can lower your APR to fourteen percent."

"Just like that, huh? Because I called."

"Yes."

Thinking of Suze, I say, "Well, why wouldn't I just switch to another card? I get a million of these things in the mail that tell me they'll give me zero percent."

I want to tell her I've been a customer for sixteen years and it's outrageous to see that all my loyalty has gotten me is some jacked-up rates, but I'm sure she's heard it all and it's not her fault anyway. I save my breath in case I have to "talk to her supervisor" or some other thing I've seen people do in movies when they are upset with their customer service.

"Just hold on one more moment and let me find out if there is something else I can offer you."

I wait another minute, a minute where I'm sure she is launching a paper airplane over to a neighboring cubicle or pulling an ingrown hair out of her leg. There's just something feeble and disingenuous about the silence.

"Yes, Miss Lisick. It looks like you can apply for a new card that will give you zero percent APR for the next year."

"Reallllly?" Suddenly I'm Charles Nelson Reilly. "Zero percent for a year? And there's no annual fee?"

"No, no annual fee. Would you like me to send you this application in the mail?"

"Totally."

In under five minutes' time, I just saved myself about $80 a month. That's huge. What I try not to think about is if only I had made this call a year ago, I would have saved myself nearly $1,000. And now I also know that if I had put that $1,000 in a high-earning account, I wouldn't really need to be reading this book right now.

Suze's next step is to face your fears about money. I discover that one of mine is a classic: I'm afraid to ask questions about money because I don't know the right questions to ask. I'm embarrassed by my ignorance. When she brings in examples of IRAs and CDs and money market accounts, my eyes go glazy. I also realize that I've somehow known my whole life that I would never invest in the stock market, most likely because my parents never did. It's risky! It's for high rollers!

Suze writes: "Money is a living entity and responds to energy, including yours, and to how you feel about yourself."

How can I convince myself that money is important, that I need to put some energy into it? Just like how Richard Simmons sees caring for your body as a matter of self-respect, Suze believes that about money. She says to look at the way that you carry your money. My bills are usually balled up in the bottom of a bag, not in the man-wallet I bought eight years ago in Guadalajara, which is mostly full of receipts from Walgreen's and local taquerias. Jack Canfield reminds me that you can't continue doing the same things and expect different results, so I need to figure out what I can do differently to start respecting the money. Maybe stop blowing through it by signing up for all these self-help programs?

It's too late to do that for this month. I've already been drawn into Suze's website. She has an event coming up in southern California called "Connect Today, Seize Tomorrow," with a roster of speakers that sounds like the setup to an elaborate joke. *So, Suze Orman, Arnold Schwarzenegger, Martha Stewart, Sarah Ferguson the Duchess of York, and the Dalai Lama walk into a convention center. . . .* When I add up how much I would have to spend on airfare, a rental car, and the convention itself, I decide to bag it. Instead, I sign up for a New York seminar called "Make Mine a Million Dollar Business." Suze is the keynote speaker, and it costs only $50 to attend. I have a JetBlue ticket to New York that will cost me $5 to reserve, and I can stay with my brother and sister-in-law for free. In this case, two days in New York will be cheaper than going down to Los Angeles for the afternoon.

The only flight I can take with the mileage program that will get me there in time is a red-eye. My last experience before the Richard Simmons cruise wasn't so bad, but that time all I had to do for a week afterward was sleep, aerobicize, and try to process the American fascination with all-you-can-eat buffets comprising SYSCO food products. This time I'll be arriving at 6:00 A.M. for a conference that begins at noon and goes until nine that night.

From what I can tell from the website, the event is something of a women's economic empowerment shindig, sponsored by OPEN from American Express, a faction dedicated to small-business owners. Suze will be addressing the crowd early in the afternoon.

I get off the plane at JFK, groggy and congested, and head to my brother's place. They recently bought an apartment on the Upper West Side in a cool prewar building with a doorman and a view of the river. How the gulf between our lifestyles grows more canyonlike by the minute.

I arrive just as they are waking up with Theo, who's super-excited to see me. Lora makes me some eggs and then plops down in a kitchen chair and says, "I'm pregnant."

"Wow, that's so exciting!" I say, but I can tell by her face that she's not really that excited herself.

Even these guys have financial worries. The trip to Italy messed with them, too. (Then again, they were also the ones picking up checks for meals and ordering exquisite wine from the local *enoteca* for everyone, while I bummed sunscreen.) Lora is worried about how they are going to pay for Theo's preschool and the new baby's day care so she can go back to work.

The nanny comes for Theo, Chris and Lora go off to work, and I crawl into bed for a pre-Suze nap. It's an experience, with a soft gray flannel padded headboard and mounds of fluffy white pillows that must equal those in luxury hotels. The comforter is apparently made from the flesh of a thousand angels.

I lie there, almost floating, thinking of some icky territory Suze gets into in her book. She talks about how many people believe they don't deserve to have money. Oh, my guts. This strikes a pathetic chord in me, a chord from some glum emo song. Though I will swear up and down that believing you don't deserve something is weak and sorry, there is a very real voice telling me I should remain satisfied with what I have and not get greedy. I shouldn't be trying to get more of *anything*, should I? I'm plenty comfortable. The bills may get paid late, but they'll eventually get paid. I can sleep in a luxury bed at my brother's house every once in a while and drink champagne at Bloomingdale's with my friend. I just got back from Italy, for pete's sake. Life is pretty great. I'm getting wound up now, as every conversation I've ever had about class politics echoes in my head. I need to convince myself that getting a fifteen-day disconnection notice from the electric company definitely means you don't have too much money yet.

Then I remember Step 4. It's where I finally feel like I am getting somewhere philosophically with Suze. While reading the chapter "Being Responsible to Those You Love," it occurs to me that I need to change the way I think about taking charge of my finances. If my incentives are splurging to take the car to the Touchless Car Wash or getting new sheets, I will never make headway because ultimately I don't care that much about those things (though they would be nice). I need to start thinking about it as a way to help Gus and Eli and our family. One of Suze's big chestnuts is "People first, then money, then things."

But, fuck. What about the older chestnut "Do what you love and the money will follow"? I've been hammering on that one for a while, and it's not working out so well. I decide to give Suze's version a whirl, to focus on the people I love so that I can provide for them. Like a man in a movie from the 1950s.

When I wake up from my nap, I put on the same pair of pants I wore in Chicago, which are also the same ones I wore to work at the open mansion with Arline. My nice pants. A gift from Lora. I take the subway to the Hammerstein Ballroom, which is a beautiful building, a 1906 opera and vaudeville house that in recent years has seen the likes of Iron Maiden, Ashlee Simpson, and Radiohead. Today, however, the headlining act is Suze Orman, personal finance pop star.

I wait in line to receive my name tag, which I immediately place around my neck before I can think too much about it. HELLO, MY NAME IS BETH, my name tag says, and I decide not to argue. I've come a long way on this one this year. No one hands me a tote bag for my growing collection, but at fifty bucks a head, I realize we aren't really at tote bag level here. There is a nice pen, though. And an American Express spiral-bound notebook. Mints.

The lobby is packed, mostly with women, who represent all manner of what I imagine to be the spectrum of lady entrepreneurs. There are fashionistas in stiletto boots and tight trousers, handsome man-ladies in suits, big-haired mall rats in too-short skirts, doughy frumps in early-adapter polyester. I actually hear a lady yell into her BlackBerry, "Rachel! The prototype has to be done by tonight or we are *fucked*!"

Businesspeople. So serious!

The main floor isn't open yet, so I head up to the balcony. A woman passing by on the stairs is chewing. Could there possibly be free food? Oh, please let there be free food. I see tables of boxed salads and grab one, bolstering myself for another cruise-ship moment as I sit down at a six-top with only one other woman. I pop open the top of my salad dressing container and send a greasy, garlicky slop of it down the front of my pants. The lady at my table looks up for a second, clearly relieved it was me and not her. I mean, I understand that reaction, but her obvious relief is a bit disarming. I return with a fistful of napkins and get to blotting with some water just as two other women are sitting down.

"I'm Sheryl," the relieved one says to them, buttering a piece of bread. "I am a CPA with a strong legal background."

She says she's here today because she wants to start her own business selling things on the Internet. She says this last word like she is just getting used to the feeling it makes in her mouth.

"What kinds of things?" the one with a gray bob asks politely. Her name tag says JUDITH.

"Antique things. Collectibles. I want to call it Sheryl's Stamps and Collectibles," she says. "Or maybe just Sheryl's Collectibles. What do you think?"

Everyone murmurs politely except for me. I'm not feeling excessively kind today.

"Well, I definitely want to use my name," she goes on. "Sheryl. It's a fairly popular name, but it seems like a good idea to personalize something if it's going to be on the Internet." In-ter-net.

I chew slowly. The stain on my pants isn't going away.

A new woman joins the table, a stationery impresario named Mimi.

"Hi, I'm Sheryl," Sheryl says. "I'm a CPA with a strong legal background."

Mimi says she does business all over the country and is here today for the "inspiration" and "networking opportunities." It becomes obvious that we're not providing her with either. Maybe it's the way she quickly fans her business cards on the table before taking off without finishing her cookie.

"You know who's terrible," Sheryl says, putting a card in her billfold. "Martha Stewart."

"Oh, yeah," Judith says. "Awful."

"Why don't you like her?" I ask. I am intentionally goading them.

"She was horrible back before she was even famous! My friend Marie's daughter used to live near her."

"She doesn't really help anyone," Judith says. "She just makes people feel bad. Not like Suze."

"I gave up on the self-help stuff," Sheryl says, swatting her hand in front of her face. It's that gesture of old people when they mean *Phooey!* "I took all my self-help books, and I burned them in a huge bonfire!"

"You did?" I'm intrigued. I love picturing Sheryl's expensive and monumental blaze. It sounds like the best idea she ever had.

"Well," Judith says rather authoritatively, "we should all do some more networking before the program starts."

"I'm going up to QVC," Sheryl announces and heads out to find the shopping channel's table.

The main floor is now open, and I find a seat as close to the stage as I can get, about ten rows back. The woman sitting next to me looks like the actress Claire Danes and is here from Carmel, California, to find out about starting a greeting card company with her mother. She shows me her prototypes. The cards she's done have a kind of *Sex and the City* girly flair, and her mom's cards are watercolor landscapes. There's absolutely no reason they wouldn't sell to somebody.

"I'm just hoping to do a little networking here," she says. God, she is really beautiful. Her mouth is like a giant invitation to the most fun dance party ever.

"Oh, wait!" I say, remembering Mimi's brief cameo at my lunch table. I dig the card from my bag. "This lady is some kind of stationery bigwig. Something about regional something-something and most of the southern states."

I get excited for a second that I am networking, *I'm really doing it!* until I realize that I am doing other people's networking. That's fine, too. I like being helpful. Anyway, I haven't figured out who would qualify as a prime networking suspect for me.

"I'm Craig," a suave guy in a business suit sitting next to Claire says. "I'm a personal coach."

I squeal inside. They are everywhere. They're coming for me.

He says he's here to support his friend, a matchmaker, who will be taking part in the contest later on. Contest? I look around.

What am I doing here again? Oh, right. It takes me a second to remember. Money. Safe to say that everybody in here is trying to get some.

There are a few more minutes until the program starts, and Craig, who is indeed very affable, asks me if I've seen *The Secret*.

"No, I haven't seen it yet. I've been wanting to, but I don't want to pay for it."

"So you know what it is?" he asks. "You know about *The Secret*?"

"Yeah, I got an e-mail about it from Jack Canfield."

Claire is intrigued.

"What's the secret?" she asks, her eyes like two limpid pools of blue.

And so another strain of viral marketing is passed on like a chancre.

When the program starts, I notice some hefty security guys casing the joint. They're backstage, posted at the sides of the audience, talking into their cuffs and tilting their chins to the ceiling. Our host for the day is CNN's Valerie Morris, who is so charming and at ease with the thousand-person crowd, she must have been born on the stage of a theater emceeing a seminar for women entrepreneurs.

We find out that all the excitement and extra security today is for the surprise guest, who happens to be right in the middle of a reelection campaign: Senator Hillary Rodham Clinton!

The crowd goes nuts. She makes a brief but passionate speech, entirely without notes or flubs, addressing the importance of women in business. *Hey! That's us!* When she leaves the stage, a palpable rush of fiery energy goes with her.

And now it's time for the contest. Women business owners from all over the country will be competing for professional mentoring, coaching, and $50,000 of capital. Seated in a lineup onstage, they will each approach the mic and have exactly one minute to give their "elevator pitches" to a panel of judges. Valerie tells everybody to take "a nice deep cleansing breath" and we're off.

One lady has a chain of airport spas, another operates a race-car driving course. There is a natural pet food company, a background-checking business, a woman who makes T-shirts with the New York City subway line logos on them, and Mary Ardapple of Apple's Bakery in Peoria ("Where smiles are made from scratch!"). There is a woman who has patented an "ornament safe" for your Christmas ornaments (the opening line to her pitch is: "Has tree decorating become a chore?") and a clothing designer in Brooklyn who found her niche making hostess gowns for Orthodox Jewish women but is now branching out into "appropriate loungewear" for mastectomy patients and plus-size women. It's fascinating. I love seeing people talk about what they're passionate about, even if they are hustling for money in the process. The enthusiasm in the room is contagious. I only wish John Gray were here to see all these testosterone-riddled Venusians kicking ass.

And now it's Suze's turn in the spotlight. For her entrance, the house speakers crank out a song called "I Wanna Be Rich."

I want money lots and lots of money
So don't be asking me why
I wanna be rich

She strides across the stage, soaking in the outrageous applause. Her outfit is kind of confusing. It's a long gray coat over a pair of pants, but it looks like she is wearing bulky bulletproof thermal underwear underneath. A white scarf is tied tightly around her neck and tucked into the front of the jacket, ascot-style. When the applause dies down, she bestows upon the crowd that most clichéd of celebrity greetings, the yoga bow. Palms pressed together, fingertips touching her chin, she closes her eyes, and nods her head forward.

Namaste, Suze.

Like many of the self-help experts I've been introduced to this year, Suze Orman has a "defining story." For many years, she was a waitress at the Buttercup Bakery in Berkeley, a place I drive by a few times a week after I drop Gus off at school. She was making about $400 a month and eventually wanted to open her own restaurant. Some of her loyal clientele pitched in and loaned her $50,000 to be paid back whenever she could. She took it to a broker at Merrill Lynch who, within a few months, had lost every penny of it. So what did our scrappy heroine do? She marched right back into the Lynch offices wearing a pair of red-and-white-striped Sassoon pants tucked into white cowboy boots and demanded they give her a job (which they did, after giving her shit about her outfit). Pretty awesome. I especially love the details about the pants because I think I had those pants when I was in junior high.

I'd read this story in her book and am kind of surprised to hear her tell it to the "Make Mine a Million Dollar Business" audience. *The Nine Steps* was published nearly ten years ago, and considering how many public speaking events she has each year, it feels like I'm on the receiving end of an overrehearsed actor's monologue. I don't want to get too down on Suze—she seems really busy and everything—but I was expecting more than just a recapitulation of her personal rags-to-riches tale.

The audience loves her, though. She is lovable in that "funny-auntie-who-takes-no-guff" way.

"I. Never. Got. Married," she says in her trademark clipped manner. "That's why I have money."

Big laughs, elbows in the ribs all around.

"I'm going to be fifty-six. I look good, don't I?"

Hoots of approval.

At one point, she brings her voice down to a whisper and hisses, "Do. You. Hear. Me. Ladies?"

Thunderous whooping.

What's wrong with me? I really liked her book and learned a lot from it, and yet this kind of feel-good camaraderie makes my spine turn to steel, makes me snap closed like a jewel case. It's tempting not to stand up and shout, "Tell everybody about the credit card thing, Suze! And also about how they should think about making money as a way to help other people!"

She gets me back again by the end, leaving us with a Gandhi quote: "We need to be the change we want to see in the world."

This, in essence, is Stephen Covey's idea of the trim tab.

I duck out to meet Lora and her friends for dinner without waiting around to see who's going to win the fifty grand. There is a big advertising convention in town, the reservation is for a super-chichi place, and I've been alerted not to worry about money, as the corporate credit cards will be coming out in droves.

I get out of the subway and walk through the West Village, checking out all the fancy shops and pricey restaurants, admiring the awesome street style of the teenagers and drug addicts. I sublimate my desire to make fun of the people lining up to get cupcakes from the trendy bakery because I admit that I wouldn't mind a delicious cupcake myself.

I think about how Suze's approach is extremely accessible to the average working joe, but how so many of her tips don't compute in my world at all. She talks about "regular" expenditures like pet grooming, gym memberships, manicures, haircuts, and, my favorite, window washing. I feel like if I could afford regular window washing, manicures, and haircuts, I might as well also own a yacht.

Even when I did her exercise of figuring out all of our expenses for the last two years, I couldn't complete the second part of it because it's impossible for us to figure out how much money we have coming in or when on earth it will arrive. If I add up all the banana jobs, teaching gigs, speaking engagements, storytelling shows, stage-managing work, freelance writing assignments, my one voice-over triumph, art auctioneering, open house policing, and focus group participation, the quiet glamour of one steady paycheck looms large.

So I go and eat. I eat the liver of ducks and cheese made from Spanish goats' milk and slices of a cow's shoulder and an obscene amount of lobster. I drink liquor that's so top-shelf I've never even heard of it before, in cocktails that were invented on-site. And I pay nothing.

Money is still so mysterious to me. The swipe of a card, $700 gone, all in the bellies of a girls' night out.

When I get back home, I go on another voice-over audition. I spend $3.10 each way so I can walk into a booth, the same booth that at least twenty-five women with distinctive voices have already walked into that morning, affix the headphones snugly around my ears, adjust the microphone and the spit guard, and yank the music stand up. Then I look through the thick glass, and when the cheery young agent gives me the signal, a truly professional jab into the air with an index finger, like she's ringing the most sensitive doorbell ever made, I lean into the mic and say in a horribly stilted monotone, "BETH." I really stress the final tongue cooler. Pause. Then: "LISICK." Trying not to be sibilant.

God, this irritates me. My voice is the exact one that my parents use on the outgoing message of their joint cell phone. The one that is followed by the canned lady who says, "is not available to take your call right now." A voice that suggests the speaker is under heavy duress translating their very own name into the faceless robotic machine of technology. Strained.

I read the script. "For a healthy start, think smart. Kellogg's Smart Start."

And then I get back on the BART, another $3.10 is deducted from my card, and I sit on the near-empty train. A lady, the M–F tranny kind, comes to sit down next to me.

"Where do I get off for Oakland?" she asks. Her blond hair is tied back with a purple batik scarf. She has kind of a Stevie Nicks thing going on that suits her. "I'm trying to buy pot at the medical marijuana place."

I give her directions to where she wants to go, and she thanks me profusely. She says she's been having a rough go of it in San Francisco.

"Everybody in Cleveland told me to come out to San Francisco, that everyone was so welcoming to trannies here, but I don't think that's true at all."

"I'm sorry," I say quietly. "How long have you been here?"

"Just a week, but it's really been tough. I'm living in a terrible SRO hotel in the Tenderloin, and I can't find a job."

We talk the whole way through the tunnel under the bay, and she shows me her artist portfolio, which is full of sci-fi and fantasy drawings. They're pretty cool in an epic, junior high notebook sort of way, but when she asks me if I know where she could sell them, I honestly have no idea.

"I'm sorry I can't help you," I say.

"You *are* helping." The way she says it, so sincerely, makes me want to escort her off the train, buy her all the medical marijuana she needs, and help her find a decent place to live, a job, and a few friends. Maybe spring for a new macramé belt to go with her peasant blouse. Helping other people, even a little bit, always feels great. There's no denying it.

I think of Suze Orman's words and try hard to believe them: helping yourself can help others.

November

YOU ARE NOT HERE

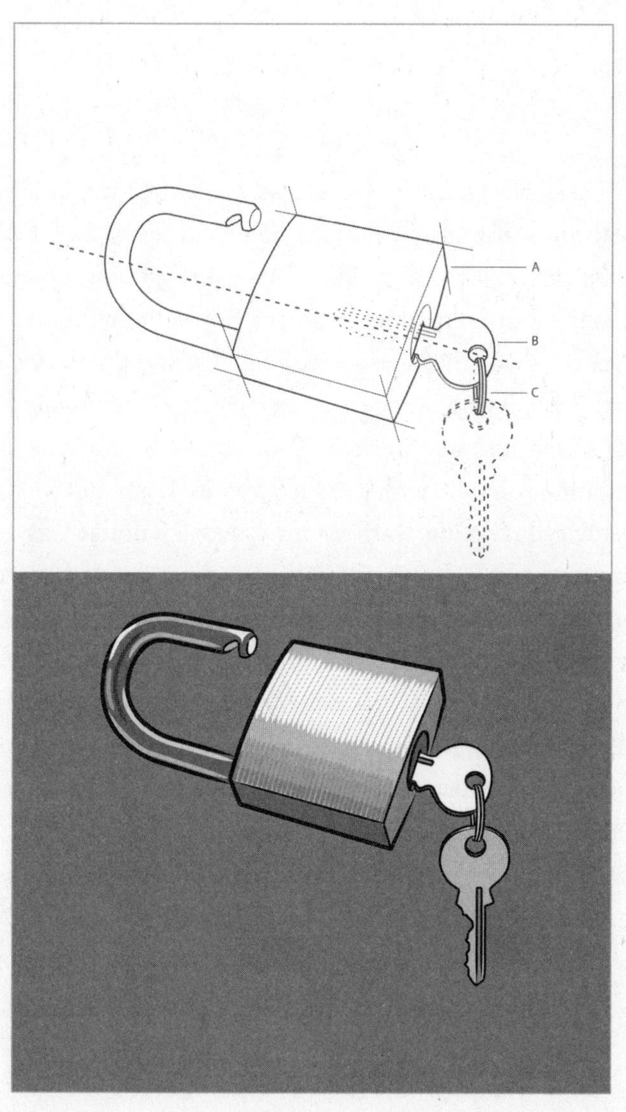

I didn't even see the car coming at us. Gus and I were on our way home from a friend's afternoon baby shower in San Francisco and had just exited the freeway. We were driving up Ashby, a fairly busy four-lane street near our house, going about thirty-five miles per hour through a green light, when this black Dodge Magnum T-boned us on the passenger side. We careened into a spin, smacking into another car in the opposite lane, the air bags went off, filling the car with a cloud of white dust, and we came to a rest facing oncoming traffic. Our trusty Hyundai was totaled, but besides a few rugburn-type things on my arms from the air bags punching out, we escaped unharmed.

There were a couple of eerie things about the accident, aside from the fact that the driver wasn't drunk, just convinced he had a green light (although there were about a dozen witnesses who stepped forward afterward and said otherwise). Gus normally sits in the backseat on the passenger side, right near the site of the impact. That day we had been bringing his old high chair as a gift for our friends (they requested hand-me-downs, I swear), and that was the place it fit best. I could push the front passenger seat all the way forward and fold it over to make room, which put Gus directly behind me. When we got in the car to go back home, without the high chair, we left his car seat where it was instead of moving it. Also weird was that the date of the accident happened to be the anniversary of the death of Eli's beloved grandfather Gus, our Gus's namesake.

I'm not superstitious or easily freaked out, but it did get me thinking, as such an incident will do, about Things.

Before I had a kid, the idea of my own death never really bothered me that much. Ever since I can remember, I figured that when you die, only one of two things could possibly happen: nothing or everything. Even though I was raised in the Catholic Church, I never believed that the afterlife, if it existed, would involve so much red tape. (And who that's decent would have such a cruddy attitude about women and girls anyway.) Early on, I told myself that you're born, you try to be good, then you die. After that, either nothing or everything happens, but you can't know. So relax.

Once, in second grade, I was standing on the playground watching some girls whisper and laugh at me. In that moment, I thought, *When I'm dead, if I still feel like it, I can find out what they are saying about me.* The solace came from the fact that eventually, if it turned out that people didn't just lie in the ground rotting, all the mysteries of the universe would be known by me, including, if I so desired, the fact that Kim Kamen told Alison McCormick and Denise Reeves that she thought my new haircut looked like a mushroom.

To say that my exploration ended there is not much of an understatement. I am kind of a spiritual midget, I know. It's always bothered me a little, mostly because people all over the world seem to really get into it. Spirituality. Who knows, maybe it would turn out like Antonioni films or Sri Lankan food did. Yet another thing that's been doing just fine without me, but could eventually add some more wattage to my world. I did read Plato's *Allegory of the Cave* in high school. Perhaps it's time I found out what's making those shadows on the wall.

It's a crowded field for soul jockeys right now, but the name I associate most with the mind-body-spirit scene is Deepak Chopra. Just to flesh out my ignorance more fully, this is what I knew about Deepak Chopra prior to this month: He is from India. He has written a lot of books. He has a spa in San Diego. He's into sex. He is a "pop culture" spiritual leader, the guy who made Eastern philosophy accessible to Westerners.

That last one just kills me. I know nothing about the man, I have not read a single one of his twenty-six books, I've never heard him speak, plus I know next to nothing about Eastern philosophy or religion in the first place, but somehow I have written off Deepak Chopra as being "spirituality lite."

No, sorry, Mr. Chopra, I'm going to go straight to the masters if you don't mind. Let me pick up the Vedanta and Bhagavad Gita source books in a decent translation and really dig into this.

One of my hugest annoyances in life is when people act like they know what they're talking about when they don't. It's a credible thing to get annoyed by, but it used to paralyze me when I was in school. I didn't want to be that person. I would sit there astounded that a nineteen-year-old was attempting to discuss Kierkegaard after reading the same excerpted essay from the photocopied class reader that I did. Or, who wants to sum up affirmative action in the next three minutes before class is over? And someone would raise their hand and report what was in our textbook. I mean, I know you have to start somewhere, but attempting to enter a world you have no information about or relationship with is always a dicey dive.

Roll up the door to the comfort zone, I'm pulling out tonight!

One of the reasons Chopra particularly intimidates me, as opposed to John Gray or Suze Orman, is precisely because he's on the spirituality beat. I've had lots of successful relationships, I deal with money every day, but the meaning of life? Death? How can I dip my toe into Deepak's oeuvre as it enters its third decade of existence?

I suck it up and buy his latest, *Life After Death: The Burden of Proof*, which has been hailed as an intellectual and spiritual tour de force. Deepak has taken his training as a scientist, doctor, and philosopher and written, as the jacket says, "a must-read for everyone who will die." Now that's a target audience. Somebody in the publicity department knew what they were doing on that one.

By page 5 of the introduction, I've already discovered that one of the tenets of karma in Dharmic religions like Hinduism and Buddhism is very similar to my childhood version of the "everything" death. He writes: "After we die, we remain self-motivated. A soul moves according to its desire from one astral plane to another, projecting as in a dream whatever sights and people, guides and astral entities it needs for its own advancement." From these different astral planes, which occur only in the imagination, you become separate from your body.

The strange thing is that this happens to me about once a month when I'm dreaming. I will be asleep and start to rise out of my body. I can look down and see myself in bed, and that's when I realize that I am having a dream. Usually I head straight for our bedroom window. There's an odd sort of squeezing sensation, like a really tight hug, as I pass through the glass pane, and then I'm free to fly around for a while before waking up or going on to another dream. In the past couple years, when I'm aware I'm dreaming, I can somehow tell myself to have sex. Flying and sex, that's all I've been able to do so far. Not that I'm complaining, though it would be cool if one night I could eat an entire five-course meal at the French Laundry or swim with dolphins.

I realize this probably sounds super-weird, but it's been happening to me for so long that it seems seminormal. (It happened occasionally when I was a kid, but I could only move around the inside of my house.) I've told Eli and a few of my friends about it, always referring to it as "lucid dreaming," a relatively common phenomenon. Reading Deepak's book makes me think about it differently. Call it Philosophy 101, but maybe this dream state could also be some sort of fancy astral plane stuff. I'm not saying that I would ever fool myself into believing that I really made sweet love to Steve Buscemi a few weeks ago, but it's fun in a slightly spiritual or perhaps borderline psychotic way to imagine Steve and I having a connection, even if it was not on this astral plane. By the way, we also share the same birthday. (Okay, so I have a thing for Steve Buscemi.) It makes me wonder if nuns and priests are onto this as a way to cope with the celibacy situation. Prisoners, monks, married people, listen up. This is a really safe way to get some action or see the outside world if you're cloistered or incarcerated.

While still in the intro, I find out that Deepak also methodically reviews the events of his day before falling asleep every night. Just like Jack Canfield and me! And even more, Deepak calls it a "spiritual practice." Who knew? I had simply been thinking of it as a kind of non-habit-forming Tylenol PM. Sheep for self-helpers.

The book goes back and forth, chapter to chapter, between Deepak's ideas about death and narratives of the myths and stories that were told to him as a child. He encourages us to look at death as an elusive, invisible miracle, as a fulfillment of our purpose here on earth. "The other side," he says, is actually very close to us right now, and if you know yourself better and expand your own consciousness, you can begin to understand the concept of eternity. Ultimately, death is about what you can become.

I'm driving on the freeway the next day, thinking about how comforting these ideas on death are, how they make me more unafraid of it, mine and others', than I've ever been. There's a song playing on the college station with the chorus "All things go, All things go," which is a semi-plate-o'-shrimp moment in itself, when a good friend calls me. She has terrible news about her childhood friend, an acquaintance of mine. I had just seen him when I went to New York for the Suze Orman thing last month. She tells me that he and his family were in a horrible car wreck. I pull the car over and sob my brains out.

I want to write to him and say something meaningful. I want to share some of the words I read last night, with hopes that they can bring comfort, but there is no way. Maybe Deepak himself could pull it off, but you can't tell someone who just lost a family member that he must have fulfilled his purpose here on earth. I settle for saying, "I'm so sorry" and "I can't imagine" and "I'm thinking of you."

Though it's tempting to convince myself that I really need to fly down to San Diego and attend a retreat at the Chopra Center, I can't justify spending money I don't have on this personal growth stuff anymore. No matter how curious I am about an Ayurvedic spa treatment or SynchroDestiny seminar, Suze Orman's voice is in my ear, clear as an air horn, spoiling the mood. My own consciousness also has a few words to say about it, "totally unnecessary" being two of them. Plus, Deepak is speaking at the Commonwealth Club in San Francisco for fifteen bucks, though at this point I'm not even willing to spend that. I find a phone number and weasel onto the press list.

It's a rainy afternoon, and the room is crowded with damp people looking for some lunch hour enlightenment. Beats going to the food court at the new mall down the street where Bloomingdale's just opened. The woman next to me totally "pays it forward" by offering to bring me back a glass of water when she gets hers. I'm about to pay it forward to my neighbor by giving him my water and getting another one, but the sound of a pounding gavel plunks me back in my seat. Next time, friend. Next time. Or maybe the guy next to him just paid him forward for me by handing him that Kleenex after he sneezed. Maybe now I owe that guy one. I feel like I'm going to need a dauber for my universal scorecard.

I catch a glimpse of Deepak, and I must say, there is something extremely vital and serene about him. It really puts things into perspective, comparing his utter calm to many of the stressed-out, bunched-up, preoccupied attendees collapsing into their chairs like shell-shocked rats. There's a brightness to him. He's like platinum in a sea of dented tin. Or maybe that's just what happens when you're a millionaire with access to good spa treatments.

He steps up to the podium to a huge round of applause and says that the things he wants to talk about today are:

1. What is our essential nature as consciousness?
2. Where is consciousness located?
3. Why do we have reason to believe that this essential part of us is not subject to what we call "death"? The miracle of death, he says, is that the real you does not die.

"So that's what I want to talk about in the remaining twenty-five minutes," he says, laughing. Everybody chuckles a bit, but we quickly put a lid on it. It's pretty clear that he will probably blow our minds with all he can fit in that short amount of time.

He has us close our eyes and visualize a sunset, a red rose, a candle in a dark room. Then he asks us to hear in our consciousness the sound of a newborn crying or a dog barking. Now taste a strawberry, lick a lemon. Were we able to have those experiences? The resounding affirmative murmur of the room says yes. Yet, he points out, if someone went inside our brains, they wouldn't see a picture of a sunset or hear the baby. What they would see would be the plus and minus charges that translate the experiences in our consciousness.

He then quotes astrophysicist Sir Arthur Eddington, winner of the Gold Medal of the Royal Astronomical Society in 1924, for grins. Speaking of the uncertainty principle in quantum physics, Eddington said: "Something unknown is doing we don't know what."

A keeper of a line, for sure.

Then Deepak starts to lose me. He says the essential nature of the physical world is that it's not physical at all. He uses the Internet, e-mail, cell phones, radio, and TV as examples. Fair enough, but what about concrete objects like podiums or, observing the man two rows in front of me, hair plugs?

"The essential stuff of the universe is non-stuff," he says. "It's not physical. . . . Everything is a fluctuation of subatomic particles that are not things. They are fluctuations of energy and information in a huge void."

He pulls out that old trick about how, in the deeper reality, he's not even really here right now. None of us is. Oh no, you didn't, Mary! I hate when they do this. It reminds me of being in the dorms at college, or something out of a scene in an independent film from the early '90s. None of us is really here?

I come back, though. This part I get: he talks about how the universe appears to be continuous, but it is really all of these electromagnetic charges going on and off. He compares it to a movie. It looks like something continuous, but it's really a series of individual frames. The discontinuity is something that becomes continuity in consciousness, and the world as we see it, as we piece it together, is in fact created inside our consciousness.

But where is this consciousness? Can you find it inside your body?

He uses the example of a surgeon stimulating part of someone's brain to make the person's arm move up. The doctor then tells the patient not to allow him to keep moving his arm up. Even as the doctor is physically manipulating the brain to make the arm move up, the patient can override that and make the decision to move his own arm down. Somebody or something more powerful is telling the brain not to move the arm. Who is the interpreter behind the scenes? Who is the choice-maker?

Every thought you have, he says, is either a choice or an interpretation. "The essential you," he says, "the choice-maker and interpreter, cannot be found in the brain or the body, and the reason that it cannot . . . is because it does not reside in the brain or the body."

He quotes Hindu Vedanta philosophy, saying, "We are not in the world, the world is in us. We are not in the body, the body is in us."

It's a cool idea, that your consciousness lives outside of you and therefore will live on after your body gives out. It also sounds a bit like wishful thinking, a palatable way for people to accept their inevitable demise.

"Death is the ticket to life," he says, finishing the lecture. "Get in touch with the part of yourself which is timeless."

The last part sounds a little like an advertisement for a watch, or yet another mandate from the diamond industry about how to prove your love to an attractive person with tousled hair, but I kind of get it.

A question-and-answer session follows, and Deepak becomes even more charming as he casually fields inquiries from the audience. I'm surprised to discover that he doesn't think of himself as a spiritual leader at all, that he calls himself an "explorer of the domain of consciousness." He says he started meditating one day in order to quit smoking and somehow wound up where he is now.

He tells a story about his father. He was a cardiologist in good health, eighty-six years old, who had a regular day, saw a bunch of patients, and went home. Later that night, he was watching George W. Bush being inaugurated on CNN and said, "I think I'm leaving," and promptly closed his eyes and died in meditation. "Very consciously," Deepak says.

The noontime San Francisco Commonwealth Club audience gets quite a kick out of this. Many, I'm sure, are wishing they had done the same.

Like many of my gurus this year, he's all for having intentions and paying attention to what you want. "Whatever is imagined," he says, "eventually shows up."

There's something about that that's both liberating and terrifying.

At the end of the hour, with the rain still beating down outside the windows, my conscious mind is left with an almighty *Huh, very interesting indeed*. As we are the only sentient beings conscious of being conscious (Covey also talks about this "self-awareness," this ability to think about your own thought process), it seems necessary for survival that we be able to turn off this mechanism on occasion. The constant din of the consciousness, as I've been discovering, is taxing.

There appear to be two modalities of self-help. One focuses on what has gone wrong and how to try to make it right, and the other chooses to start with what is right and build from that. Could the consciousness be trained to focus only on the positive and the improvement upon it? Because the negative is often needed to appreciate the positive, why would we ever want to ax it out completely? Or perhaps it is like when someone loses his sight after being able to see for many years. He's already established the reference points and can expand from there. If you've been through hell, can you just decide not to act like you've been through hell anymore?

Thanksgiving dinner is at our house this year, for the first time ever. My parents have been busy with a lot of health issues, and

I think my mom's happy to have the year off. Forty consecutive years of providing the horn o' plenty and the lady deserves a break. We keep it pretty simple—mashed potatoes, Brussels sprouts, yams, and salad as sides—and while the pies are baking, Eli, Gus, and I take a family bike ride to the flower shop to get something festive for the table. It feels huge that we have $10 to spend on flowers. Eli has taken the job in San Francisco and even though the pay's not great, it's steady.

What we just sprung on my parents yesterday is that after Thanksgiving dinner we're going to drive down to Santa Barbara. One of Eli's best friends is in from New York, visiting his family for the holiday weekend. It'll have to be a really quick trip. The drive is about five and a half hours, we won't be done with dinner until at least six, and Eli's got to be at the studio Saturday morning at ten. I was on the fence about getting into Santa Barbara at 11:00 P.M., going to sleep, and getting back in the car the next afternoon, but there is one factor that pushes me over the edge. The friend we're visiting is the one whose dad is Jack Canfield.

After dinner, we throw a change of clothes for everybody into Gus's little suitcase, grab our toothbrushes, and head south on the 101. The sun goes down, and it feels like we're in a spaceship. You can barely feel anything in this new car we got. It's like we're in a bubble. I've always loved driving because what is expected of you is so clear. Even if you're just a passenger, as I am tonight, your job description is easy: talk, listen, pick some music, help navigate. The moon, a fragile nail clipping of a thing, follows us as we go. For about a hundred miles we keep pace with a guy in a minivan, his wheelchair visible through the back windows, as he accelerates and breaks with hand gears. It makes me happy to think that you could have no legs at all and still be able to drive a car. At one point, as we loop around near Pismo Beach, I see him pack a small pipe and hold it up toward me as if to say "Cheers!" We smile and wave as he turns off.

When we reach Santa Barbara, we exit the freeway and drive under an iron archway with a sign that says HOPE RANCH. It's like a gated community, but without the gate. The roads are twisty and pleasantly rural, with many of the homes barely visible down long driveways and wooded paths. We find the address we're looking for and pull into the drive, but it's hard to figure out where to park. There are so many cars in the driveway. (One being a Honda Element wrapped in a Segway Human Transporter ad. Awesome.) The front of the property is landscaped with palms and ferns and bamboo. Tree branches encircle a column, climbing to the eaves of an overhang, and spiritual-looking statuary serenely watches over the wide front steps. The only sound is the light trickle of water from a fountain. I instantly feel like I'm in Hawaii or at a very, very upscale Thai restaurant.

Gus wakes as I lift him out of his seat, looks around, and says, "Are we at a hotel?"

"We're at Uncle Oran's dad's house," Eli says. "We're at a mansion."

Oran walks down the drive to meet us, the orange glow from his cigarette between his fingers. I wonder if being with his family stresses him out. I wonder if he takes a lot of smoke breaks while he's here.

Some of the Thanksgiving guests are still sitting around the kitchen talking. Jack's wife, Inga, is there, but we hear that Jack has retired for the evening to practice piano.

I lay Gus down to sleep in a king-size bed in a guest room and soon drift off myself to the murmur of Oran's and Eli's voices out in the living room. So many of Eli's friends have moved away from San Francisco, and he works so much, that this is a rare opportunity. Something as simple as having a conversation with a friend has become a special event worth driving over three hundred miles for.

Morning fills the room, golden and luxurious. Gus and I get

up and explore the grounds while everyone is still sleeping. The area around the house and guesthouse, where the pool and Jacuzzi are, feel sublimely tropical. Even as a California native, I can't believe it's the end of November. We run down a path and find a barn. There's a stable down there, and cute little ponies! A hawk circles overhead. So this is the place Jack was talking about in his book. I can see why you might want to toot your horn about it.

Eventually, we go back up to get some breakfast. The house feels lazy and homey. Like the regular home of a nice family, just extremely large and expensive. One by one, everybody wakes up and wanders into the kitchen, pulling up bar stools around the island. Inga comes out, then Oran, then Eli. When Jack emerges, I'm embarrassed to look at him at first. I say hi and quickly look away as he goes into the fridge for some berries. Eli and Oran are talking about movies, and Jack joins in, saying he just went to see *Borat* the other day. Gus is sitting on my lap coloring while I'm telling Inga about my attempts at self-help.

"Hey, Jack," she says. "You gotta hear this."

I feel my cheeks get hot.

"Beth, tell him what you're doing."

I explain the whole thing to him, rapidly at first, to get it over with, and he seems very interested. He's the kind of person who really listens, who really focuses. It feels like he's trying to put himself in my shoes and understand an outsider's perspective on his life's work. It reminds me of sassy Judy Henrichs and her "Active Listening" class at the FranklinCovey symposium.

He wants to know which people I've been following. When I mention John Gray, and how when I saw him in Atlanta I felt like he was performing for the crowd more than really talking to us, Jacks stands up for him. Of course they're friends.

"Maybe he didn't feel safe," Jack says.

"Maybe that was it," I answer, eager to switch topics. Though

I could launch into a play-by-play of the infomercial I witnessed, I don't want to dis anybody's friend.

I ask him what he's working on. He's just released a new book called *You've Got to Read This Book*, which is a collection of essays by people writing about the books that changed their lives. A cool idea. His contributors include activists, publishers, healers, entrepreneurs, coaches. Even Kenny Loggins.

"I'll get a copy of that for you before you leave," he says. "And have you seen *The Secret*? I can get you a copy of that, too."

The Secret. The film I've been hearing about all year. I knew if I waited long enough, it would somehow find its way to me, saving me $4.95.

Jack pops a few blueberries in his mouth and explains his approach to his work.

"What I really like to do is read all sorts of things, everything." I had seen his enormous library earlier that morning. "And then put it out there for other people to read. To make this stuff accessible to everyone."

I am guessing that part of that sentiment is in his mission statement, that idea of interpreting other people's ideas and philosophies and bringing them to the largest audience possible.

"I've never had an original idea in my life!" he says, laughing.

I tell him I've had an interesting year, a hard year in some ways, because I became so aware of all my faults and kept fighting the urge to resist.

"You seem like an optimistic, positive person, and I bet you get a lot of good energy back from people," he says.

I let the smile creep across my face. It's not every day you receive affirmations about your energy from America's "Number One Success Coach." And maybe he's right. Jack would probably know from positive energy, what with all the professional feng shui in his house.

Before we take off, he loads me up with a bunch of books and the audio CD of *The Success Principles* and, yes, *The Secret*. Then I remember that I brought his book with me in case I got the nerve to have him sign it.

I hand it over to him, and he laughs. There are at least fifty Post-it notes, covered in scrawls, hanging out of the pages. Inga brings him a special pen, and he sits in his foyer, taking time with the inscription.

When we get back in the car to head home, I open it up.

> Beth—
>
> Love, joy, and great success with your new book! May these principles and strategies help you create the life of your dreams!
>
> Jack Canfield

I hold the book in my lap for a while, thinking about the expression "life of your dreams" with my new Choprian understanding of the dream world. Jack's book did turn out to play a big part in that, more than I ever imagined, a matrix that stayed with me all year.

I try to remember Jack's and Deepak's advice and wisdom, even when seemingly "off the clock" at a book festival in Las Vegas. Chuck "Fight Club" Palahniuk is the keynote speaker at the UNLV student union. I haven't read any of his books, but when his last one, called *Haunted*, came out, there were reports of people fainting or barfing at his readings because the material was so graphic and unsettling. I'm curious if it was just hype. Plus, there's a rumor going around among us lesser-known writers that he's getting paid $10,000 for this talk. I was pleased as punch to receive my check that covered air travel and my hotel, but ten grand launches you into motivational speaker territory. Going back to my "career" dilemma, I can't visualize ever being in such a position myself. What $10,000 experience is he going to deliver?

Some of the other authors and I sit in the second row, close to the wooden risers that have been jammed together to create a stage. There is a podium and a few large cardboard boxes off to the side. Chuck makes his way to the front rolling a fairly large suitcase with him. It seems awkward, but I assume he might have to go to the airport right afterward. Either that or he's like this guy I used to work with, so severely attached to his stuff that he couldn't even take his backpack off while going into the office bathroom to take a shit.

Chuck's look is surprising to me. Not rakish or any species of hip, and far from the stereotype of the schlubby writer, he appears extremely efficient and tidy. His neat haircut, smooth shave, ramrod spine, and starched white shirt actually kind of creep me out. He's like some of the business guys at the FranklinCovey symposium except that all of Chuck's obsessions about identity, brutality, and instinct are available for purchase.

He takes the stage and quickly unzips the suitcase for the big reveal. As hundreds of his Las Vegas fan base await, he unveils scores of airplane-size bottles of liquor. Vodka, gin, rum, tequila. He begins hurling them out to the crowd. He's cradling them in his arms and power-pitching bottles across the room. They just keep flying. People are going crazy. Eventually, he has to ask for help from some of the college kids.

The energy in that first ten minutes is absolutely bonkers, comparable to one of the Crimpshrine shows I witnessed at Gilman Street in the late '80s. Kids are cracking open multiple bottles of whatever and swigging them down. Chuck Palahniuk is now a hero, bathed in the white-hot light of adulation. His eyes shine.

He tells a story of working at a movie theater as a teenager. They made him wear a space suit, which the banana in me loves. We're all laughing about the absurdity of it when he reaches into his suitcase and pulls out the very same space suit he used to wear! When the theater was being sold, they tracked him down and asked him if he wanted it. He tries it on for us, pivoting a bit in the aisles to yelps of approval.

Instead of reading from one of his books, he tells story after story, each more outrageous than the next. He says one of the main reasons he writes is so he can travel the world and hear more stories. We hear about eight-year-old Brownies masturbating with heating pads, pug dogs eating Kleenex laced with HIV-positive semen, miscarried fetuses preserved in bottles of vodka, and French veterinary students being sewn inside horse stomachs while they were blacked out. There is something a bit evil about him, something diabolical. The crowd, mostly white people under thirty, is rapt.

He's got about seven stories related to severed limbs. While he's telling these, he rips open the boxes that have been sitting next to him on the stage and starts flinging out arms and legs, rubber ones with fake bloodied stumps. He's beaming, throwing body parts. An hour into his talk, he shows no signs of stopping.

He starts talking about liminality right around the time the mini-bottle of Cuervo I drank kicks in. Though it would be so much easier to write off his whole presentation as schtick, the idea he speaks of, that of being in limbo, at the threshold of something new, is intriguing. Characterized by disorientation, a liminoid experience differs from a liminal one in that it doesn't necessarily involve the resolution of a personal crisis. I start wondering whether perhaps an entire calendar year could be liminoid. Sure feels like it.

It also dawns on me that Chuck has a lot in common with many of the motivational speakers I've seen this year. And it's not just his price tag. (Though now it's obvious where a lot of the money went. Limbs and liquor are expensive.) He's getting paid to create liminoid experiences for large audiences. I think of Suze telling the story of losing all her money, or John Gray talking about his father being found in the trunk of the car. Julia Cameron prescribes them with her "artist dates." The cruise with Richard was like a week of sailing liminoid seas. The participant is reeled into the liminal zone that these speakers create and once there, if hooked, will go just about anywhere with them. Buy the book, get the CD, keep trying to recapture the magic of the first time they brought you there.

It makes sense. Liminoid experiences are some of the things I cherish most in my life. The feeling of being neither here nor there. Going up that escalator at Bloomingdale's, taking that long walk in Chicago, watching the dancers at the Clermont Lounge in Atlanta, driving to Santa Barbara. I like being in places where I have no reference point, where nothing concrete is expected of me.

Going on its third frenzied hour, the talk is far from over when I leave. The city of Las Vegas, this absurd and deeply human construction, envelops me. Fake boobs and oxygen tubes, wasted tourists and sad-sack locals. Every third person making a joke about "what happens in Vegas. . . ." I reach into my new bag of spirituality tricks and imagine an astral plane, an illusory world that contains all the things I like about Vegas. The neon sign graveyard, the Hoover Dam, how I always find money on the floor of cabs and casinos. One of my favorite people in the world was born and raised here. I am grasping.

Instead of making me feel better, this process of strategizing about how to cope with reality makes me feel soft and dumb, the opposite of being alive. I shake it off by engaging in a marathon air hockey tournament with so much abandon that I walk away bruised. I hit the sack. The blackout curtains are shut. The room is silent. After recounting the day's events, I will myself to have transcendent dreams, but nothing magical happens. I'm just dead to the world. Not that there's anything wrong with being dead.

December

THE EXISTENCE OF GOD

When I was in high school, my friend Amy and I used to do some babysitting for this family around the corner. In a neighborhood populated with station wagons and basketball hoops, these people were glamorous. The husband had a blond "Dry Look" hairdo and drove a red Corvette. The mom was also blond, pretty, and stayed at home caring for their adorable baby girl. We liked the mom a lot, she was sweet, but we couldn't get over how cheesy the husband was. He was a Realtor who wore creased jeans with loafers and yelled a lot. On his bookshelf was a spin-off of the then-popular "One-Minute Manager" business book series called *The One-Minute Dad.* We loved that one. Apparently, somebody's time was pretty valuable.

Occasionally they would hire us to help out at their dinner parties, '80s home-entertaining wonders with crepes and quiche and lots of chablis. I'll never forget one night when Amy came home from working at one and immediately called me, breathless. She said one of the dinner guests that evening was none other than Sylvia Brown, a local psychic who appeared on the Bay Area morning show *People Are Talking.* Turns out, while clearing away the plates from the dining room table, Amy decided to break down some boundaries of her service position.

"Will I pass geometry this semester?" Amy asked her, with perhaps a hint of desperation in her voice.

"Just barely," Sylvia rasped.

Later in the evening, she was going around the room telling all the guests what they had been in their past lives. She divined that Amy had once been an English maid who married into royalty. Amy was floored. When she was a little kid, to pass the time doing her family's dishes after dinner, she created an elaborate fantasy about being a maid in an English castle. She would stand at the sink, imagining her life with the demanding king and queen who would punish her if she wasn't done quickly. So whether Sylvia picked up on Amy's fantasy world or her "past life" or was just riffing on watching her clear plates at a dinner party, Sylvia made quite an impression on us as teenagers. Creatures that exotic rarely made pit stops in our vanilla burb.

As my year comes to a close, I decide to check back in with my cynicism. How I've missed it. Having given so many things the benefit of the doubt, I'm looking for a canary in a coal-mine experience. How deep have I gotten myself into this? That's when I notice that Sylvia, who has now become a world-renowned psychic, *New York Times* bestselling author, and millionaire, is on tour for the paperback release of her latest book, *If You Could See What I See*. She also added an "e" to her last name at some point along the way, becoming Sylvia Browne. Whether the name change has to do with a sticky legal situation written up in the papers in the early '90s (which involved the phrases "grand theft," "investment fraud," and "probation") is a little murky.

I show up at the Masonic Auditorium on San Francisco's Nob Hill, right across from Grace Cathedral, just in time. I've always loved the juxtaposition of these two institutions, surrounded by their twin spiritual force fields, situated at the highest point on California Street. The auditorium is a stately building, a serious structure, and yet somehow when I walk into the enormous white marble lobby, I immediately think "Reno" or "state fair." This didn't happen when I saw jazz pianist McCoy Tyner here years ago. I guess it must be the people. This is an unfortunate development, my unflattering read on the crowd, seeing as I made such a big deal about how all the Carnival Cruisers weren't "midwestern." There is such a feeling of immense despair among all the crushed velvet and frizzy way-too-long hair and severe eyeliner that makes me think of a carnival fairway and games of chance. Considering the evening's entertainment is three hours of talking to the dead, it makes sense that many of the people here are probably bummed out and desperate.

The venue seats over three thousand people, and while it's not sold out, it is pretty well packed. I was waffling between shelling out $75 for a main-floor seat, to be closer to the action, and saving $25 by sitting in the balcony, but luckily the fates stepped in. Just as I'm told that the main floor is sold out, a woman smelling like smoked nuts approaches my right shoulder.

"I can give you a blue-section ticket for fifty dollars," she whispers.

I hate myself for being suspicious, but I blame it on the carny vibe.

"Oh, let me see!" I say, inspecting the ticket like a U.S. border agent looking at a brown person's passport. "How do I know this is for the blue section?" I am staying upbeat, pretending like I'm just confused, instead of convinced that she's on the short con.

"Let's walk in together," she says, smiling. Surely she's been taken for a ride or two in her fifty years and recognizes the familiar musk of apprehension. "My daughter couldn't make it," she explains hoarsely, tossing a cigarette lighter into her purple suede satchel. "I thought I was going to lose the money because I was too embarrassed to talk to anyone and see if they wanted it." I'm flattered to seem approachable.

We hand our tickets to the doorman with no problem, and I

thank her. A quick trip down to the basement bathroom underscores my first impressions. It smells like farts and feet and popcorn down here. A drunk girl in her early twenties has just vomited into a toilet and is cracking up with her friend as she rinses her mouth out. "We're gonna get Nicky to talk to us tonight and tell us how fucked up this shit is!"

The opening act is already on. It's a Scottish guy named Gordon Smith, also known as "the psychic barber." I guess he used to be a barber. Even though his hair is severely overstyled and his shirt too far unbuttoned, his charisma slices through it on impact. Part of it is just the accent, I realize. A Scottish person could cut your tongue out and stuff it into a bottle of Laphroaig and still you would hope they were free for dinner later that evening. He roams the stage in order to follow the energy of the "spirit world," which he pronounces "speddit woold." He's saying stuff like, "A little doggie is running around my feet right now. I can see him running around. Hi, doggie!" and then turning to someone in the audience and saying, "Did your father Richard have a little dog? Because the dog is with him now and they are very happy."

And the rub of it is that the woman he's speaking to will, without a doubt, respond into the microphone that has been quickly placed in front of her face by one of the attractive roving assistants, "Yes, he did! My father Richard had a terrier named Ringo!" And the audience erupts into applause.

Not to brag, but I feel like I could spot an actor or a plant a mile away. What's happening seems to be "real." It seems inconceivable to me that the entire show would be a farce, that from city to city they would hire new actors to sign confidentiality agreements, and that no one would spill their guts in a tabloid or on their blog. Time after time, Gordon delivers. Skeptics call this practice "cold reading," the act of picking up on appearance and body language as one hedges guesses about a subject. At one point, Gordon follows the energy up to the balcony where a voice, wavery and hyperventilating, replies that, no, the necklace she is currently wearing around her neck is not significant to her dead father. But Gordon isn't convinced.

"He keeps saying something about the necklace. He wants to talk about the necklace. Are you carrying a picture of him with you?"

"In my pocket!" the woman says. "I have a locket with a picture of him in my pocket. The clasp broke, so I'm not wearing it."

"Well, that would be a necklace then," Gordon chides. The audience *tsk-tsks* her a bit for not realizing the significance of the necklace right away.

"It's in my pocket," the woman says again, on the verge of tears now. "That's incredible."

"But the fact that I'm currently talking to your dead father isn't?" he laughs, and the crowd busts up.

"I'm sorry," Gordon says. "I don't mean to be flippant, but they want to make you laugh. They really do."

Wrapping up, Gordon graciously thanks us and reiterates that he wants to use his powers for good deeds. By working as a medium, he wants to make people feel at peace with the death of their loved ones. I believe him. And I'm sure he's making a shitload of dough.

At the intermission, I wander out into the lobby, where the credit card machines are practically melting holes into collapsible tables. In addition to Sylvia's massive bibliography and discography, including a children's book she's written with her son Chris Dufresne (also conveniently psychic) called *Animals on the Other Side*, there is an official Sylvia Browne Latte Cup for $10.

With the headliner about to take the stage, many of the audience members furiously stub out their cigarettes and wrap up their transactions. By way of introduction, the emcee announces that she has some very exciting news. This December, Sylvia will make her debut on daytime TV's *The Young and the Restless*. The audience goes wild. I guess the guru–soap opera connections don't stop with Richard Simmons, who got his start on *General Hospital*. Turns out Sylvia also has a cruise and a line of jewelry.

"Isn't that incredible?" the emcee brays into the mic, as if cracking the casting call for *The Young and the Restless* was more mystical than convening with the dead on a daily basis for the past forty years.

Sylvia, clad in a flouncy lime green blouse, walks onto the stage, and it is standing O time. A woman's voice rises up from the crowd, "I love you, Sylvia!!" and it is then that I realize who Sylvia reminds me of. Courtney Love, age seventy. Her voice is beyond raspy; it's more "violently throaty." She makes no bones about it that her work leaves her exhausted. Her world-weariness is her trademark.

"I always ask Francine if there is heroin on the other side. Or at least liquor." Francine is her spirit guide.

Sylvia Browne may be a psychic, but she is at least half stand-up comic. Her opening remarks are an absolute comedy monologue, one that she delivers with utter effortlessness.

"I think we should boycott hotels," she says, super-droll. There are a few whoops in the audience, but I can't imagine why. Do they already know this bit?

"Did you ever notice that when you step out of the bathtub in a hotel there is always a full-length mirror right there? I'm looking at myself going, 'What part of the body is *that*?' " Beat. "And then you turn around and . . ." Beat. She waves a hand in front of her face, looking disgusted. The crowd busts up. She takes in the energy and picks up her pace.

"And you men out there . . ." (oh my God, she's really going there) ". . . I know when you sit down and go 'Ow!' " She mimes sitting down and then quickly jumping to her feet. "I know what you're sitting down on!"

"People say, 'If I had my life to live over again.' You know what?

Stupid. That's stupid." It's clear that this is her catchphrase. "You'd do the exact same thing and you know it. Stupid."

She's seated in a white chair with a fan blowing on her face, sending her blond hair back in little wisps.

"Martyrs. Hate 'em. A martyr can only nail one of his hands down himself, you know? Let him hang there! You need to live your life with as little guilt as possible."

"Get this," she continues. "I went to Kenya and they said, 'What did you think of all the black people?' and I said, 'I didn't see any.'" She bristles. "Racists. Homophobes. It's like, you know what, you used to be all of them in a past life, and if you don't shut up you'll be one in the next. So *shut up*!"

I am quickly falling for Sylvia.

"And these people call themselves Christian," she spits. "The Bible says we're not supposed to judge, but you know who you *can* judge? You can judge the people that judge. I've read all twenty-six versions of the Bible, and that's what I think."

She then moves into her final joke, one of the oldest in the world, but it still gets a big laugh. She says when she was in Catholic school the girls weren't allowed to wear patent leather shoes because the boys could look up their skirts and see their underwear.

"No, they can't!" she says she told the nuns. "Because I'm not wearing any!"

With her closer successfully delivered, Sylvia turns serious. She takes an extended pause and looks over the crowd.

"You're everything to me," she says. She has none of the desperation John Gray had in Atlanta, and nowhere near the histrionics of Richard Simmons.

She begins speaking about the disabled, calling them "angels" and "advanced beings." Of course, I've heard this theory before and always found it incredibly mawkish. I tell my brain to can it for a second, to please halt the cringe mechanism in my body so that

I can at least consider it. The disabled as angels. I think of the disabled people I have known. Dru Dougherty, my neighbor growing up. If you've ever known someone with Down's syndrome, it is hard to argue that they're not pretty angelic. I think of my brother Paul, who has cerebral palsy, with his steel-trap memory and off-kilter sense of humor. How he reads reference books and the TV guide cover to cover, and owns every edition of the World Almanac from 1980 to the present. I think of the way he hovers around the world, like ozone, instead of really inhabiting it. I come out of my haze just in time to hear Sylvia saying, "Like people with Down's syndrome or cerebral palsy." Wasn't I just thinking that? Please make Sylvia Browne not be reading my mind.

Then she tosses in the doozy of the evening.

"The world is coming to a close, people."

This elicits a substantial amount of head-nodding and affirmative murmuring. Like this information was possibly in the newspaper that morning, not on the front page so that *everyone* would be talking about it, but maybe in a local section next to a story about the lane closures on Interstate 80 near the Carquinez Bridge.

"About a hundred more years." She rethinks it. "More like ninety-five. It's just that we are seeing more people on their last lives than ever before. Believe me, you don't want to come down to this hellhole anymore."

There is some laughter, and then silence as it looks, from the JumboTron anyway, that Sylvia is "seeing" something. Her mouth drops open, and she mouths, barely audible, the word *fuck*.

Sylvia's theory is that the closest thing to the existence of hell is the world we're living in right now.

"God's not going to send you to hell," she says. "This is hell. When you look in a newborn baby's eyes, they're thinking, 'Oh shit. I'm in this hellhole again.' It is a look of utter depression. God is not mysterious. People say, 'But, Sylvia, I prayed and prayed to

God, and he didn't answer my prayer.' And I say, 'Yes, he did.'" Beat. "He said *no*.

"I don't want to get too political, but our boys and women in Iraq are saints, and it's time for them to come home. We need our gas prices to go down. We need health care. We need to take care of our homeless. I just wish Bush knew how to speak the language. Take what you want from what I say and leave the rest. I hate people cramming stuff down your throat. But the more spiritually attuned you are, the easier you go at the end."

I think of Eli's grandfather Gus and Deepak's dad.

"And there's only one dumb question. People ask it on *Montel* all the time." The mention of his name gets applause.

"I love Montel. I've been with him for seventeen years. Longer than most marriages."

She fingers her necklace and then runs her hand across her décolletage as if she were applying sunscreen.

"People always ask, 'Are they happy?'" Beat. "So stupid. Of course they're happy. Everybody's happy on the other side."

What about evil people?

In an ominous monotone, she states, "Dark entities will be absorbed."

Sylvia moves into the guided meditation portion of the program. We are instructed to sit up straight, close our eyes, and rest our hands, palms up, in our laps. I am torn between documenting her meditation, being the only person in the hall with my eyes open, scribbling, or going with the flow. I decide to surrender and am soon trying to picture the "silver columns of God" surrounding me. Corinthian? Doric? Over the next ten minutes, there is a lot of talk about columns and light. White light, gold light, purple light, and green light, all surrounding my body. I can't stay in the meditation. I am picturing myself surrounded by the colored light, but I am also picturing everybody in the Masonic Auditorium surrounded by colored lights. We're glowing like aliens.

Afterward, I do feel rejuvenated, partially because my mind has been given a rest from the asphyxiating two-fer of Sylvia's sarcastic quips and the audience's sycophantic worship. That is the part I hate about these gurus. How everyone gets all brown-nosey around them. It's like when I went to a Tom Waits concert and people chuckled at every single thing that came out of his mouth.

"Can I get a glass of water?"

Ha-ha. Isn't he a genius? He wants water!

It's time for Sylvia to select members of the audience to speak with. We were all given numbered wristbands upon entering, and now she will randomly select numbers out of a basket. This part seems to go on forever. It is a special torture, hearing that voice of hers go on and on. Blue section 095478, green section 079321, green section again 679321, blue section 388642, blue section again 876011.

When she finally finishes, there are nearly fifty people lined up at the microphones to get their one-on-one time with Sylvia. Or one-on-two, to be fair to Francine the spirit guide.

The next hour is alternately fascinating and grim. A sobbing woman asks about her brother who was killed by a drunk driver, a sniffling girl wants to know if her father committed suicide or was murdered.

"How is my son's life going to turn out?" a woman asks.

"Fine, if you stop worrying about him. Next!"

"My mother died last year, and I want to know if she is happy."

Uh-oh. She asked the only dumb question. Here comes the hammer. Sylvia just shakes her head while the crowd silently chastises this lady for her poor listening skills.

"Next!"

"In 2004 I watched my mother bleed to death."

Sylvia responds, "Why is your brother grabbing his chest?"

Body-racking sobs ensue. "Because my father's best friend stabbed him in the heart."

After watching more than a dozen scenes like this, I make the very conscious decision to get up and leave. This enormous auditorium is a place for people who are in a lot of pain, the downtrodden looking for a thread of hope, people who want to believe they are currently living in hell, that it can't get any worse than this.

It's an interesting concept, that one. It would sure explain a lot. I think about it as I walk past the Masonic symbol of the all-seeing eye, out the door, and then run into a grieving friend who just returned from his seventeen-year-old cousin's funeral. It could explain war, genocide, disease, even a meal I had at an airport Chili's where the waitperson confided that the burgers could now only be prepared medium-well or well-done as a guarantee that no one would get *E. coli*. And then she carded a *sixty-year-old* woman who ordered a glass of wine because of official restaurant policy. What kind of world is that? Where meat is presumed to be poisonous and a senior citizen can't order a glass of house chardonnay without revealing her age? Look at Darfur, Iraq, Hurricane Katrina, and the recent announcement that there is going to be a movie based on Thomas Kinkade's blockbuster painting *Christmas Cottage*.

Two nights after I see Sylvia, I'm putting Gus to bed. We finally got him to fall asleep on his own, but sometimes he'll call out to us when he's still awake. It's usually nothing, a stalling technique framed as an important question like "Is tomorrow Thursday?" or "Which pajamas am I wearing? I forgot."

"Mama," he says. "You need to come in here."

He's already gotten up to pee, asked for a Band-Aid, and requested a glass of water since I've said good night. I pull my hands out of the dishwater and dry them on my pants.

I walk into his room, keeping my cool by trying to sound childishly mystified instead. "What on this great big giant green earth could you want now?"

"I'm scared," he says. "What happens when you die and turn to dust?" His voice is quiet and shaky. He really does sound scared.

"Mommy, I don't want to die and turn to dust and go down in the ground."

I sit down on the bed and rub his back, saying he doesn't have to worry about dying for a long time, that he has nothing to be scared of. In the back of my mind, I'm thinking of Sylvia and her prediction of ninety-five more years on earth. I can't possibly lean into his soft, small ear and say, "You'll be fine, baby. A psychic Mommy paid fifty dollars to see at the Masonic Auditorium says it will be your children and grandchildren who might die in a skin-stripping fireball of chemical explosions that destroys all human life and leaves the planet smoldering."

He falls asleep, and then I see the final evidence that we actually are living in hell. On a show called *Dr. 90210* there is a good-looking couple in their twenties who are both getting cosmetic genital surgery so they can be pretty down there, too. In the four years they've been together, they haven't ever had sex with the lights on or during the day because they both are convinced they have unattractive genitalia.

Stupid.

While I'm relieved to get back in touch with my sarcasm, there is no denying that the synchronicities, the plate o' shrimp moments, seem to be everywhere. It's almost as if they're reaching a crescendo to send me out of my year in style. I've found I can barely have a conversation, turn on the radio, or walk out of my house without getting some kind of message that relates to my self-help journey.

In a pre-Christmas cleaning frenzy, I go to the corner to dump some more old clothes in the bright green donation bin, but it's suddenly gone. The thing was half the size of a Dumpster. It's been there for years. Just yesterday I noticed it because it was overflowing. When I walk inside the store to ask what happened to it, a guy buying a forty-ouncer is saying to the cashier, "People who love think they live in a loving world. People who hate think they live in a hater's world."

Mohammed the owner nods his head.

"But it's all the same world, man. Think about it."

I go home and look up the recycled clothing nonprofit, Gaia, online and discover that it is affiliated with something called the Tvind network, described in a recent court case in Denmark as a $500 million maze of scam charities and companies active in fifty-five countries. (On the east coast, the bins are yellow and say Planet Aid.) The *Guardian* (U.K.) describes the founder of the "cult-like organisation," Amdi Pedersen of Denmark, as a "hippie guru" who has a decades-long history of being investigated for fraud. Allegedly, Tvind is in the highly profitable international rag-picking business and claims to use its donated clothes to finance environmental projects, though a consumer website called the Charity Industry Observer stated that tax filings show only 4 percent of Tvind's revenues were donated to charity.

(At the time of editing this book, a watchdog website, Tvind Alert, was reporting that Danish police were attempting to serve papers on Pedersen in connection with plans by prosecutors to appeal Pedersen's acquittal of fraud charges relating to the charity. His whereabouts are unknown.)

So for the past few years I've been donating all of my family's used clothing to a multimillionaire scam artist guru, whose donation bin happens to disappear the month my year of multimillionaire gurus comes to a close.

Gus is in the bath one night, and as I'm running around trying to clean the house, I'm thinking about all the things I didn't accomplish this year. I wanted to do a lot of practical things like paint the living room and get an earthquake preparedness kit together. Not fifteen minutes later, there's an earthquake centered in Berkeley. Over the next week, as I continue to put off buying batteries and bottles of water, we have three more decent-sized earthquakes in a row, all centered a few miles from my house.

We go to a birthday party at a bowling alley. I'm talking to this writer I've never met, and I mention the Richard Simmons cruise.

"It's the weirdest thing," he says. "One time a Richard Simmons video came on TV, and I saw this guy in the background that I used to know. I hadn't seen him in twenty-five years, and I hardly recognized him because he had lost so much weight, but it was definitely this guy I knew when I lived in Mississippi."

"That's funny," I say.

"I wrote a story about him once because he was just so cool. He took me to see *Superman* when I was thirteen years old. I met him at the 7-Eleven. He was a clerk there, and I went in all the time to buy candy, and we became friends. He had been on *The Price Is Right* and won a Chrysler LeBaron that he drove around. We were kind of an odd couple. He was this huge older black guy, and I was this skinny white kid."

"Wait a minute." There were only a couple black people on Richard's cruise and only one black man. "What was his name?"

"Elijah," Eric says. "I kept his name in the story the same because it seemed so biblical."

"Wow! I met him!" I say. "He was on my cruise! Elijah was on my Richard Simmons cruise. He lost, like, three hundred pounds. I can't believe I met a friend of yours from Mississippi, from over twenty years ago, on a Richard Simmons cruise."

A few days before Christmas, I give my neighbor a ride to the BART station. She comments on our new car, and I tell her about the accident. "The reason you didn't get hurt is because you're good people," she says. "Do you believe in angels?"

No one has ever, seriously or jokingly, asked me if I believed in angels. And it's not often I get asked a question that I've never been asked before.

"Um, I don't know," I answer diplomatically.

"I'm telling you that you're alive right now because of the angels watching over you."

Eli crawls into bed one night and rubs my shoulder.

"Are you awake?"

"What is it?"

"I have to tell you something really insane about this job."

"What?" I roll over and open my eyes. I know he wouldn't be waking me up unless it was something really good.

"The guy who started the company used to do cassette tape duplication in L.A. in the eighties."

I cannot possibly guess where this would be going.

"And there was some guy who used to keep coming in and getting more copies of his tapes made. He was selling so many of them that my boss figured he must be onto something. He decided the guy should be on television and made his first infomercial."

"Who was it?"

Eli is laughing really hard at this point, dragging it out to heighten the suspense.

He brings his nose to my nose and spills it in a whisper. "Tony Robbins!"

"No! That's crazy."

"Yes! They are really good friends. I guess he comes into the office whenever he's in town. And . . . ," he says. "And guess who else he's made videos for?"

"Who?"

"Richard Simmons!"

It's uncanny. My husband, the musician and recording engineer, who has a degree in electronic music and composition from a small women's college, has suddenly started working for a company affiliated with Tony Robbins and Richard Simmons.

I lie awake for the next two hours reeling over all the coincidences, going back months, beginning to understand, just a little bit, what people mean when they say that everything is connected. The circle as an object of nature, the idealization of pure mathematics, a symbol of how everything in my life seems to come back to Richard Simmons (with his "round" hair and signature move called the "Angel"). Jack Canfield's insomnia trick isn't even working on this one. Finally, it occurs to me that I have the power to turn the synchronicities off if I want. After all, I made them appear in the first place by spending so much energy focusing on this stuff, it makes sense that now I could shut it down. I make out the shape of the $100,000 bill, still taped on the wall next to the bed, a little bent around the corners, as Eli snores away, oblivious to my Herculean brain chatter. I drift off after coming to the realization that this lattice of coincidence doesn't mean that anyone is sending me "signs" or "messages"; it doesn't even mean that I've gone crazy. I decide that it is simply evidence that there is something cool and mysterious about being alive. A random element that can shock and surprise. Something I normally don't think about every day. An element that may as well, for convenience sake, be referred to as God. Possibly.

Meanwhile, my lucid dreaming is off the chain. Early this morning, I see myself in a forest. I'm lying down on my back, looking up at dozens of redwood trees, the branches interlocking high. I suddenly become aware of the dampness seeping into my clothes from the forest floor and realize that I am in a dream. That's when I decide to fly. Instead of flying, however, my body slowly starts levitating. I rise up in between the mighty brown trunks, and as I am approaching the branches I realize it's going to hurt to pass through them. I tell myself to make it not hurt, and I pass through them as if they are invisible. A series of lights starts flashing around me, like big flashbulbs, until I am past the tree line. Now I rise into the black sky, and the lights shimmer and turn into stars. I flip myself over and start to fly, feeling tiny and safe and incredibly calm as some gentle force pulls me into outer space by a single vertebra. I am so high that I can see the curve of the earth. It's one of the best dreams I've ever had.

Today is December 31. I lost the coin toss, so guess who's cleaning the toilet for the party. Even though there are still a million things I could improve about my life, and I'm so relieved this year is finally over, I'm pretty happy. For the first time ever, I made a conscious decision to step out of my regular way of living, a low-impact go-with-the-flow system, and try to think in a different way, a way that often made me cringe and shudder and question if I had any integrity. Back in January, I thought it would be the funniest thing if I didn't improve at all, if I came to the conclusion that self-help programs were mostly a bunch of crap. But, despite the fact that this year was one of the hardest and most confusing ever, I no longer believe that. Completely. I mean, it's hard to deny that something definitely happened to me and that most of it was positive. (Whether I could have achieved the same ends by tackling something else I thought was stupid, like bungee jumping or bikini boot camp, I don't know.) We'll see if any of the programs stick with me, but right now there are some more concrete goals to attend to. Like I've got just under nine hours to learn to do the splits.

AFTERWORD: JULY 30, 2007

I handed out bananas at the finish line of the San Francisco Marathon yesterday, dressed in my banana suit. What I imagined would be an experience akin to watching a triumphant Nike commercial turned out to be way more grisly and human. People were cramping up, falling down, wailing, dazed. Faces were crusted with dried salt, snot poured out of nostrils, and chafed nipples bled through T-shirts, sending twin trails of rust dripping down chests like the Virgin's tears. More than a few people appeared to have leaked from their bowels into their shorts. *Why would anyone do this?,* I rhetorically asked a pigeon as I rearranged my face-hole. And then a runner, who had been doubled-over and heaving in the gutter, stood up, looked at my outfit, put his hand on my shoulder, and said, "And I thought *I* was having a rough day. You went to college for that?"

This exchange is a distilled version of my experience with self-help. This baffling assessment. Because it's our nature to take stabs at being better or happier people, we constantly design our own hoops and hurdles to see what we're capable of. In this version, the guy has his marathon and I have my banana suit. We may be humming along just fine for a while, but we also can't help but compare our tests and goals to those of other people. This is when "experts" come in handy. It seems like, at its best, self-help is probably supposed to remind us that we can be strong and in control, that we can do anything. The problem with this is that we are human. All we're ever going to do is stumble around. Sometimes we hit the sweet spot, and the rest of the time we spend trying to unravel the formula for how to hit the next one.

ACKNOWLEDGMENTS

A huge thank-you to all of the publishing people who helped me help myself with this thing: Anna Bliss; Judith Regan; Sarah Burningham; Jennifer Schulkind; my editor, Mauro DiPreta; and all the kindhearted folks at the Levine Greenberg Literary Agency, including Daniel Greenberg, Jim Levine, and, most especially, my agent, Arielle Eckstut.

Thanks to all of the self-help gurus whose books I read and whose seminars, lectures, symposiums, plenary sessions, performances, and fitness cruises I attended. It is a brave and strange thing you do, and it was a curious pleasure to participate in your life's work.

Titanium Empowerment Winners Circle Forever: Stephen T. Brophy, Marc Capelle, Eli Crews, Dayvid Figler, Matt Greenberg, Tara Jepsen, Dan Kennedy, Arline Klatte, Chris Lisick, Paul Lisick, Ron and Anne Lisick, Tucker Malarkey, Lisa Margonelli, Chris Mittelstaedt and the Fruit Guys, Frank Portman, Jan Richman, Mary Roach, Lora Schulson, Dave Spalding, Penelope Starr, and Kirby Walker.